Additional Praise ~~for~~ *the Platform*

"*The Age of the Platform* is not a light or easy book because business today is neither light nor easy. Through the book's framework, Simon asks tough questions and makes readers think long and hard about whether their current business models meet the new realities of the 21st century."

—*Barbara Weltman, host of* Build Your Business Radio
and author of J.K. Lasser's Small Business Taxes

"Profound. Important. A groundbreaking text."

—*Jay Miletsky, Founder and CEO, MyPod Studios
and author of* Perspectives on Marketing

"Finally, someone who gets it! In this powerful new book, Simon's analysis and synthesis help businesses of all kinds understand today's adapt-or-die business world."

—*Natalie MacNeil, Emmy* Award-winning *producer
at Imaginarius and author of* She Takes on the World

"Provocative and useful—a rare combination."

—*Amy Wohl, author of* Succeeding at SaaS: Computing
in the Cloud *and Editor, Amy Wohl's Opinions*

"An incisive look at people, companies, trends, and events that have done nothing less than redefine business and consumerism over the last decade. Simon has written an essential text for any business that aspires to successfully build and operate a winning platform."

—*Damien Santer, CEO, Praxis BT*

THE AGE OF THE PLATFORM

"Essential reading on the state of business today – and where it is going. Ignore this book at your own peril."

—**Adrian C. Ott**, award-winning author, *The 24-Hour Customer*

How Amazon, Apple, Facebook, and Google Have Redefined Business

PHIL SIMON

Foreword by Mitch Joel
President of Twist Image and author of *Six Pixels of Separation*

Motion Publishing, LLC
Las Vegas, Nevada

© 2011 by Phil Simon

All Rights Reserved. No part of this work covered by the copyright herein may be reproduced, transmitted, stored, or used in any form or by any means graphic, electronic, or mechanical, including but not limited to photocopying, recording, scanning, digitizing, taping, Web distribution, information networks, or information storage and retrieval systems, except as permitted under Section 107 or 108 of the 1976 U.S. Copyright Act, without the prior written permission of the publisher.

www.motionpub.com

Published by Motion Publishing, LLC
Las Vegas, Nevada

Although the author and publisher have made every effort to ensure the accuracy and completeness of information contained in this book, we assume no responsibility for errors, inaccuracies, omissions, or any inconsistency herein. Any slights of people, places, or organizations are unintentional.

ISBN: 978-0-9829302-5-0
LCCN: 2011938398

First printing: 2011
Printed in the United States of America

Editor: Sue Collier

Interior Design and Layout: Juanita Dix

Electronic Book Design: Kristen Eckstein

Cover Designer: Luke Fletcher

Indexer: Johanna VanHoose Dinse

Proofreader: Marlowe Shaeffer

Book Website Developer: Shiri Amram

Definition: The Platform

An extremely valuable and powerful ecosystem that quickly and easily scales, morphs, and incorporates new features (called *planks* in this book), users, customers, vendors, and partners. Today, the most powerful platforms are rooted in equally powerful technologies—and their intelligent usage. In other words, they differ from traditional platforms in that they are not predicated on physical assets, land, and natural resources.

Today, the most vibrant platforms embrace third-party collaboration. The companies behind these platforms seek to foster symbiotic and mutually beneficial relationships with users, customers, partners, vendors, developers, and the community at large.

Even though a great deal of potential commercial appeal and applications inhere in them, platforms do not exist simply as a means for companies to hawk their wares. At their core, platforms today are primarily about consumer utility and communications. Finally, because consumers' tastes change much faster than businesses' tastes, platforms today must adapt quickly—or face obsolescence.

—*from Chapter 2, discussed in more detail in Part II of book*

To my favorite tweeps:

Dawn Westerberg (@dwesterberg) and Dharmesh Shah (@dharmesh).

Thank you for believing in this book.

And to the eternal spirit of Steve Jobs.

TABLE OF CONTENTS

IN GRATITUDE   xi
FOREWORD   xv
INTRODUCTION   xix

PART I: THE RISE OF THE PLATFORM AGE

1: THE INTERNET: WHERE ARE WE NOW?   1
Web 1.0 (1993 to early 2005) ● Web 2.0 (Mid-2005 to Present)
● It's Not All Rosy: The Downsides of Technology Gone Wild ● Summary
and Conclusion

2: PLATFORMS: DEFINITIONS, HISTORY, AND ECONOMICS   21
The Need for Platforms ● Defining the Platform ● The Platform As a
Business Model ● Platforms and Technology: Then and Now ● Powerful
Platforms vs. Monopolies ● Barriers to Entry ● Types of Traditional
Monopolies ● Platforms Are Not Monopolies—Natural or Otherwise
● Summary and Conclusion

PART II: THE GANG OF FOUR:
THE LEADERS OF THE PLATFORM AGE

3: A MERE BOOKSTORE NO MORE   43
Get Big Fast ● The Planks: How Amazon Built Its Platform ● Missteps
and Conflicts ● The Future of the Amazon Platform

4: BEYOND THE COMPUTER   67
Pushing the Envelope ● The Planks: How Apple Built Its Platform
● Getting More Social ● Missteps and Detractors ● The Future of the
Apple Platform

5: THE KING OF SOCIAL   89
A Rapid Ascent ● Lessons from Friendster: Scale, Speed, and Paranoia
● The Planks: How Facebook Built Its Platform ● Missteps ● The Future
of the Facebook Platform

6: FROM SEARCH TO UBIQUITY   113
A Brief History ● The Planks: How Google Built Its Platform ● Missteps
● 2011: The State of Google ● The Future of the Google Platform

PART III: SYNTHESIS:
UNDERSTANDING THE POWER OF THE PLATFORM

7: THE DNA: PLATFORM COMPONENTS AND CHARACTERISTICS   133
Platforms Evolve—and So Do the Companies Behind Them ● The Ability
to Scale ● Dynamic Stability and Change-Tolerant Organizations ● Heavy
Reliance on Data and Technology ● The New Blueprint for Innovation

● Loyal and Vocal Communities ● A Dual Focus: Customers and Users ● Simplicity ● Platforms Are Not Businesses ● Extensive Borrowing from Other Platforms ● Powerful Platforms Often Spawn Imitators ● Iconic and Visionary Leaders ● Platforms Synthesize ● Switching Platforms Is Difficult—by Design ● Platforms Collide ● Platforms Are Inherently Political ● Summary and Conclusion

8: GIMME THE PRIZE! THE BENEFITS OF PLATFORMS   153
Risk Mitigation and Increased Diversification ● Brand Building and Extension ● The Creation of Virtual Barriers to Entry ● Greasing the Wheels: Increased Innovation ● Accidental Lines of Business ● Reaching the Overwhelmed Consumer ● Superior Understanding of Customer and User Bases ● Increased Organizational Agility ● Preemptive Strikes ● Summary and Conclusion

9: SLINGS AND ARROWS: THE PERILS OF PLATFORMS   169
The Limitations of Platforms ● Platform Abuse, Scams, and Misconduct ● Increased Government Scrutiny ● Keeping Secrets ● Angering Others ● Increased Competition ● Planks Beware: From Partner to Rival ● When the Mighty Fall: The Ephemeral Nature of Platforms ● Summary and Conclusion

10: THE HOW: TIPS FOR BUILDING A PLATFORM   191
Act Small ● Be Open and Collaborative ● Seek Intelligent Acquisitions, Extensions, and Directions ● Make Little Bets: Encourage Experimentation ● Fail Forward and Embrace Uncertainty ● Overshoot ● Know When to Punt ● Breadth Trumps Depth ● Embrace Risk and Uncertainty ● Move Quickly and Decisively When Spotting a Niche ● Use Existing Planks ● Temper Expectations ● Summary and Conclusion

PART IV: LOOKING FORWARD

11: THE CANDIDATES: TODAY'S EMERGING PLATFORMS   221
Who Knew? ● Foursquare ● Twitter ● WordPress ● Groupon ● Adobe ● Salesforce.com and Force.com ● LinkedIn ● Quora ● Summary

12: CODA: A GLIMPSE OF WHAT'S BEYOND   237
Web 3.0 and Beyond ● Continued Growth and Evolution ● Technology and Greenfield Organizations ● Next Steps

FURTHER READINGS AND RESOURCES   249
BOOK SPONSORS   256
A HUMBLE REQUEST FROM THE AUTHOR   259
ENDNOTES   261
INDEX   269
ABOUT THE AUTHOR   277
OTHER BOOKS BY PHIL SIMON   278

"An idea that is not dangerous is unworthy of being called an idea at all."
—*Oscar Wilde*

IN GRATITUDE

While writing a book may be an inherently selfish endeavor, no book comes together without the help of others.

Kudos to the remarkable group of people I collectively call *Team Simon*. I am extremely lucky to have worked with the following talented individuals: my book designer and eleventh-hour savior Juanita Dix, my amazing proofreader and sounding board Marlowe Shaeffer, my cover designer—and fellow *Big Lebowski* nut—Luke Fletcher, my marketing guru TJ McCue, my eBook specialist and muse Kristen Eckstein, my conscientious indexer Johnna VanHoose Dinse, my exceptional web developers Angela Bowman and Shiri Amram, and voiceover artist extraordinaire Lisa Scott.

Adrian Ott was beyond generous with her time. Despite her hectic schedule, she served as an invaluable sounding board and critical eye during the book's development stages—and I am forever grateful for her cover endorsement.

My technology mentor, the über-smart Bob Charette, has been a veritable fountain of knowledge over the past two years.

Special props to Jim Harris, Ivana Taylor, Stacey Cornelius, Michele Welch, Donna Papacosta, Chuck Martin, and David Freedman for listening to me and offering essential input at different stages of the writing and publishing processes. Mitch Joel wrote an inspirational foreword.

A tip of the hat to Jill Dyché; Tony Fisher; Jane Applegate; Chuck Martin; Melinda Emerson; Regina Cardona; Ellen French; Dick and Bonnie Denby; Justin Amendola; Scott "Caddy" Erichsen; Mike McDonald; Kristen Eckstein; Bo Burlingham; Rose Aulik; Vinnie Mirchandani; Thor and Keri Sandell; Steve "Winning Ugly" Katz; Michael, Penelope, and Chloe DeAngelo; Brian and Heather

Morgan and their three adorable kids; Karen Gill; John Spatola; Joanne Lam; Marc Paolella; Matt Carlson; and Angela Bowman. Next up are the usual suspects: my longtime Carnegie Mellon friends Scott Berkun, David Sandberg, Michael Viola, Joe Mirza, and Chris "Tripped Over the Blue Line" McGee.

My heroes from Rush (Geddy, Alex, and Neil), Dream Theater (Jordan, John, John, Mike, and James), and Porcupine Tree (Steven, Colin, Gavin, John, and Richard) have given me many years of creative inspiration through their music. Keep on keepin' on!

Seth Godin's writing and speaking is a similar source of remarkable energy and wisdom. Vince Gillian and the entire ensemble of *Breaking Bad* make me want to do great work.

Next up: my parents. I'm not here without you.

THE KICKSTARTER CROWD

I am indebted to the following individuals who supported this book: Aaron Curtis; Aaron Goldfarb; Adam Heller; Alan Berkson; Amy Wohl; Andrew Gossen; Barbara S. Green; Benny Alexander; Bill Hinsley; Blair Richwood; Brenda Bush Johannesen; Brian L. Hill; Brian Morgan; Brian Rosenberg; Brian Weber; Bruce F. Webster; Carol Morgan Cox; Casey Wiesel; Chris C. Ducker; Colin Hickey; Cori Chavez; Crysta Anderson; Dalton Cervo; Damien Santer; Daniel Lynton; Daragh O'Brien; Daria Steigman; David Berger; David Rogers; Dawn Westerberg; Deb Ondo; Deborah Major; Dharmesh Shah; Don Frederiksen; Dwayne Thompson; Erika McAnn; Frank Johnson; Gary Silberman; Geri Rosman; Heather Etchings; Ina Mutschelknaus; Ivana Taylor; Janet Stewart; Jacek Rawicki; Jack Spain; Jacqueline Roberts; Jaime Fitzgerald; Jane Applegate; Janet Boyer; Jay Baer; Jay Miletsky; Jean-Baptiste Collinet; Jennie Mustafa-Julock; Jennifer J. Cullari; Jeremy Benson; Jim Harris; Jim Kukral; John Glover; John Lauermann; Jon P. Yarger; Julie Hunt; Karin Socaransky; Kathy Lynn Johnson; Kenneth Weil; Kevin Brennan; Kirsten Knipp; Larry Goldberg; Lauren Anderson; Les Tuerk; Lisa Bambauer-West; Loraine Lawson; Louis Rosas-Guyon; Marc Paolella; Marisa Smith;

Mark Allen; Mark Hayes; Mark Jones, Jr.; Mark Nowotarski; Mark Unwin; Matt Mansfield; Matthew Hanover; Megan Atkinson; Megan Torrance; Melissa Armstrong; Michele Welch; Mikael Vaede; Mike McDonald; Mike Ryan; Mike West; Naynish Jhaveri; Nikos Acuna; Nina Kaufman; Noah Fine; Patrick Foley; Patrick Mooney; Paul Spiegelman; Penelope, Michael, and Chloe DeAngelo; Phil Montero; Ravi K. Vajjah; Rich Murnane; Rik van der Schalie; Rob Bell; Rob Croll; Rob Paller; Robert Brands; Sally Cooper; Sarah Worsham; Scott Ryan Jones; Shane Petty; Shiri Amram; Stacey Cornelius; Stephen Putman; TC Coleman; Terri Rylander; Tim Vink; Tim Ware; TJ McCue; Todd Hamilton; Tom Bardzell; Tom McClintock; Tony Marciante; Tor Iver Wilhelmsen; Tracy Austin; Whurley; William McKnight; and Yvonne Dillard.

FOREWORD

It's All About the Platform

It's not uncommon to hear me (along with some of my other New Media pundits) debate the notion of "What is a book in 2011?" While the topic might send many people straight for the pillow, it is actually quite fascinating. Consider that a book is no longer just words printed on paper and bound together in a text-based format that is void of advertising. A book typically contains much more in-depth content than a magazine or newspaper. Suddenly—through the digitization of everything—books look more like video games in their digital format. The actual text can be modified by size, style, and color, and embedded within the book is a myriad of multimedia—from images and videos to interactive components and beyond. At the end of the day, it's getting harder and harder to tell the difference between a book and a website.

Talk about change. Fast change.

Beyond the debate of "What is a book in 2011?" comes the discussion about which platform will win the book wars. Will it be Amazon's Kindle? Apple's iBooks? Barnes & Noble's Nook? Kobo? A new platform we haven't seen yet? Sadly, the discourse has been largely misplaced. Far too many people are focusing on the hardware instead of the platform behind the hardware. Amazon made a bold move fast when it introduced its Kindle app for smartphones and tablets. Suddenly, you didn't need a physical Kindle ebook reader to buy and read books. What's more, the content could be completely asynchronous (meaning if you read a page on your iPad and then started to read your book some time later on your iPhone, the apps were all synchronized and knew where you left off).

Currently, the ebook reader wars are about the hardware. In the end, however, we'll wind up discovering that it's all about the platform: whichever brand can create the winning platform for the consumer.

In this instance, it's about making the most books available for the best price with the optimal functionality in as many places as the consumer would like to be able to access their literature.

Once in a while, we all buy into the hype. It's just human nature. Much like rubbernecking, if everyone else is checking something out, we feel like we have to as well—you know, just to make sure we're not missing out on anything important or interesting. We're like this in our personal lives, and we're like this in business as well.

PRIORITIES

At least in business, it's critical that we spend our precious time where it truly matters. We need to prioritize to determine which platforms really benefit our businesses, consumers, competitors, partners, and the industry at large. As big as both Facebook and Twitter are, there are plenty of people (and potential consumers) who are simply not that interested in what they have to offer. Perish the thought! Shortly after Twitter reached the tipping point, I saw the statistic that 60 percent of Twitter users quit within their first month of using the service. Does that mean Twitter isn't a good platform for your business?

Not necessarily. People quit Twitter in droves because using it effectively takes time and effort—as do most of the newer online social networking platforms. Yes, new media is amazing because of the interactivity of it all. But we all need to remember that most people are not used to interactive media—let alone having to take part in the creation of content, the sharing of it, and beyond. And then there are those who like old media just fine, thank you very much.

Pushing forward, we need to get beyond the hype to get to the real application and power of these platforms for business.

BEYOND THE SHINY OBJECT SYNDROME

And that's exactly where *The Age of the Platform* kicks in. Before Google+ it was all about Twitter. Even while Twitter was all the rage, it was also all about Facebook. Before Facebook it was all about MySpace. During the MySpace craze, it was also all about *Second Life*. And that's just the past four years or so. That's what trends are about, whether we're talking new media, music, fashion—something new comes along and we are distracted long enough to lose interest in what happened before. This is also known as *shiny object syndrome*.

Hype does not make a platform functional; it can only take a platform so far, perhaps to the level of intriguing curiosity.

What exactly makes a great platform? It's about what your business puts into its platform and what your consumers and/or business partners get out of it.

And that's the point. A platform either fits into an overall corporate strategy or it doesn't. Let's say that you're on Twitter because everyone else is. This "me too" strategy is hardly viable in the long-term. It's certainly unlikely to maximize the use of platforms for your business. What if you spend all of your time on Facebook because it is hot at the moment? You do this even though you may be more likely to find the kind of people with whom you should really be connecting on *Second Life*. Not all platforms are created equal. There's no reason that you should mindlessly follow the masses.

IT'S THE PLATFORM

It's tempting to stick with what has always worked best for you, but today it's critical to explore new platforms—and to build your own. As obvious as this sounds, it's amazing to see how many businesses refuse to experiment with new technologies and media. They're afraid of new platforms.

To some extent, this is entirely understandable. Everything continues to digitize, morph, and evolve. As I see every day in my role as president of Twist Image, the online landscape befuddles the vast majority of businesspeople. Thankfully, Phil provides some desperately needed clarity around platforms and how your business can benefit from them.

Get ready for *The Age of the Platform*—an important and timely explanation of a new way of doing business. This is a book about the present, the future, your business, and the industry you serve. And it couldn't have come at a better time.

Today, more than ever, it's all about the platform.

Mitch Joel
President of Twist Image and author of Six Pixels of Separation
October 2011

INTRODUCTION

The Gang of Four

There are many smart people out there—and few are smarter than Eric Schmidt.

Even before joining Google as chairman in August 2001, Schmidt was long regarded as one of the most respected, knowledgeable, and prescient technology minds on the planet. Among his many accolades, in 2007 *PC World* named him the most important person on the web—along with Google co-founders Larry Page and Sergey Brin.[1] Today, there are few more astute observers in the field. When he talks, people listen.

Schmidt was talking on May 31, 2011. He had the floor at the D9 Conference in Rancho Palos Verdes, California. In broad terms, he discussed today's rapidly moving, tech-heavy economic climate. Beyond generalities, though, Schmidt remarked that a small cadre of companies was growing at unprecedented rates, reaching scales that could only be described as extraordinary. Moreover, this growth had "not been possible before."[2] Schmidt named four companies that stood apart from the crowd: Apple, Amazon, Facebook, and Google. He collectively referred to these companies as *the Gang of Four*.

Today the Gang of Four is light years ahead of its peers. And this lead is not just in one vital area, such as technology. In incredibly short periods of time, Apple, Amazon, Facebook, and Google have done truly amazing things. They have built valuable brands, released popular products and services, cultivated widespread followings, and generated enormous shareholder value and profits. They have quickly risen to prominence, in the process becoming the envy of thousands of organizations. They have been able to innovate and launch products, services, and even entire lines of business at unprecedented rates. As we'll see in this book, the source of these companies' competitive advantages stems from many things, including profound customer insights enabled by troves of data, immensely valuable partnerships, highly adaptive cultures, and the intelligent use of technology.

BIG COMPANY SYNDROME

Historically, as large companies have grown to such dizzying heights, they have begun to show signs of fissure and eventual decline. Examples abound. IBM struggled mightily in the late 1980s and early 1990s. To be fair, it was able to successfully redefine itself as a service-oriented company, a turnaround that has been nothing short of astounding. Kodak was woefully unprepared for the rise of digital cameras and printing. More recently, many iconic organizations have lost their leads, sometimes in just a few years. Microsoft comes to mind and is discussed at length in Chapter 9 of this book.

It doesn't take a genius to recognize the symptoms or diagnose the disease. After some degree of success, large organizations begin to tread water. Over the course of, say, five years, they start to exhibit the signs of stereotypical risk-averse, monolithic organizations. Again, this is well-trodden ground. Many books have been written about how size tends to encumber organizations, along with attendant bureaucracy and other baggage. Call it *big company syndrome.*

The Gang of Four, however, appears to be largely symptom-free. Each company continues to hire thousands of new employees, enter new and often challenging markets, forge new partnerships, and launch entirely new lines of business. These companies are doing much more than avoiding the traditional perils of growth, nor are they simply maintaining previous levels of performance. They are somehow *increasing* their organizational pace of innovation.

Disclaimer

I have no axe to grind with Microsoft, IBM, MySpace, AOL, Yahoo!, and other technology companies that have recently fallen from grace. On the contrary, I admire each company's accomplishments and innovations. As we will see in Chapter 1, we would not be where we are today if Microsoft had not pushed for common computing standards, Yahoo! had not broken new ground with portals, AOL had not taken dial-up to the masses, and MySpace had not introduced the idea of a social network to millions. In many important ways, these companies paved the way for the Gang of Four.

I only highlight the missteps of these organizations to underscore one of the key points in this book: *Platforms—even great ones—do not guarantee long-term success*. In other words, the platform is no silver bullet, and we can learn a great deal from the declines of these companies—and their platforms.

What's more, I have great admiration for Amazon, Apple, Facebook, and Google—and the leaders behind them. However, I do not mean to imply that the Gang of Four can do no wrong. In Part II of this book, I catalog some fairly large tactical and strategic blunders made by these companies. Throughout the book, I have endeavored to strike a balance between the good and the bad.

Let me be clear: Microsoft, Yahoo!, and their struggling counterparts are not bad or incompetent organizations. Nor are Amazon, Apple, Facebook, and Google above reproach. They are not run by inherently better or smarter people. But the fact remains: Each member of the Gang of Four has done an excellent job of building and managing its platform. And this is the main reason that each has enjoyed so much success over the last five years.

Bezos, Zuckerberg, and company have learned a great deal from tech pioneers like Bill Gates and Jerry Yang. But now the pendulum has swung the other way. Current management at many organizations—including Microsoft, Yahoo!, and other besieged companies—would do well to study the success of Amazon, Apple, Facebook, and Google. Hence the need for this book.

GET BIG FAST

> "At electric speed, all forms are pushed to the limits of their potential."
> —*Marshall McLuhan*

In general, the Gang of Four is doing what top management gurus have been espousing for years. Specifically, these companies are embracing intelligent risk. They aren't afraid of failure, experimentation, and change. Innovation depends on this type of mentality. At least in part, each company has moved away from its original and core business model—often multiple times—sprouting in different and unexpected directions: horizontally, vertically, and *even diagonally*. Each company has entered new markets, and in some cases, created markets where none had previously existed.

That's one explanation. But it's actually not the underlying reason for the massive and sustained success of these companies. Rather, they are winning because they are following an entirely new blueprint and business model. They have spent a great deal of time and money building extremely powerful and valuable ecosystems, partnerships, and communities. This new model hinges on powerful ecosystems that, in turn, fuel astounding levels of innovation, profits, and growth. In the understated words of Eric Schmidt at the D9 Conference mentioned earlier, Amazon, Apple, Facebook, and Google "are exploiting platform strategies really well."[3]

Without question, the Gang of Four has built the world's most valuable and powerful business platforms. In so doing, these companies have done nothing short of redefine business. Collectively, they have introduced the platform as the most important business model of the 21st century. And they have spawned a litany of imitators. Thousands of companies are:

- ❏ Building their own platforms
- ❏ Creating valuable planks that complement existing platforms
- ❏ Modifying their business models to incorporate platforms
- ❏ Becoming platform partners

Welcome to the Age of the Platform.

FORESIGHT IN AN ERA OF CONSTANT MOTION

It isn't easy to conceive of, build, and continuously adapt a platform. If it were, then everyone would be doing it. Amazon, Apple, Facebook, and Google would be commonplace, not exceptional. Expenses aside for a moment, creating a robust platform does not just hinge on consistently developing great products or services. Rather, it requires a completely different mind-set. It must be at the core of a company's business model. Companies must not only exist, but they must thrive in a state of constant motion. They must embrace *dynamic stability* (discussed in Chapter 7). They need to constantly reevaluate and redefine basic precepts such as:

- ❏ What they currently do
- ❏ How they do it
- ❏ What they *could* do
- ❏ How they could do it
- ❏ With whom they do it
- ❏ How each piece interacts with other parts of its ecosystem and the world at large

As Part II of this book will show, building such a platform requires many things. There is no five-step program or quick how-to guide. At the top of the list are amazing foresight, organizational agility, and the courage to let third parties participate in a business frequently, and in some very unconventional and collaborative ways. Insular companies are unlikely to build a great platform.

Book Back Story

As 2011 progressed, I began to feel a compelling need to write a book about the platform as an important and new business model. As I will explain shortly, I have learned from personal experience that building a platform is not only beneficial, but also imperative for many companies' survival. I look at myself as a case in point: In a relatively short period of time, I redefined my business and launched completely new products and services. How did I do this? In short, I built my own platform.

By way of background, from 2002 until 2008 with a few brief exceptions, my entire livelihood was tied to one fairly specific type of work: enterprise resource planning (ERP) consulting. Even that type of relatively provincial work involves a wide variety of people and technical skills. Let's just say, however, that more than 99 percent of all companies never considered engaging me. And probably 99.99 percent did not need me at any given time.

Despite this significant limitation, by 2008 I had started to come into my own. That year, I knocked the ball out of the park, making more money than at any other point in my life (nearly $250,000). I had concurrently balanced several difficult projects and had taken just one week off. For me, 2008 was the very definition of the "feast" year about which independent consultants like me dreamed—as in feast or famine. By any measure, I should have been ecstatic.

Yet, at least professionally, I was quite concerned. At the time, I was 36 years old. As I gave my accountant my third-quarter financial statements to prepare my taxes, I told myself: I had better enjoy this while it lasts, because it just couldn't get any better. I couldn't raise my rates forever and there were only so many hours in a year. Plus, rarely does an independent

(continued)

consultant like me move seamlessly from one project to another for an entire year as I just did. Downtime was a given in any economy, and ours was getting worse.

I knew that I needed to diversify and establish myself in different lines of business—or face dire consequences. But somehow that didn't seem sufficient. I strongly suspected that I would have to refine my entire business model—and maybe even blow it up. In the long-term, this shift was necessary, but there was a short-term problem: No one cared. The world at large was not terribly interested in my decision to enter new lines of business—nor were many of my clients for that matter. If I was going to be successful in diversifying and mitigating my own risk, I would have to build my own *platform*.

Simon 2.0

Fast forward to mid-2011. As I send my same accountant my quarterly financial reports, "Simon, Inc." barely resembles the company of less than three years ago. That same type of consulting that generated more than $200,000 in revenue for me in 2008 is now barely a line item on my P&L statement. I had completely transformed my business. In part by accident and in part by design, over the next three years I launched entirely new lines of business. I earned money via services such as website design, writing, book coaching, marketing, and other areas for which I had no formal training. I made money from book royalties and mobile app sales. I also started a publishing company and a public speaking practice. In large part, I would have not been able to pay my bills and continue working for myself if I had not built an effective platform.

As we'll see later in the book, platforms are not elixirs. You still have to do the work. In my case, I had to develop a new brand and offer services that people would want—and pay for.

For three reasons, I'm glad that I started diversifying and building my platform when I did. First, I was beginning to tire of

(continued)

working on the same types of highly contentious projects. Second, I wanted to tackle new challenges and continue my own professional development. Third and most important, my shift turned out to be an economic imperative. In hindsight, my timing could not have been better. By early 2009, ERP consulting had slowed to a trickle, and many of my colleagues had either lost their jobs or could not find work. Although I have yet to replicate the financial success of 2008 (and may never do so), my platform-based business model is much more sound and resilient to risk. I start each year with a fair amount of base income from my writing and speaking clients. What's more, book sales generate passive income for me. Unlike years past, I no longer start at zero every January. As my platform continues to evolve in new and unexpected ways, it generates new income and opportunities for me.

Why These Four Companies?

As mentioned previously, I have been self-employed for most of the last 10 years. I am also a student of both technology and business—perhaps *sponge* is a better word. I am constantly absorbing information from myriad sources about technology and business trends, events, and issues. Like any solopreneur, I have my ups and downs.

If I have a bad quarter—or *three*, as I did in 2009—I wonder what I would do if I had to close my own little shop and work for a large company. And assuming it was my choice, where would I like to work? It would have to be a company that was:

- ❏ Doing extremely interesting and innovative things, especially with respect to emerging technologies
- ❏ Adapting extremely well and quickly to change
- ❏ Routinely introducing compelling new offerings
- ❏ Working with partners in very exciting ways.

Which ones fit the bill? Which large companies are doing the most exciting things?

To me—and I don't think I'm alone here—the answer is clear: Amazon, Apple, Facebook, and Google. I certainly didn't need Eric Schmidt to tell me as much. These four companies occupy elite status because of the popularity, reach, and power of their platforms. I knew that their extensive and successful use of platforms warranted a book. Against that backdrop, I started writing *The Age of the Platform* in April 2011.

In this book, I certainly don't contend that Amazon, Apple, Facebook, and Google are the only companies that understand the notion and importance of *platforms*—or at least make that claim. (Chapter 10 provides examples of lesser-known platforms, and Chapter 11 covers powerful emerging platforms.) I focus on the Gang of Four in this book because their platforms are so popular and robust. What's more, these four can teach businesses of all types and sizes many valuable lessons. To my knowledge, no existing book has looked at each of these dynamic organizations through the lens of the platform.

> **Very large companies such as Google and small companies like mine have embraced platforms—and seen amazing results. As a business model, the platform is size- and industry-agnostic.**

I make no secret of my admiration for Amazon, Apple, Facebook, and Google—and the leaders behind these amazing companies. Yet, I have another reason for profiling them. Millions of people and small businesses concurrently do business with the Gang of Four in a wide variety of capacities. That is, we have *symbiotic* relationships with them. For instance, we earn money from Amazon as affiliates and then buy books on the site. We sell games and productivity apps on Apple's App Store and then spend money on an iPad or a MacBook Pro.

WHY BUY THIS BOOK?

This book is first and foremost about the platform as a business model. It explains how Amazon, Apple, Facebook, and Google have built dynamic and powerful ecosystems. Next, it provides lessons for creating and expanding your own platforms—and utilizing existing ones. Finally, it looks at the candidates for the next great platforms.

You might be asking yourself:

- ❑ Just what is a platform, anyway?
- ❑ Why are planks so important to platforms?
- ❑ Why does my law firm or accounting practice or widget factory need a platform?
- ❑ What can my business and I possibly learn from the platforms of Amazon, Apple, Facebook, and Google?
- ❑ How is my small business remotely similar to these companies?

These are all fair questions. After all, relatively few businesses can spend billions or even millions of dollars on acquisitions—and afford to be wrong. Only a fraction of all companies have this type of liquidity and size. In fact, fewer than 1,000 American companies employ more than 10,000 people, according to the 2008 U.S. Census.[4] In all likelihood, your business cannot be compared to Amazon, Apple, Facebook, and Google.

But let me draw a few analogies here. One should not embark on a career in acting with the expectation of becoming the next Robert De Niro, Al Pacino, or Meryl Streep. Foolish is the guitarist who starts a band with the hope of selling more records than the Beatles. The upstart novelist who expects to be the next John Grisham or Stephen King had better not quit her day job. Ditto the teenager who picks up a tennis racket with dreams of being Roger Federer incarnate. The odds that any of these things will happen are beyond remote.

We can still learn a great deal from these extremely talented and successful people. Iconic actors, artists, musicians, writers, and athletes have achieved their levels of prominence because they are doing so many things right. Luck and innate ability can only explain so much. I can't hit a forehand like Roger Federer, but I certainly can learn a few things by watching him on the court.

The same principle applies to the business world. It may not be realistic to *compare* your company to Amazon, Apple, Facebook, and Google, but you can still learn a great deal from them and their platforms. And your business can benefit from these lessons. In a nutshell, these are the goals of this book.

> Aside from examining the platforms of Amazon, Apple, Facebook, and Google, this book profiles a number of smaller companies that have built impressive platforms.

THE STRUCTURE OF THIS BOOK

The Age of the Platform is organized into four parts. Part I provides the framework and background for the remainder of the book. It takes a look at the technological, societal, and economic trends and developments that have led to the emergence of the modern-day platform. A number of key trends and events have allowed Amazon, Apple, Facebook, and Google to build powerful platforms. Before examining each company and its platform, we need to consider the context in which it is operating.

Part II looks at today's great platforms and the companies behind them. We'll see how external parties such as customers, users, developers, partners, and vendors extend platforms' reach. The focus is on the Gang of Four. Besides providing brief histories of these organizations, Part II examines how they have created such transformative platforms—and why they are generating such incredible results. It shows that, by building powerful platforms, Amazon, Apple, Facebook, and Google have become admired and valuable companies. Part II explores how these companies benefit immensely from their platforms—*and of equal importance, allow their partners to benefit as well.* Moreover, companies don't build powerful platforms by doing only one thing—even if they do that thing really well.

Part III takes a step back. It synthesizes the lessons of the previous four chapters. It looks at the components, characteristics, benefits, and perils of the platforms. Part III concludes by providing lessons for building your own platforms.

Part IV looks at the powerful platforms of the future, provides a brief synopsis of the book, and boldly offers a few predictions.

WHAT WILL I LEARN BY READING THIS BOOK?

That is probably the burning question in your mind right now. You will gain a profound understanding of the importance of the platform. You'll learn how the Gang of Four—and other companies—is utilizing these ecosystems in all sorts of innovative ways.

> **"Give me the place to stand, and I shall move the earth."**
> —*Archimedes*

Granted, this knowledge alone will *not* enable your company to usurp Google in search. Although your company might sell more stuff *on* Amazon's platform, it will not sell more stuff *than* Amazon. Neither scenario is realistic, and I am not a fan of business books that make grandiose promises such as these. But this much I vow: After reading this book, you will know why platforms matter today more than ever. And you'll understand the importance of how platforms are changing business in many profound ways.

Let's go!

PART I
THE RISE
OF THE PLATFORM AGE

Part I provides the book's background and establishes its framework. It takes a look at the technological, societal, and economic trends and developments that have led to the emergence of the modern-day platform.

It examines why the platforms of Amazon, Apple, Facebook, and Google are so powerful. However, before looking at each company and its platform, we need to consider the context in which it operates.

Chapter One—The Internet: Where Are We Now?

Chapter Two—Platforms: Definitions, History, and Economics

ONE

The Internet: Where Are We Now?

L et's begin our journey with a high-level summary of the last three decades of what we now call the Internet.* To paraphrase the 1968 Virginia Slims ad, we've come a long way, baby. In relatively short periods of time, entire industries have been shattered. New ones have come and gone. These advancements and changes have been nothing less than astounding, causing seismic shifts in many areas of society beyond the business world. Moreover, each trend and development has brought us to where we are now: the Age of the Platform.

But we can only understand this new age—and how we arrived here—by first taking a look at where we have been. Let's start.

WEB 1.0 (1993 TO EARLY 2005)

> "The first rule of any technology used in a business is that automation applied to an efficient operation will magnify the efficiency. The second is the automation applied to an inefficient operation will magnify the inefficiency."
> —*Bill Gates*

In 1993, the National Center for Supercomputing Applications (NCSA) released Mosaic (soon to be rebranded as Netscape), the first web browser and the progenitor of the Internet. As the 1990s progressed, the Internet quickly gained traction. Early adopters

---

* The predecessor to the Internet was called the ARPANET (Advanced Research Projects Agency Network). ARPA was created by the United States Department of Defense during the Cold War.

took to creating their own primitive web pages, browsing exist-ing pages, and sending email and, later, instant messages (IMs). Netscape's initial public offering (IPO) in August 1995 served as a wake-up call to the world. In 1996, company co-founder Marc Andreessen found himself on the cover of *Time* magazine. The Internet had arrived.

By the late 1990s, many of the kinks of ecommerce had been ironed out. Companies such as Yahoo!, go.com, Excite@home, and America Online (AOL) evangelized the flexibility and power of web portals. These soon became all the rage, a fact reflected in these companies' astronomical valuations and stock prices. Beyond providing the ability to browse the web, portals let users easily view and customize their email, news, stock prices, informa-tion, weather, and entertainment. Finally, we had one-stop shopping.

The great Internet bubble had arrived. All kinds of startups launched, promising to remove friction and rewire every industry imaginable, including:

- ❏ Grocery delivery (Webvan)
- ❏ Government (govWorks, profiled in the Machiavellian 2001 documentary *Startup.com)*
- ❏ Branded fashion apparel (boo.com)
- ❏ Telephony (Vonage, one of the pioneers of Voice Over Internet Protocol [VOIP])

Google then changed the game with exponentially better search. As Chapter 6 will explain, a few years later, the company found a way to turn eyeballs and clicks into actual dollars—lots of them. And it wasn't just 20-something dot-com paper billionaires espousing the virtues of ecommerce. Consider the following quote from a February 2000 piece in the *Economist*:

> The Internet seems to be creating the possibility of a perma-nent worldwide bazaar in which no prices are ever fixed for long, all information is instantly available, and buyers and sell-ers spend their lives haggling to try to get the best deals.[5]

Boom! There Goes the Dynamite

By the early 2000s, early adoption of the Internet gave way to its eventual maturation. Because of tenuous business models and excessive hype, the vast majority of dot-coms had imploded by 2001. "New economy" evangelists were proven wrong. Employees at dead startups packed up their offices, and a few remaining companies (Amazon, eBay, Google, etc.) emerged as victors of round one of the Internet Age. Historians noted that the same thing has happened many times before. For instance, in the early 1900s, more than 2,000 firms produced one or more automobiles.[6] Those that couldn't compete with the largest manufacturers were eventually weeded out.

In the early days of the Internet, few people trusted websites to store their credit card information, hold their money, and pay their bills. Online banking was still considered risky. By the end of Web 1.0, however, much of the fear surrounding certain aspects of the Internet had abated. For millions of folks, it was no longer weird to buy things online. Ecommerce was here to stay. In 2005, the Pew Internet and American Life Project reported that 53 million people, or 44 percent of Internet users and one-quarter of all adults, used online banking. Those figures amounted to an increase of 47 percent compared to late 2002,[7] a trend that has continued. Today, more than 75 percent of all Americans pay at least some of their bills online.[8]

Let's now move to the second incarnation of the web, as it has either directly or indirectly brought about the powerful platforms of today.

WEB 2.0 (MID-2005 TO PRESENT)

The mid-2000s saw a new breed of web services begin to take root—many of which have enabled the Age of the Platform. To be sure, many businesses began to embrace web services to expedite the deployment of powerful new offerings. But make no mistake: Web 2.0 is all about consumers. They are leading the way.

At first, social networking websites such as MySpace, Friendster, and classmates.com allowed individuals to easily find and connect with one another. For the first time, people could share and exchange information *en masse*. Blogging exploded in popularity, buoyed by user-friendly sites such as LiveJournal, OpenDiary, WordPress, Blogger, and TypePad. YouTube allowed nontechnical folks to easily publish videos that ran the gamut, some of which "went viral" and attracted millions of views.

Over the past five years, we have seen many *revolutionary* (not evolutionary) changes. The rise of the platform is just one of them. Data storage and personal computers have continued to drop in price. Mobility has exploded and smartphones are nothing short of portable mini-computers. Free software has continued to proliferate. The advent and mass adoption of broadband and mobile technologies have enormous impacts on many aspects of contemporary life for both businesses and consumers. Ditto the explosion of social media and networking sites. In late 2010, Facebook surpassed mighty Google as the premier property on the web.[9] (We'll return to Faceboo frequently in this book.)

Regardless of the precise year in which this occurred, one thing is certain: Today we have firmly entered the second iteration of the web. Monikers such as *the social web* and *Web 2.0** quickly became common parlance in technology circles. It's clear that the days of *occasionally* using the Internet for simple email and web browsing are gone forever, looking almost quaint in comparison to today's cavalcade of activity on the Net. From a technology perspective, we are living in a vastly different world compared to just 10 years ago. It has been transformed by the Internet, which we are constantly using. The full promise of the web has finally arrived.

Social Revolutions and Citizen Journalists

One could write a very big book on just the geopolitical examples the world has seen during the first half of 2011. The near-constant

---

* Tim O'Reilly, founder of the eponymous O'Reilly Media, coined the term at the O'Reilly Media Web 2.0 conference in late 2004.

stream of information on Twitter caused the fall of dictatorships and civil unrest in Libya, Egypt, Iraq, and Tunisia.[10] Citizen journalists are now "reporting" major stories well before established news mediums, such as the US Airways plane with 155 passengers forced to land in the Hudson River outside of New York City.

Collaboration across borders means that organizations can access an entire planet of available and inexpensive human resources for a wide array of different projects. People can search many books previously only available in libraries (via Google Books). Blogging, podcasting, and online videos have taken off, giving anybody the ability to broadcast to the world.

The Consumerization of IT

> "I think there is a world market for maybe five computers."
> —*Thomas Watson, president of IBM, 1943*

In her 1998 book, *Where Wizards Stay Up Late: The Origins of the Internet,* Katie Hafner describes what was considered high-tech in the 1960s. Back then, few people actually worked on computers—and fewer still actually owned them. Those who conceived of the Internet worked on massive and very expensive mainframe computers in large government buildings. They could only connect via complicated programming. Computers just didn't talk to one another 50 years ago.

From a technological perspective (as well as social and economic ones), the 1960s seem quaint in comparison to today. Those same clunky mainframes contain fractions of the compute power of a modern-day smartphone. Aside from being exponentially more powerful thanks to Moore's Law,* computers as we know them are also less expensive and more useful. It should be no surprise, then, that they are much more prevalent.

---

* The basic rule states that the number of transistors on a chip doubles every 24 months. It has been the guiding principle of the high-tech industry since it was coined by Intel co-founder Gordon Moore in 1965. See *www.tinyurl.com/greatplatforms-9.*

Up until relatively recently, the vast majority of people used "technology," or at least the most advanced technologies, while at work. This is no longer the case. Long gone are the days in which one would only use a computer—or sophisticated technology in general—while on the clock. Today, technology of all kinds permeates the home, a trend that some have dubbed the *Consumerization of IT*, a term first popularized by Douglas Neal and John Taylor at CSC's Leading Edge Forum in 2001.

Blurring of the Lines: The Rise of the Prosumer

Generally speaking, the quality and power of technology at home has at least pulled even with technology at work—if not surpassed it. What's more, billions of people constantly use a wide array of devices and apps well after they leave the office. The distinction between "at home" and "at work" has blurred, if not become meaningless. One can just about work anywhere these days, spawning the terms *virtual* or *distributed companies*. And the very notion of a computer is changing before our eyes. Smartphones and tablets are replacing desktops and laptops as the primary means by which people connect to the Internet and do much of their work.

Today, the lines between consumer and business markets are very fuzzy. Amazon, Apple, Google, and others established themselves as not just consumer product and service companies. They all now offer business services as well—and have for some time. Even Facebook, through its business fan pages and applications, is no longer a pure consumer play.

Along these lines, we've seen the rise of the *prosumer*. The term has taken on multiple meanings—and not all of them are in synch. On TechCrunch, Duncan Riley defines the word as "a combination of producer and consumer that perfectly describe the millions of participants in the Web 2.0 revolution."[11] While some see it as a professional–consumer hybrid, it reflects a more active consumer. No longer is the average customer willing to wait for established brands and companies to "get with the times." Individuals are no longer passive; they are becoming more involved in the production of goods and services. This is why terms like *crowdsourcing* have gone mainstream.

Freemium

In 2006, *Wired* editor-in-chief Chris Anderson penned the best-selling book, *The Long Tail: Why the Future of Business Is Selling Less of More*. In it, he explains that unlimited shelf space allows even niche books, movies, albums, and other products to exist—and profitably. The digital revolution means that stores are no longer constrained by physical shelf space and inventory.

In July 2009, Anderson wrote an equally groundbreaking text. In *Free: The Future of a Radical Price*, Anderson reveals how many companies today are succeeding by, somewhat paradoxically, giving away their products and services. Lest you think that freemium is only for obscure companies, consider that (to varying extents) Google, Facebook, Apple, Pandora, Vimeo, Flickr, LinkedIn, Skype, and a bevy of others have embraced this revolutionary business model. In a nutshell, the logic behind freemium is twofold. Many users will enjoy the free and limited products and services. Given that, a respectable percentage of users will become customers— that is, they will upgrade to paid offerings.

At least that's the theory. Freemium is a risky gambit and whether an individual organization will ultimately survive by adopting the model is anybody's guess. To be sure, freemium is no silver bullet. First, as behavioral economists have discovered, consumers are more likely to use something if they've paid for it. Second, it doesn't work for every type of product, service, and company. Some companies have abandoned the freemium experiment. For instance, in April 2010, social networking site Ning announced that it was "killing off its free product, forcing existing free networks to either make the change to premium accounts or migrate their networks elsewhere."[12] Ning executives decided that the company should embrace a "less is more" strategy—that is, it would be better off with fewer paid *customers* than with a mob of unpaid users.

Abandoning freemium seems to have paid dividends for Ning, although the company is rumored to be shopping itself to potential buyers. In August 2011, Kara Swisher of All Things D observed that, "since its business shift a year ago…it has had 400 percent year-on-year revenue growth, going from 17,000 to more than 100,000 subscribers and with 60 million monthly active users."[13]

The Monetization Challenge

Freemium has intensified an already extremely competitive environment for many businesses. At one point or another, most Internet companies have struggled with turning clicks, eyeballs, and page views into actual revenue—and, ultimately, profits. The dot-com implosion weeded out companies with suspect business models, although some question today whether we're entering a new tech bubble. At the same time, though, Web 2.0 companies have also had to answer the same question for their investors, whether they are venture capital (VC) firms or angels: *How are you going to make money?*

Today, this simple question is often not easy to answer. As companies such as MySpace have shown, millions of users do not necessarily equate to millions of dollars. We'll see in Part II of the book how Facebook and Google have successfully overcome the challenges associated with indirect monetization.

The Digital Revolution

The dramatic changes brought about by the explosion of the Internet are difficult to understate. Many industries and companies were entirely unprepared. They hemmed, hawed, or completely missed the boat as their business models imploded. Relatively few companies immediately understood consumers' desire to "go digital." For instance, because it was late to the digital camera game, Kodak is now a shell of its former self. Travel agents as we knew them even 20 years ago are essentially extinct. And then there's the music industry, the quintessential case study in how *not* to adapt to a brave new world.

In his excellent 2009 book, *Ripped: How the Wired Generation Revolutionized Music*, Greg Kot details how the Recording Industry Association of America (RIAA) fought digital music services like Napster tooth and nail. Rather than offering a viable electronic alternative to their extremely lucrative compact discs (CDs), the RIAA sued individual consumers for copyright violation. To be fair, the RIAA wasn't alone here. Successful bands like Metallica faced tremendous heat for their "anti-fan" stances against piracy. Although in the end these entities were legally correct, they clearly lost the PR battle.

Today, music sales are a fraction of what they were even 10 years ago. David Goldman of CNN Money noted that "total revenue from U.S. music sales and licensing plunged to $6.3 billion in 2009, according to Forrester Research. In 1999, that revenue figure topped $14.6 billion."[14] Although reports vary, it is estimated that 40 songs are illegally downloaded for every one purchased legally. While Napster may no longer be the elephant in the room, it spawned myriad imitators. Today, BitTorrent—along with high-speed Internet connections—makes it remarkably easy to download illegal music, books, movies, and software applications. The future of movie theaters, as well as traditional books, bookstores, and CDs is also in doubt.

The Death of Old Media

On the television front, DVRs have allowed people to essentially pause live TV and skip bothersome commercials. This has enormous implications for how companies tell consumers about new products. And, lamentably, hallowed industries such as newspapers are on the verge of extinction because of sites such as Craigslist.

The deaths of many major newspapers serve as particularly instructive events. Not surprisingly, there's even a website devoted to the topic. Newspaper Death Watch[15] tracks the latest casualties under an "R.I.P." heading.

Even those that have weathered the storm have had to reinvent themselves—or face extinction. Stalwarts such as the *Wall Street*

Journal and the *New York Times* have experimented with different types of pay walls. Results have been mixed. Whether many people ultimately will pay for premium content is anyone's guess. (I have my doubts.) At the very least, it's an uncertain proposition in an era in which many people expect everything to be free. The bottom line is that people increasingly want to consume their own personalized content in an easy, integrated, and on-demand fashion.

Later in this book, we'll see how Amazon, Apple, Facebook, and Google have taken advantage of this trend. They have gained at the expense of newspapers, the RIAA, MySpace, Yahoo!, Microsoft, and other industries and companies slow to adapt to changing realities.

A Brave New (Mobile) World

Cell phones have made people reachable virtually everywhere at anytime. Cheap digital storage, WiFi, and smartphones equipped with digital cameras and recorders mean that people can broadcast as much of their lives as they want in real time. In his 2011 book, *The Third Screen: Marketing to Your Customers in a World Gone Mobile*, Chuck Martin writes about a new, "untethered" customer freed from the chains of TVs, desktops, and even laptops. She is capable of taking her very personalized computing experience with her wherever she goes and whenever she wants. This has enormous implications for marketers.

Powerful new tablet computers have brought *apps* into the vernacular. Relative to three years ago, today it is remarkably simple to create a mobile application. Sites such as BiznessApps[16] allow nontechnical folks to build mobile applications through a web-based interface in a matter of minutes. This will only continue.

Free and open source software development kits (SDKs) allow people to develop mobile websites and applications for specific devices and operating systems. Examples of SDKs include the

Windows 7 SDK, the Mac OS X SDK, and the iPhone SDK. More than 200 million people use Facebook every day via mobile devices.[17]

The Ease of Experimentation

One of my favorite axioms is "fast, cheap, and good: pick any two of the three." While I would argue that this still holds, these days, development can be remarkably fast and cheap. Never before has it been easier for companies of all sizes to experiment with new offerings. Consider that sites such as eLance[18] allow individuals and companies to easily connect with talented developers and build just about anything imaginable for reasonable prices. As marketing guru and bestselling author Seth Godin has remarked, even a site as ostensibly complicated as Groupon would be, at least from a technology perspective, relatively inexpensive to create—maybe $30,000. The genius of Groupon isn't the technology; *it's in the idea and benefits behind the technology.*

And as we'll see in Part II of the book, many companies and individuals are experimenting in many different ways. Never before has it been so easy to reach others via different platforms—and not just for large companies. Consider that author Gary Vaynerchuk held a contest to design the cover of his 2011 book, *The Thank You Economy*. He received hundreds of responses.

The Explosion in Content

While Web 1.0 allowed us to *view* content, the arrival of Web 2.0 lets us easily *create and distribute* professional-grade content. These days, anyone can create and share videos. You can be up and running with your own podcast or radio show in minutes using sites like BlogTalkRadio.[19] Even for the masses, creating physical books and ebooks has never been easier. Ditto movies. No longer do record companies control which music is released. Blogging makes reaching the world remarkably easy, at least in theory.

Not everyone appreciates this new democratized world. In his controversial 2007 book, *The Cult of the Amateur*, Andrew Keen argues for the return of the gatekeepers. His central contention is that publishers, record companies, and their ilk served a critical function in society: They set standards and ensured a certain level of professionalism. Thanks to the Internet and its bevy of tools, those standards have eroded.

Like many people, I don't entirely agree with Keen, but he's right on at least several points. For one, it's remarkably easy to bypass traditional gatekeepers these days. Also, not all content generated by "the masses" is particularly polished. Sometimes the prevalence of bad content can make it hard for customers to find the good stuff, even when assisted by sophisticated ratings systems from sites like Amazon and Netflix. (We'll see later in this book how the Gang of Four has been able to manage the content explosion through the use of powerful technologies.)

The Multihub Universe

> **"There is no reason anyone would want a computer in their home."**
> —*Ken Olsen, founder of Digital Equipment Corporation, 1977*

Fifteen years ago, when Microsoft ruled the world, it was all about the personal computer (PC). Today, PCs still matter, but they share the spotlight—as well as consumers' attention—with smartphones, increasingly smart TVs, a growing array of tablets, and other evolving electronic devices. Part II of the book explains how the most powerful platforms transcend multiple devices.

Maybe Ken Olsen was right after all—but just way ahead of his time. For many people, no longer is the PC the epicenter of the home computing experience.

The Cloud Goes Mainstream

Beyond specific events, Web 2.0 has given people the ability to access their music, videos, pictures, and contacts anywhere at any time through "the cloud." The rise of mobility and the untethered customer (mentioned earlier in this chapter) have accelerated the adoption of cloud-based services, such as streaming video and music.

Now, let's switch gears and explore some of the challenges posed by this massive technology explosion. In the words of noted technologist Melvin Kranzberg, "Technology is neither good nor bad; nor is it neutral."

IT'S NOT ALL ROSY: THE DOWNSIDES OF TECHNOLOGY GONE WILD

Let's be clear here: Technology is a net positive. Recent technological advancements have transformed society on many levels, and mostly for the better. I have a hard time finding common ground with those who refuse to acknowledge as much.

By the same token, it is foolish to ignore the significant economic, social, legal, privacy, and ethical problems often posed—or exacerbated—by these new technologies. At present, many people, groups, organizations, and institutions are simply incapable of dealing with the rapidity and enormity of these changes.

A Flat World and the New Normal

As discussed previously, over the last few years we have seen the deployment of incredibly powerful collaborative tools as well as an unprecedented increase in the speed of technology adoption. Against this backdrop, we now live in a flat world, to paraphrase journalist and author Tom Friedman's groundbreaking book, originally released in 2005. In *The World Is Flat*, Friedman persuasively argues that technology has leveled the playing field. Businesses now compete with one another *no matter where they are*. This does not augur well for niche businesses in "developed" countries, especially those that compete solely on the basis of cost. The arrival of the flat world means that many people with dated skills face bleak economic futures. Many businesses and employees will have to retool—and soon.

And then the Great Recession happened. The flat world was no longer a theoretical construct. It was here. Amidst the most severe economic crisis in generations, pundits began to talk about the *New Normal*, a phrase coined in May 2009 by Mohamed El-Erian and his colleagues at Pacific Investment Management Company (PIMCO). The New Normal instantly entered the zeitgeist. In an interview with *USA Today*, El-Erian explained what he meant:

> The basic premise is that we are in the midst of a major national and global realignment. The main catalyst was the financial crisis of 2008, but the underlying factors have been there for a while. The question is: What does the world look like post-realignment? The world is on a bumpy journey to a new destination and the New Normal.[20]

Author Seth Godin has written extensively about the challenges and opportunities of our day. The following text, taken from his blog, is particularly apropos:

> We're realizing that the industrial revolution is fading. The 80-year long run that brought ever-increasing productivity (and along with it, well-paying jobs for an ever-expanding middle class) is ending.
>
> For a while, politicians and organizations promised that things would get back to normal. Those promises aren't enough, though, and it's clear to many that this might be the new normal. In fact, it is the new normal.[21]

When the Great Recession finally ends, we are not returning to the simpler times of the 2000s, much less the 1950s. We had better get used to an era of near-constant change and ubiquitous global competition.

The Erosion of the Local Advantage

The flat world and the new normal mean that widespread disintermediation is taking place right now—and has been for quite some time. Consider a few examples.

Accountants in India

American accountants used to feel safe, in part because it took them years to understand the nuances and rules of the byzantine U.S. tax code. Beyond intimate knowledge, accountants' jobs have historically been safe for another reason. No sane American citizen would send her sensitive financial information overseas to be analyzed by people who didn't even speak the language, much less understand complicated terms like *itemized deductions*. For Jane Q. Public, it was worth paying $2,000 to have her taxes done right every year. Why risk an IRS audit?

Now Jane can have her cake and eat it too. Foreign tax professionals who understand the U.S. tax code can accurately do her taxes and save Jane $1,000 in the process. It's happening right now and has been for some time. In fact, as many as 360,000 U.S. tax returns were prepared in India in 2006, according to a report by Pune-based ValueNotes, a leading provider of business intelligence and research.[22] Why would this trend abate?

This is bad news for people like my friend Lenny. Now in his early 60s, he has run a pretty successful accounting practice for the past 30 years. He doesn't "do" the Internet. So close to retirement, he follows the tried and true maxim, "If it ain't broke, don't fix it."*

Lenny has spent years building his small business. He is counting on the loyalty of his current and longtime customers to help him weather the current economic storm. In a few years, he will retire to Florida. Because he is so close to retirement, he will probably survive the globalization of the economy. But what about accountants who are 10 years younger?

Let's return to Jane. She doesn't have a strong relationship with a particular accounting firm or individual accountant. What happens when she tells friends or colleagues that she used an Indian

---

* At a fundamental level, many people fight change, especially after reaching a certain age. My grandfather smoked two packs of cigarettes per day despite his doctors telling him for years to quit. He didn't care and lived until he was 92.

firm? What happens if they go that route as well—and are just as happy with the results as Jane is? What if, no matter how much U.S. consumers like the idea of "buying American," the cost savings become too much to ignore?

People like Lenny are a dying breed.

The Zappos Effect

For decades, local shoe stores had it made. They even survived the explosion of ecommerce sites. Sure, from the inception of the web, some traditional retail companies such as Lands' End embraced the notion of selling clothes online, but shoes just seemed too personal and difficult to view and buy on a website. Unlike CDs or books or pet supplies, no one would ever want to buy shoes online. Or so the thinking went.

Then along came Zappos. Founder Tony Hsieh turned the entire local shoe store model on its head. He realized that local stores were actually at a major disadvantage. Stores meant managing multiple real estate leases, staffing issues and costs, inventory management headaches, and a bevy of other problems. He started Zappos because he knew that he could use the Internet to circumvent those problems. To boot (pun intended), he threw in a liberal return policy and killer customer service.

Hsieh's idea was crazy but it worked—really well. Hsieh sold his company to Amazon for nearly $1 billion in mid-2009.[23]

Zappos illustrates a critical point: Today, competition can come from just about anywhere at any time. No business is completely safe, especially in the long-term. Being local no longer guarantees that you can count on patronage from folks around the corner. This erosion of a local advantage is huge. It's one of the reasons that Groupon and LivingSocial are currently enjoying so much success—and why Google, Facebook, and countless others are trying to get in on the action.

The Futility of Planning

"The reason that everybody likes planning is that nobody has to do anything."
—Jerry Brown

Our world moves too fast these days for most businesses to follow anything resembling a five-year plan. I chuckle when I think of senior executives in large companies acting as if they can predict the future with some degree of certainty. Oppression in Egypt continued essentially unabated for decades. Then, thanks to Twitter, the Internet, and mobile phones, the dictatorship fell in a matter of weeks. Who predicted that one?

I have always been conflicted about the word "plan." Perhaps because of the years I spent working on large-scale IT projects, I never agreed with the level of certitude that supposed experts would ascribe to different aspects of complex projects. While I recognize and firmly agree with the need for estimates, how can anyone know precisely how long a task or event would take and how much it would cost?

Today, nobody knows.

Unpredictable Profits

For years, companies such as General Electric (GE) have faced accusations that they have managed their earnings.[24] That is, they would allegedly employ a wide variety of accounting tricks to produce a steady income stream. Wall Street would reward these companies because they showed consistent revenues and profit over a long period of time.

Or so the thinking went.

Accounting shenanigans aside, it has never been more difficult for companies to predict their performance and profits. Faced with increasing global competition and a deluge of technology, how can even company insiders possibly know how a business will perform at the beginning of any year? We live in chaotic times that make it nearly impossible to predict how a company is going to do. In publicly traded organizations, company officers often struggle to provide guidance to analysts on earnings.

Today, the exceptions prove the rule. Consider Oracle, an enormous enterprise software and service company. It posted nearly $27 billion in revenue in 2010.[25] Like any company, its profitability ebbs and flows. Oracle closes new deals every year—and loses other clients to competition and increasingly viable open source alternatives. But unlike many companies, Oracle has a greater degree of predictability vis-à-vis its revenue and profits.

Although it won't divulge profit margins by service and offering, much of the company's revenue stems from lucrative annual maintenance and support contracts. At least in the short-term, Oracle knows that this revenue isn't going anywhere. Oracle's software isn't cheap, and not surprisingly, most of the company's customers are quite large and relatively conservative. As such, they don't want to rock the boat with their back office systems, customer relationship management (CRM) applications, and powerful databases. Of course, Oracle knows this and in 2009 raised the prices for its support programs.

In other words, Oracle has the benefit of relatively predictable profits through *vendor lock-in* and multiyear contracts. Before Oracle starts each new fiscal year, its senior leadership has at least a ballpark idea, if not a very good one, about how much money it will make.

Of course, on a number of levels, your business is probably nothing like Oracle. Even Google faces much more uncertainty vis-à-vis profits, as its AdWords customers can easily manipulate (read: lower) their weekly, monthly, and annual spends. AdWords does not require rigid long-term contracts. If it did, it never would have exploded to begin with.

The underlying point is that most businesses these days operate under a cloud of uncertainty. Relatively few enjoy any degree of revenue and profit predictability. Hopefully, your clients like working with you, but are they locked in? Probably not. Should a competitor come along with (significantly) lower rates or a better product, are you confident that your clients will stick with you?

Sexting and the Death of Privacy

Not all of the changes sparked by technology are good ones. For instance, it's now easier than ever for just about anyone to engage in—or be affected by—inappropriate behavior. In June 2011, New York Congressman Anthony Weiner had to resign amid a salacious scandal. Weiner sent a link via Twitter to an online photo showing his erect penis concealed by briefs to a 21-year-old woman in Bellingham, Washington. In April 2009, 18-year-old Phillip Alpert of Orlando, Florida, was convicted of "sexting" a naked picture sent to him by his 16-year-old girlfriend. He was sentenced to five years in prison and required to register as a sex offender.[26]

Some have asked if we are seeing the death of privacy. In March 2009, the Philadelphia Eagles of the National Football League (NFL) fired stadium operator Dan Leone for posting disparaging remarks about the organization on Facebook. Somewhat ironically, Marissa Anastasio-Leone started a Facebook group intent on making the Eagles give her husband his job back. (We'll see throughout this book the unique opportunities and challenges presented by our web-centric world, including the politics of platforms, covered in Chapter 7.)

Security continues to be an issue. In August 2007, Albert Gonzalez was charged with stealing more than 130 million credit card numbers, the largest hack of its kind to date. In April 2009, Philip Markoff used the popular website Craigslist to solicit the services of model Julissa Brisman, whom he then murdered.[27] Markoff allegedly attacked at least two more women he met through Craigslist.

Faced with growing privacy concerns, Google had to blur the faces of individuals on its Google Maps application.[28] Google has become so powerful that even nonhackers can discover intimate details about almost anyone. For instance, in preparing for a 2005 interview with Google's then-CEO Eric Schmidt, it took CNET reporter Elinor Mills all of 30 minutes to discover Schmidt's home address, net worth, political fundraising activities, and hobbies. For all of his evangelizing about the value of readily accessible information, Schmidt was not amused.

And this was back in 2005! Imagine what Mills could dig up on Schmidt today. Social media is evolving in completely unexpected ways. We are sharing more information—and more *personal* information—faster and more frequently than ever, the ramifications of which fall well beyond the scope of this book. Books, articles, and TV shows lament the death of privacy.

Constant Connectivity: Are We Ever Off the Grid?

Thanks to smartphones, we can all be connected all the time. In fact, many of us are forced to go "off the grid"—the implication being that we're always online and connected. Professional sports organizations such as the NBA and NFL have actually had to create and enforce policies surrounding athletes' use of Twitter during games. Some people text so much that the term *texting intervention* has actually entered the vernacular. In fact, in 2005, a man in India texted 182,689 messages in a single month.

SUMMARY AND CONCLUSION

This chapter has provided a very brief synopsis of the technological advancements over the past 20 years—and many of their intended and unintended repercussions. It has laid out the good, the bad, and the ugly.

Now that we have provided the requisite backdrop, we are ready to move on. The next chapter defines the *platform*, introduces it as a new business model, and discusses the economics behind it.

TWO

....

Platforms: Definitions, History, and Economics

Our journey continues with a detailed discussion of the rise of the platform. This chapter provides a definition of the platform, develops it as a business model, and considers its historical context. Platforms have always been highly dependent on the available and affordable technologies of their times, something certainly true today. Finally, the chapter compares and contrasts powerful platforms with traditional monopolies.

THE NEED FOR PLATFORMS

Why are platforms more important today than 10 years ago? Why have platforms become almost irreplaceable parts of our lives? These are essential questions to answer before going much further.

Today, we are constantly connected—and have to consciously decide to go "off the grid." We spend most of our waking hours looking at some type of screen—more than 8.5 hours on any given day, according to a 2009 study by the Council for Research Excellence.[29] That number will only increase, as smartphones improve and ereaders like the Kindle continue to replace physical books and magazines. Cloud computing has given us the ability to access our data and apps wherever we are; no longer are we chained to desktops. Tablets such as the iPad mean that we can take our digital lives with us everywhere.

If the changes wrought by technology were temporary, then perhaps they could be easily dismissed as flashes in the pan. However, technology's march is certainly not abating; in fact, it is intensifying. For this very reason, people need simple, secure, powerful, integrated, and user-friendly ways to create, consume, purchase, share, and manage their content. They need to connect with others—easily and often. For all of these reasons, they need platforms.

DEFINING THE PLATFORM

Inasmuch as this is a book about platforms, it is now time to formally define this book's most important concept. The *Oxford English Dictionary* offers four definitions of the word *platform:*

1. A raised level surface on which people or things stand.
2. The declared policy of a political party or group.
3. A very thick sole on a shoe.
4. (Computing) A standard for the hardware of a computer system, which determines the kinds of software it can run.

Although the term has recently entered the business zeitgeist, it is hardly a new concept. Types of past platforms include:

❏ **Physical and infrastructure:** Highways, airports, and railroad systems allow people to physically meet.
❏ **Technology:** Landlines, cell phones, and the Internet allow people to communicate with one another.
❏ **Media:** Newspapers, radio, and television allow people to consume content—and advertisers to reach the masses.

At a very high level, platforms simply allow people to reach and connect with one another and obtain information. Through platforms, businesses can connect with current and prospective customers. Consumers can purchase goods and services. Governments can connect with their citizenry.

This text defines a platform as an extremely valuable and powerful ecosystem that quickly and easily scales, morphs, and incorporates new features (called *planks* in this book), users, customers, vendors,

(continued)

and partners. Today, the most powerful platforms are rooted in equally powerful technologies—and their intelligent usage. In other words, they differ from traditional platforms in that they are not predicated on physical assets, land, and natural resources.

The most vibrant platforms embrace third-party collaboration. The companies behind these platforms seek to foster symbiotic and mutually beneficial relationships with users, customers, partners, vendors, developers, and the community at large.

Even though a great deal of potential commercial appeal and applications inhere in them, platforms do not exist simply as a means for companies to hawk their wares. At their core, platforms today are primarily about consumer utility and communications.

Finally, because consumers' tastes change much faster than businesses' tastes, platforms today must adapt very quickly—or face obsolescence.

Platforms comprise individual components, features, products, and services—collectively referred to in this book as planks. Put simply, without planks, there are no platforms. We'll cover planks in much more depth later in this book. For now, suffice it to say two things. First, useful and popular planks give platforms their power. Second, today a company's platform need not consist of only its own tools, applications, and innovations. On the contrary, platforms can easily and quickly integrate extremely powerful planks from the outside—that is, developers, partners, prosumers, and other third parties.

THE PLATFORM AS A BUSINESS MODEL

As we'll see throughout this book, the platform is becoming one of the most important business models of the new millennium—and with good reason. Buoyed by the success of Amazon, Apple, Facebook, and Google, many exciting new companies are hitching their wagons on the platform. In fact, the stated goal of many startups today, at incubators such as Y Combinator,[30] is to do one of the following:

❏   Become a platform, preferably a powerful one.

❏   Build a useful and complementary *plank*—that is, a product, service, or community that integrates with an existing platform, or better yet, *platforms*.

But make no mistake: The platform is not the exclusive purview of startups or small companies. Many large businesses are trying to reinvent themselves along platform lines. They are adopting more collaborative business models, embracing new partnerships and ecosystems, and building their own platforms and planks.

So, how is the platform today different from that of yesteryear? Table 2.1 represents the Age of the Platform across a number of key dimensions.

Attributes	Pre-Platform Age	Platform Age
Target Market	Predominantly business-oriented. Planks used in an office by employees on a single device (PC).	Both business- *and* consumer-oriented. Planks used everywhere by everyone on multiple devices.
Ecosystems	Stable. Primarily comprising relatively few arms-length resellers and strategic partners.	Vibrant, robust, dynamic. Comprising individual developers and small partners. Partnerships and communities quickly form, change, and dissolve.
Collaboration	"We'll buy you or we'll crush you." Fixed pie. Competition-based.	"We want to work with you." Grow the pie together. Cooperation-based.
Technology	Mostly closed source or proprietary, sometimes available via expensive licensing.	Mostly open source and less proprietary. Often takes form of a free development kit or an API.
Innovation	Top down. Internal or via acquisition. Usually slow.	Bottom up. External or partner-based or -assisted. Much faster.
Marketing	Centralized single company campaigns, rigidly coordinated and controlled.	Comarketing and partner-driven campaigns. More independent, organic, and decentralized.

Table 2.1: Dimensions of the Platform Age

Note the general nature of the descriptions in Table 2.1; they certainly do not apply to every company, product, service, and industry. For instance, it's not as if Microsoft never penetrated consumer markets. And Apple isn't always terribly collaborative, as executives from Adobe Systems will attest, a subject discussed more in Chapters 4 and 11.

What does the platform look like as a business model? How exactly does it generate revenue and ultimately profits? And how do platforms grow and add more planks? The answers to these questions are represented visually in Figure 2.1.

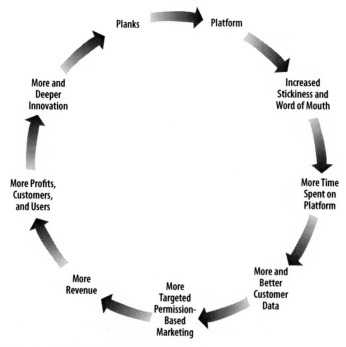

Figure 2.1: The Platform As a Business Model

As Figure 2.1 illustrates, a platform starts with planks; a platform has no value without them. For instance, people had never heard of Google until word spread that it was a superior search engine. By the same token, if Google were a one-trick pony and only offered search, people couldn't use it for anything else.

We'll explore platform components and characteristics in more depth in Chapter 7.

Platforms and Network Effects

In 1975, we saw the advent of the fax machine. As it became more popular, it became more much valuable. Ditto the introduction of telephones, stock exchanges, and even infrastructure investments. With respect to the latter, consider that the U.S. government spent untold billions of dollars building the national highway system because it would spur a great deal of commerce. This would not have happened if only a small fraction of the population drove on these new roads.

Each of the above is an example of a *network effect*, and network effects are crucial in understanding the power of the platform. Like fax machines and roads, platforms become *exponentially* more popular as they become more popular. Reflexively, platform popularity begets more popularity, planks, value, and power. Platforms are subject to—and benefit from—network effects. For instance, as we'll see in Chapter 5, because of network effects, it was actually easier for Facebook to add its second million users than its first million.

PLATFORMS AND TECHNOLOGY: THEN AND NOW

While mind-boggling at the time, the technology of yester-year was simply incomparable to the technology of today. For instance, the Ford Model T was a technological and manufacturing marvel in 1908. Today, however, it couldn't hold a candle to my relatively modest Acura 2010 TSX, much less a $100,000 luxury car with a supercharged engine and every conceivable bell and whistle.

The Model T and my Acura TSX are both cars, but that's where the similarities end.

And the same holds true when comparing the historical platforms to those of today. No, its notion isn't new by any stretch. However, today's most powerful platforms differ from their predecessors—and not just in terms of technology. In the words of Vinnie Mirchandani, founder of the technology consulting firm Deal Architect and author of the 2010 book, *The New Polymath: Profiles in Compound-Technology Innovations*:

> Every successful technology platform has had a thick application catalog around it. You can even go back to the 1980s when IBM introduced minicomputers such as the AS/400. In the end, though, customers always buy applications, not base technology. This hasn't changed. Compared to thirty years ago, the difference today is twofold. First, AppStores and ecosystems are being fueled by entire communities consisting of hundreds of thousands of mom and pop stores and entrepreneurs. Second, apps today are priced to sell billions of copies via high-speed downloads. The sheer scale is unprecedented.[31]

Mirchandani echoes Eric Schmidt's sentiments referenced in the Introduction. Today, technology-based platforms are much more powerful than ever—in part because computers are faster, broadband and mobility have exploded, the Internet has evolved and matured, and we have become more connected than ever.

Can and Must

Part II of this book explains in depth how the platforms of Amazon and Apple *can* meet a diverse set of customers' purchasing and entertainment needs—and the needs of millions of other consumers. Users *can* do many different things on the Facebook platform beyond poking their high school classmates. Through the Google platform, millions *can* compose email messages; listen to music; make phone calls; do research; make purchases; create web pages, web-based surveys, and spreadsheets; and do about 100 other things.

Of course, we should never mistake *can* for *must*. We consumers don't have to buy anything on Amazon, much less everything. Despite its robust catalog, Apple's iTunes does not sell every song customers want. Some people choose not to use Facebook. And no one has to use Google Sites[32] to build web pages or YouTube to upload videos. The point is that anyone can—and many do. (We'll cover much more about these companies in Part II of the book.)

Platforms, Different Eras, and the Role of Technology

It's often difficult comparing companies across eras, especially when those comparisons involve the most advanced technology of their day. In looking at the most important platforms of today, we must analyze the Gang of Four within the appropriate historical contexts. To paraphrase James A. Baldwin, we are trapped in history and history is trapped in us.

With that out of the way, let me repeat a point made on page xxi: Amazon, Apple, Facebook, and Google are not objectively "better" platforms and companies than their predecessors, such as IBM, Microsoft, and AT&T. That second group of companies (and others) built the most powerful platforms *of their times*. Foolish is the person who forgets those last three words. Compared to years past, the technology of today is better, more user-friendly, and cheaper by orders of magnitude. It should be no surprise that the same can be said about the platforms of today.

To be sure, powerful technology enables powerful platforms, but it's not as if Jeff Bezos embraced cloud computing in 1988—or even 1995. He did not conceive of the Kindle when no other company was using the Internet. Even if he had conjured up the idea, these tools weren't commercially available, nor were they affordable. We are all creatures of our environments.

At the same time, though, we shouldn't minimize the contributions and foresight of Amazon, Apple, Facebook, and Google either. Even with sufficiently powerful technology, platforms are certainly not easy to build—and maintain. The intelligent use of existing technology has almost always been a necessary but insufficient condition for success in business. Put simply, good tech doesn't make up for bad management, lack of creativity, ill-advised mergers and acquisitions, poor execution, and the like.

With the necessary background out of the way, here's the bottom line. Platforms today are more important and powerful than their predecessors for several reasons. Previous platforms:

❏ Did not—*and could not*—introduce new planks nearly as fast.
❏ Were not nearly as easy—or as fun—to use. They did not attract passionate followings.
❏ Did not embrace partnerships and collaboration as much.
❏ Maybe most important, did not—and again, *could not*—provide the same level of integration.

Integration here is especially critical. Platforms allow consumers and businesses to do many different things while under one umbrella. At a minimum, platforms have obviated the need for many standalone devices, websites, and services.

For the harried people struggling to manage their increasingly chaotic lives as discussed in Chapter 1, platforms offer tremendous and extremely valuable convenience. Perhaps above all, platforms allow people to save a great deal of time.

Two additional disclaimers are in order here. First, integration and convenience alone don't butter the biscuit. As mentioned above, platforms have to provide for useful and user-friendly experiences—otherwise, they will not be used. That has not changed.

Second, not all platforms are created equal—and they never have been. Some are much more powerful, popular, and valuable than others.

POWERFUL PLATFORMS VS. MONOPOLIES

Now that we have established the definition of the platform, it's time to ask some important historical and economic questions:

- ❑ Are Apple, Amazon, Facebook, and Google simply modern-day monopolies?
- ❑ Are these companies just high-tech versions of *vertically* and *horizontally integrated* companies?
- ❑ Is the Gang of Four really following a new business model?
- ❑ If not, then why not?

These are all fair questions. Let's look at them.

The Robber Barons and Traditional Monopolies

> **"Power is my mistress. I have worked too hard at her conquest to allow anyone to take her away from me."**
> —*Napoleon Bonaparte*

Let's dust off a few tried-and-true economic principles. The *Merriam-Webster Dictionary* defines a monopoly as the "exclusive ownership through legal privilege, command of supply, or concerted action."[33] Historically, conglomerates have achieved monopolies through one of two means: horizontal and vertical integration. A complete discussion of each is certainly not warranted here. Suffice it to say that each method is based on complete control, whether it's of entire production processes (vertical) or entire markets (horizontal).

Horizontal and vertical integration will forever be associated with robber barons, such as steel magnate Andrew Carnegie, oil tycoon John D. Rockefeller, and railroad kingpin Jay Gould, men who epitomized the ruthless businessmen of their generations. If they couldn't acquire their competitors, they would simply squeeze them out. Embracing partners and mutual gain were largely foreign concepts to the robber barons. Back then, companies didn't grow via collaboration; it was kill or be killed.

Despite their charitable and philanthropic endeavors toward the end of their lives, the robber barons were utterly cutthroat. They proved that a single company could dominate a market, at least as long as that company controlled the right product. Consider oil for a moment. The transportation costs alone (and time required to deliver the product) deterred many would-be competitors. As a result, Standard Oil could get away with bloody murder—and it usually did. The demand for oil and steel was *inelastic*, in the parlance of economists. There just weren't too many substitutes for either one.

Horizontal and vertical integration can be quite dangerous and anti-competitive. Proponents of government intervention often point out the pernicious effects of monopolies on key markets, prices, and industries. Examples include steel and oil (vertical) and the consolidation of major media properties (horizontal). That doesn't mean that reaching a position of market dominance has been easy. In fact, nothing could be further from the truth.

BARRIERS TO ENTRY

The robber barons did not have the monopoly on monopolies (pun intended). More recent examples of *de facto* monopolies include large corporations such as AT&T, IBM, and Microsoft—although their company lawyers have spent tens of thousands of hours arguing those very assertions in response to lawsuits.

Whether a particular company has had a monopoly at any given point has always been an issue for the courts to decide. Those cases have been argued *ad infinitum*, and there's no point in debating them here. It is important to point out, however, that large companies with significant clout have all historically benefited from what economists call *barriers to entry*. The term means that market conditions effectively prevent meaningful competition, enhance the pricing power of existing companies, and reduce competitive behavior.

For example, let's say you and I meet on an Amtrak train and aren't happy with its level of service. We consider ourselves pretty industrious and decide to start our own private railroad company. We have great ideas, tremendous energy, and even some seed money. But the deck is still enormously stacked against us.

Existing behemoths have a vested interest in seeing us fail. If Simon Railroad has any success at all (which is incredibly unlikely), existing railroads would try to crush us by hook or by crook. If that didn't work and our company grew by leaps and bounds, our competitors would probably lobby the government about why it ought to be shut down.

The same can be said about competing with companies such as General Electric. It would be very difficult for us to start a major conglomerate with massive engines, plastics, and capital divisions. It's just too expensive, time consuming, and filled with regulatory hurdles.

Today, physical barriers to entry are still significant in the bricks-and-mortar world. But people are starting more *virtual* businesses than ever. Consider Zappos, discussed in the previous chapter. Setting up an Internet-based shop has never been easier and cheaper. Deploying email, productivity, and customer relationship management (CRM) used to require considerable technical know-how and great expense. Building websites used to be the same way. Today, these are remarkably easy and inexpensive to do.

TYPES OF TRADITIONAL MONOPOLIES

The term *monopoly* is a catch-all. Geographic monopolies stem from location-based advantages, such as a single grocery store operating in a remote area. Some companies are granted government monopolies in which they maintain exclusive permission for running water to local municipalities. These two types of monopolies are not terribly controversial.

Then there are natural monopolies, defined as "situations in which economies of scale can only be achieved under a monopoly rather than under a situation of perfect competition. This was applied to some of the nationalized industries such as electricity." [34] The very notion of a natural monopoly is quite contentious.

Adam D. Thierer of the CATO Institute, a libertarian think tank, disputes the natural monopoly. In his article, "Unnatural Monopoly: Critical Moments in the Development of the Bell System Monopoly," Thierer writes:

> For many decades, economic textbooks have held up the telecommunications industry as the ideal model of natural monopoly. A natural monopoly is said to exist when a single firm is able to control most, if not all, output and prices in a given market due to the enormous entry barriers and economies of scale associated with the industry. More specifically, a market is said to be naturally monopolistic when one firm can serve consumers at lower costs than two or more firms (Spulber 1995: 31). For example, telephone service traditionally has required laying an extensive cable network, constructing numerous call switching stations, and creating a variety of support services, before service could actually be initiated. Obviously, with such high entry costs, new firms can find it difficult to gain a toehold in the industry. Those problems are compounded by the fact that once a single firm overcomes the initial costs, their average cost of doing business drops rapidly relative to newcomers. [35]

Whether you agree with Thierer's argument probably hinges on your political leanings. However, it's hard to dispute the notion that natural monopolies have historically relied on high entry costs—that is, barriers to entry.

PLATFORMS ARE NOT MONOPOLIES—NATURAL OR OTHERWISE

On all sorts of levels, today's world is dramatically different than the world of the erstwhile robber barons—and even the heyday of Ma Bell in the mid-to-late 20th century. Of course, some things haven't changed. For example, turn on the news if you doubt that oil is still incredibly important. But how many "non-oil" companies today have the kind of reach and pricing power that Standard Oil and their ilk had in the late 19th century? Not many; oil is the exception that proves the rule. This begs the question: Are Amazon, Apple, Facebook, and Google the Carnegie Steels and Standard Oils of today?

The answer is *no*. To be sure, the Gang of Four has created extremely robust platforms. However, these platforms have not resulted in monopolies, at least in the traditional sense of the term.* The remainder of this chapter explains why.

Pricing Power

First, let's discuss for a moment the general ability of individual companies today to set their prices. With few exceptions, technology and the Internet mean that most companies' margins are under constant pressure. (As we saw in Chapter 1, some businesses even have to compete with free products.) For every company like Apple, with its 40 percent gross profit margin,[36] many more are getting by with single-digit margins—what economists would typically call *normal* profits.

Over the past 15 years, globalization and the Internet have eroded, if not eliminated, the ability for almost every company to make *super-normal profits*, especially in the long-term. Thanks to the Internet and the explosion of available information, today it's extremely easy for consumers with computers, Internet access, and a modicum of web savvy to find the lowest possible prices for just about any product or service. If I think that a book or CD or DVD is too expensive on Amazon, then I can turn to eBay or another site. Don't like what the local car dealer is charging for a 2011 Acura TSX or a BMW 325xi? No problem. You can go to edmunds.com[37] and research to your heart's content. Looking for a deal on a random

---

* It's interesting to note that some believe Apple has become a *monopsonist*—the one buyer that can control an entire market. See *http://tinyurl.com/3e8dqyg*.

product? Consider overstock.com. And let's not forget that many products are available for free as illegal versions. Music, movies, TV shows, ebooks, and other digital products come to mind.

And if you don't have a proper computer? Or you live in a developing nation? Just use a mobile device. The massive rise in cell phone usage has dramatically increased the penetration of the web.

Competition Is Everywhere

Second, let's return to the topics of technology and barriers to entry. Anyone can start an online bookstore or social network relatively easily. For the most part, the robber barons did not have to deal with competition from other industrialized nations, much less developing ones.

Our frictionless global economy means that U.S.-based companies such as Facebook and Google must contend with competition from *everywhere,* including companies based in emerging power-houses like China, India, Brazil, and Russia. In fact, those countries may offer significant advantages by virtue of lower labor costs and more favorable tax laws. (Of course, the Gang of Four capitalizes on those advantages both directly and indirectly as well.)

Elastic Demand and Necessary Evils

Demand for oil and steel was pretty inelastic 100 years ago—and remains so today. Can the same be said about a social network or a search engine? You may prefer to search the Internet with Google, but you would be able to function if it was down.

Economists often talk about *elasticity of demand*—that is, how responsive consumers are to changes in price. Elastic demands are extremely price sensitive. If the price of a Big Mac increases by 50 percent, people will buy more Whoppers. But if the same happens with gasoline, what are you going to do?

This notion of elasticity of demand has always been inextricably linked to a company's monopolistic power, especially in the short-term. Very powerful companies with significant market clout can survive events that less powerful companies cannot. For instance, Exxon is still an extremely formidable company despite the *Valdez* fiasco, and BP will survive the Deepwater Horizon explosion. Why? As horrible as these events were, as a society, we haven't been able to rid ourselves of our dependence on oil. By way of contrast, AOL did not do anything nearly as objectionable as Exxon and BP, yet today it is essentially irrelevant because we grew tired of dial-up connections and other companies surpassed their offerings. Or consider Microsoft. Learning how to use a new operating system (OS) is often much easier than finding a reasonably powerful electric car—though I hope that changes soon. Apple's iPads and iPhones might be cool, but we don't truly *need* them—and there are legitimate alternatives to each.

Technology and the Need to Keep Up

As we saw in the previous chapter, the paces of innovation and technological change are orders of magnitude faster today than they were in the 19th century. The word *frenetic* comes to mind. From this standpoint, we live in times incomparable to a century ago. Established technology platforms have fallen from grace because they have failed to keep up with consumer tastes, priced their products too high, and refused to embrace the most current technologies.

But are Exxon and BP using the most current technologies in drilling for oil? Many environmentalists doubt it, and how would we know if they are? It doesn't matter anyway. If their methods are inefficient or antiquated, then they will, like the oil companies of years past, simply pass their costs along to consumers.

Amazon, Apple, Facebook, and Google don't have the luxury of lagging. They are facing more elastic demand for their products, as discussed in the prior section. As such, they cannot be complacent and expect to maintain their positions as market leaders. The same cannot be said about monopolies—either then or now.

Levels of Hatred

> **"Competition is a sin."**
> —John D. Rockefeller

As we'll see in Part II, Amazon, Apple, Facebook, and Google do not always play nice. However, they generally don't attempt to quash real and potential partners like Rockefeller and Carnegie did—or most recently, Bill Gates. Often, the Gang of Four call these individuals and companies *partners* and work with them so everyone wins. This is a critical distinction.

Back in their day, the vast majority of politicians, journalists, labor unions, customers, and competitors alike truly hated Rockefeller, Carnegie, and the powerful, merciless companies they spawned. Think for a minute about the enormity of getting those disparate parties to agree on anything. The term *robber barons* is anything but flattering. In fact, in 1880, the tabloid *New York World* described Standard Oil as "the most cruel, impudent, pitiless, and grasping monopoly that ever fastened upon a country," according to Grant Segall's book, *John D. Rockefeller: Anointed with Oil*. Not exactly high praise.

I want to tread carefully here because my opinions are hardly universal. To be sure, Amazon, Apple, Facebook, and Google individually and collectively face many detractors*—and not just one another. It's not as if they have perfect track records over their histories. I have met and read about people with massive axes to grind against each company. In some cases, these gripes were justifiable. Despite this, many if not most of these companies' customers and users truly enjoy their products and services. While the reasons for these love affairs vary, at a high level, their offerings make their customers' and users' lives easier, more efficient, more fun, and better in some important way. Call it the *enjoyment factor*.

---

* In fact, Facebook made a 2011 *Business Insider* list of the top 19 most hated companies. See *http://tinyurl.com/geatplatforms-6*.

As a result, consumers do not vilify the Gang of Four to the same extent as modern-day behemoths such as Wal-Mart and BP. And, historically, it's hard to put Amazon, Apple, Facebook, and Google in the same boat as reviled companies of years past like Carnegie Steel and Standard Oil. Consider Apple for a moment. Many customers use the words *cult* and *love* in relation to Apple—and I'm one of them. And then there are the Apple partners and vendors who have to pay 30 percent royalties. This number may be on the high side, but the vast majority of Apple partners *voluntarily* continue to submit books, products, and apps. Ditto Amazon. Partners realize that they benefit a great deal from these symbiotic relationships.

Price Discrimination and the Death of Local

Rockefeller segmented markets to maximize profit and keep the competition at bay. Doesn't the Gang of Four have the technology to isolate customers and theoretically charge more in certain areas than others? Yes, but the Internet and today's competitive environment mean that customers can easily look and buy elsewhere if they feel they're being gouged. In fact, comparison sites such as mysimon.com make this even easier.

But there's a different type of price discrimination going on here, one that is more consumer-oriented and more democratic. The Gang of Four does not charge the same price for all of its products everywhere—nor should it. For instance, the value of a Google keyword is highly contextual and location-specific. It has no "absolute" value and *shouldn't* cost the same everywhere and at every time. Not too many people are looking to buy air conditioners in Alaska in December—and the same holds true for heaters in Phoenix in July. Price discrimination here just makes sense. And although many consumers are forced to buy gasoline, prosumers and businesses aren't *forced* to buy keywords. They do it because it's good business—and they can easily opt not to make this purchase. The days of going down to the local store to pay whatever the owner wants—or do without—are long gone.

Near-Constant Competition

Carnegie Steel and Standard Oil faced little or no competition once they achieved levels of market dominance, the same just cannot be said about the Gang of Four. Robust partner networks, a blistering pace of technological change, and low—if not non-existent—barriers to entry mean that tech-heavyweights compete against one another on a near-constant basis. In September 2011, Amazon announced plans to launch Fire, a tablet computer, putting it at odds with Apple's iPad and Google's ever-changing hardware. Although it has remained unscathed, Facebook—the king of social networks—faces constant threats from Google. Examples include Orkut, Buzz, and its +1 Button.[38] What's more, Google is constantly flirting with buying Twitter outright.

Beyond competition from one another, let's not forget that the leaders of these companies justifiably fear startups in garages. There is no guarantee that these mighty companies will remain ubiquitous or nearly as profitable. When AOL and Yahoo! became passé, consumers circumvented them much more easily than they could have found alternative energy sources. (Chapter 9 looks in more depth at the ephemeral nature of platforms.)

Today, companies such as Apple with high profit margins are the exceptions that prove the rule. Traditional monopolies have always attracted competition, but one could not easily launch a railroad, telecommunications, or oil company. That's just not true with platforms.

Welfare and Regulations

Perhaps the single best gauge of whether Amazon, Apple, Facebook, and Google are modern-day monopolies, however, is how they act. In his 2011 book, *The Rational Optimist: How Prosperity Evolves*, Matt Ridley writes:

> Like Milton Friedman, I notice that "business corporations in general are not defenders of free enterprise. On the contrary,

they are one of the chief sources of danger." They are addicted to corporate welfare, they love regulations that erect barriers to entry to their small competitors, they yearn for monopoly, and they grow flabby and inefficient with age.

We'll see in Part II of this book how none of the above statements applies to the Gang of Four.

SUMMARY AND CONCLUSION

This chapter has defined the platform as a new and important business model. It has also distinguished today's powerful platforms from the traditional monopolies of the late 19th and 20th centuries. Granted, no one can argue that Amazon, Apple, Facebook, and Google are entirely benevolent nonprofits. Each company is out to make money—and does so quite handsomely. However, each has built a platform, not a *de facto* monopoly. Part II explains how.

PART II
THE GANG OF FOUR:
THE LEADERS OF THE PLATFORM AGE

Part II explores today's most powerful platforms: Amazon, Apple, Facebook, and Google—collectively termed the *Gang of Four*. It looks at how each company built its platform, the importance of external parties, its missteps, and its lapses in judgment. We'll also examine how each company's customers, users, developers, partners, and vendors extend its platform.

Besides providing brief histories of these organizations, Part II examines how they have created such transformative platforms—and why these platforms are generating such amazing results. It shows that, by building its platforms, the Gang of Four has become an admired and incredibly valuable and powerful group of companies. Even the Pentagon seeks technology advice from some of them.[39]

We'll see how powerful platforms are not based on doing only one thing—even if the company does that one thing really well. Let's examine these amazing companies and the platforms fueling them.

By no means does each chapter in Part II provide a comprehensive history of each company. I merely pinpoint key events, achievements, and mistakes, particularly as they relate to creating platforms. Many excellent books have been written about these companies, providing much more detail about their histories.

Chapter Three—A Mere Bookstore No More

Chapter Four—Beyond the Computer

Chapter Five—The King of Social

Chapter Six—From Search to Ubiquity

THREE

A Mere Bookstore No More

J eff Bezos was working at a hedge fund in the early 1990s. By all accounts, he was making a great deal of money. He certainly didn't hate his job and he was very good at it. Many men would have been content to stand pat.

But there was just one problem: His heart really wasn't in it. Bezos was much more of a computer geek than a financial wonk. At the time, the Internet was set to explode and Bezos was getting antsy. He had heard a statistic that the Net was growing at an annual rate of 2,300 percent.* He left his lucrative Wall Street job, and in 1994, founded Amazon as an online bookstore.

It didn't take too long for Amazon to branch out beyond books— big time. The company soon began selling DVDs, CDs, MP3 downloads, computer software, groceries, video games, electronics, apparel, furniture, and toys. But as we'll see in this chapter, Amazon didn't stop there. Before looking at this company today, let's take a brief look at its past, as this now enormously successful company faced plenty of challenges along the way.

GET BIG FAST

> **"Growth is the only evidence of life."**
> —John Henry Newman

In the late 1990s, Bezos irked many Wall Street traditionalists skeptical of "the new economy" by constantly reporting *pro-forma* profits.

---

* For a quick history of Amazon and Jeff Bezos, check out the Bloomberg show *Game Changers* (http://www.bloomberg.com/video/69862112).

Without getting too technical here, pro-forma net profit excludes many normal business charges and expenses but includes interest payments. (It's kind of like playing golf but not counting the bad holes.) Semantics aside, Amazon struggled for its very survival during and immediately after the dot-com implosion:

> By the summer of 2000, Amazon's share price had dropped by almost 70 percent. Analysts began to criticize the company for venturing into too many products and spreading itself too thin. Speculation on Wall Street suggested that Amazon would file for bankruptcy or be bought out. Some even clearly warned investors to avoid buying Amazon stocks. Gloom and doom mongers gave the company various labels such as Amazon.toast or Amazon.bomb* as the collapse of the world's largest e-tailer was predicted. In early 2001, Amazon reported a huge fiscal loss of $1.4 billion—the company's worst-ever annual performance.[40]

Bezos made "Get Big Fast" Amazon's mantra. Rather than taking a conservative approach to growth, the company tried to grow as fast as possible. Moving so far so fast presented a fair share of challenges, but eventually Amazon turned the corner. In January 2002, Amazon became the first online retailer ever to post a profit.[41] The company hasn't looked back since. No longer is it criticized for its questionable accounting tactics. It's a monster likely to continue its massive growth—all thanks to shrewd moves and its robust platform.

Today, Amazon's platform is nothing less than a *force majeure*. In their 2006 bestselling book, *Wikinomics: How Mass Collaboration Changes Everything*, Don Tapscott and Anthony D. Williams explain the mechanics of the Amazon platform. They write:

> With 975,000 active seller accounts, 140,000-plus developers, and third-party sales generating 28 percent of Amazon's revenue in the second quarter of 2005 (i.e., almost half a billion

---

* On *Charlie Rose*, Bezos remarked that his favorite barb was Amazon.org—implying that the company was a nonprofit.

dollars), there is arguably no company in business today that knows how to harness a platform for participation like Amazon, so it's worthwhile taking a deeper look at their model.

Amazon's platform for participation spurs two things: innovation and viral growth. Most companies spend hundreds of millions of dollars on R&D every year with no guarantee that it will lead to the next great innovation. Amazon leverages a massive community of developers and small and medium-size businesses to delve into uncharted areas where traditional R&D models typically fail. Even better, Amazon incurs very few costs and risks—most of which are borne by outside developers who create the innovations. Apart from the costs of maintaining the Web services, it's virtually a free development model where both parties win when developer creations increase sales.

Note that *Wikinomics* was written and published before Amazon launched the Kindle, a move that grew its platform considerably—and resulted in significant additional revenue. Again, we see the expansion of the platform at work.

THE PLANKS: HOW AMAZON BUILT ITS PLATFORM

Let's now look at how Amazon created its amazing platform. The company has continued to innovate, find new revenue streams, and, in the process, disintermediate existing businesses.

The Elegant Customer Experience

During the dot-com boom, Amazon and eBay were considered competitors. Ecommerce was taking off, and as is normal in any nascent market, companies sought *first-mover advantage* (FMA). Bezos understood that FMA is not the same as being "first to market." Rather, true FMA means being the first *to make a significant move in a market*. Being first is no guarantee of permanent or even long-term success in any given market. After all, markets change and even become irrelevant. Still, head starts are almost always critical. All else equal, companies able to pounce first tend to benefit more than those slow to the gate.

In 1998, buying online was sometimes easier than going to a bricks-and-mortar store, depending on the product. That store might or might not have a product in stock, in your desired color, size, and so on. Because most people connected to the Internet via dial-up modems back then, the experience was often clunky, resulting in many incomplete transactions and frustrated users. Bezos knew that ecommerce could be vastly improved.

Depending on the type of auction, buying a product on eBay required up to 12 clicks. That is, there were 12 opportunities for a customer to change her mind. At too many points, a customer's Internet service provider (ISP) could fail to render a page or a dial-up connection might terminate. Maybe a computer would freeze up, making the would-be customer give up. In an ideal world, customers would be able to make a purchase instantly. Enter 1-Click.

1-Click

Although details are a bit sketchy, in the mid-1990s, Amazon went to work on what would become a game-changer. It sought to simplify the entire online experience by dramatically reducing the number of clicks. By early 1997, Amazon had developed technology allowing customers to make purchases with a single click of the mouse. The company quickly filed papers with the U.S. Patent and Trademark Office (USPTO).

In September 1999, the USPTO granted Amazon what would turn out to be a very controversial patent for its 1-Click technology. It has had to revisit this controversial patent several times over the past few years, and multiple lawsuits have been filed around it. In a nutshell, 1-Click allowed online shoppers to easily make purchases using a marketplace-type of forum. No longer would they need to endure time-consuming and often cumbersome shopping cart software. The time savings were extraordinary. Before 1-Click, Amazon customers needed to manually input their billing and shipping information into web pages for every purchase. Thanks to 1-Click, they could now use a previously registered and saved credit card number. They also could have their products mailed to an existing address.

Forget ease of use for a moment—although that is enormous. One-click allowed Amazon to obtain *accurate* customer payment and address information on its millions of customers. This is a major headache for large organizations. And Amazon knew which customers bought which products—and when. It's impossible to overstate the enormity of 1-Click: Amazon wouldn't be nearly as successful as it is today if it continued to force its customers to follow an eBay-like purchase process.

And, at least for Amazon, it gets better. Bezos realized that other companies would soon want similar—if not identical—technology for their own sites. In the first of what would amount to many licensing deals, Amazon licensed 1-Click ordering to Apple for use on its online store in September 2000.[42]

The Customer Experience Does Not End with the Purchase

> "We see our customers as invited guests to a party, and we are the hosts. It's our job every day to make every important aspect of the customer experience a little bit better."
> —*Jeff Bezos*

Most executives recognize that, without customers, their businesses would cease to exist. Paradoxically, however, many companies struggle with customer service. Google "United Breaks Guitars" or "Comcast sucks" and you'll find some interesting reading on how many companies have dropped the ball.

Not Amazon. From day one, Bezos emphasized the importance of taking care of the company's customers. Amazon's focus on customer service can only be described as relentless. It has always done well on customer satisfaction surveys, and Amazon recently surpassed Netflix in the Foresee Results annual Top 100 Online

Retailer Satisfaction Index.[43] Amazon does much more than espouse the virtues of customer service through hollow platitudes. For instance, the company makes returns exceptionally easy. The only gripe among many customers is that Amazon doesn't make it easy to get a human being on the phone.

In hindsight, Amazon's emphasis on customer service could not have come at a better time. Web 2.0 and social media sites have given rise to the social customer. This development has changed the consumer–business dynamic in ways never seen before. Angry customers can and do routinely air their grievances on blogs, Twitter, Facebook, and myriad other public forums. Social review sites such as Yelp and Angie's List are taking off. Also, since just about everyone has a smartphone these days, consumers need not wait until they get home to complain. While 100 percent satisfaction may not be possible, Amazon knows that angry folks let the world know—immediately, frequently, and loudly.

The Importance of Permission

In his 1999 debut book, *Permission Marketing*, Seth Godin explains the need for businesses today to receive permission from current and prospective customers. Companies now have to ask if they can market to consumers. Godin writes about the end of the 1950s era of mass marketing in which companies spent millions to plaster their ads and messages over television, radio, and print. That era is now over—and has been for quite some time.

Amazon understands this. The company makes untold amounts of money from its gentle, nonintrusive recommendations. It asks for permission to market to its customer and user bases. For instance, I typically receive weekly emails from Amazon with subjects such as *Bestselling Management Books*. These emails are helpful, relevant, and timely. How many companies can say that about their marketing efforts?

Further, Amazon understands the damaging reputational effects of spam. Too many companies make it difficult to opt out of mass communications, a problem amplified when the messages are both irrelevant and untimely. Not Amazon. At the end of each Amazon email is a simple and powerful message: "We hope you found this message to be useful. However, if you'd rather not receive future emails of this sort from Amazon.com, please opt-out *here*."

Affiliate Marketing and Amazon Associates

Early on, Jeff Bezos intelligently realized two key things:

❏ The Internet was going to be a game-changer.
❏ If customers were unhappy with Amazon, they would most surely tell others.

And the converse was also true: Happy customers may well promote Amazon to others, especially since the company offers financial incentives for doing so via affiliate links.

Delighted customers with easy means to communicate with others led Amazon to embrace the notion of affiliates: Those who would spread the word and drive traffic—and ultimately revenue—to Amazon. Today, according to its website, the company claims to have nearly one million members in its affiliate programs worldwide, making it the most successful affiliate program ever.

And Amazon makes it simple for customers—and itself, for that matter—to cash in. The company's Product Advertising application programming interface (API) allows customers to embed product links on their own websites, making money for everyone in the process. From the Amazon website:

> The Product Advertising API helps you advertise Amazon products using product search and look up capability, product information and features such as Customer Reviews, Similar Products, Wish Lists, and New and Used listings. You can make money using the Product Advertising API to advertise Amazon products in conjunction with the Amazon Associates program.

Be sure to join the Amazon Associates program to earn up to 15% in referral fees when the users you refer to Amazon sites buy qualifying products.[44]

Amazon's planks compare favorably to those of any other platform today. Bezos understands full well the Age of the Platform— that is, business today is not one-directional, nor is it a zero-sum game. Interact with consumers, users, partners, and communities and they will respond.

Technology Enables Accurate Recommendations

If you're an Amazon customer, Figure 3.1 will probably look very familiar to you:

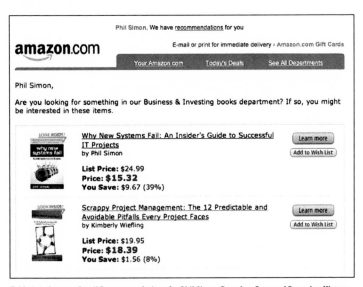

Table 3.1: Amazon Email Recommendations for Phil Simon Based on Personal Browsing History

The content of this email represents Amazon's best attempts at mass customization. The company knows I frequently go to amazon. com to check sales of my first book, *Why New Systems Fail*. (Perhaps I do this far too often, but that's an entirely different discussion.)

Amazon's technology constantly "learns" from my browsing and purchasing behavior. Again, with my permission, it regularly sends me emails with book recommendations from which I can easily opt out. But I don't. I like these gentle suggestions and frequently consider them—and I am not alone.

And Amazon's email suggestions don't stop with books. Its technology collects information on me as I view DVDs, CDs, beef jerky, toaster ovens, and other products. Surely, when viewing products on amazon.com, you've seen the phrases "Frequently Bought Together" and "Customers Who Bought This Item Also Bought." This is no coincidence.

How does Amazon make all of this magic happen behind the scenes? Amazon keeps its specific applications and technologies under tight wraps—and for good reason. This much I can tell you without fear of contradiction: Amazon's technology operates on two levels. First, there's the transactional level. When customers make purchases on amazon.com, they interact with the company's operational data management system. This system provides master product data about every product that Amazon sells. To make a purchase, customers must enter accurate billing and shipping details in order to authorize the online sales to deliver the product.

However, *by themselves*, even best-of-breed transactional systems and processes cannot easily display product recommendations likely to result in additional purchases. Here, Amazon's second level of technology comes into play. The company employs powerful analytical systems that sift through an enormous amount of data to provide relevant product suggestions to its customers. Frequently termed *business intelligence*, this software is able to quickly associate ostensibly disparate products with one another, discovering previously unknown relationships in the process. For instance, people who buy Rush records are likely to buy music by Pink Floyd.

Aside from knowing what to suggest, Amazon's systems know what not to recommend. Fans of Metallica are unlikely to consider purchasing the latest Lady Gaga album. And this is just within music. The combinations within—and across—product groups are limitless.

The Power of Defaults, Ease of Use, and Impulse Buys

Few companies make shopping as easy as Amazon does. In a July 2011 *Wired* article entitled "You Are Being Gamed," Dan Ariely shows how companies such as Amazon, Netflix, and Apple manipulate customers into making decisions that they otherwise would not make. Ariely explains:

> Eliminating small frictions can radically alter one's decisions. An elegant demonstration of this comes from research by Eric Johnson and Dan Goldstein, who asked people whether they wanted to opt out of organ donation (i.e., starting with the choice preset at "donate") instead of asking whether they wanted to donate (presetting at "don't donate"). That switch caused the pro-donation response to rise from around 40 percent to more than 80 percent. This is the power of defaults: We have a marked tendency to take the path of least resistance.

> For many of us, Amazon.com functions as a default because it has all our credit cards and addresses on file. If we asked people how much they would pay to save the time needed to retype that information on another site, they'd most likely say, "Not much." Most of us don't value our time so highly. But during the few seconds in which we make our buying decisions, when we are not thinking very deeply, the barrier to entering that data seems too forbidding and we default to Amazon.

> Amazon also created two smart solutions to the problem of shipping cost, which has always been one of the biggest psychological hurdles to buying online. The first is Super Saver Shipping, which sets a $25 threshold to qualify for free shipping. This turns a lot of one-item purchases into two-item sprees, as people add an extra book or CD just to avoid shipping costs.

Ariely goes on to explain how Amazon Prime's cheap and fast shipping causes shoppers to buy considerably more than they normally would. And he correctly observes several other things in this *Wired* article. First, everything Amazon does—and how the company does it—is by design. Amazon is hardly unique here. Its actions are analogous to those of many companies looking to maximize profit, as books such as Paco Underhill's classic *Why We Buy: The Science of Shopping* manifest. For instance, grocery stores place milk in the back and put high-margin items near the register. They make it reasonably difficult for customers to run in and run out. Customers in the store for longer periods of time are more likely to purchase more things; they have more time to make impulse buys.

Second, Amazon understands that default settings are incredibly important, especially for today's extremely busy consumer. Most people do not adjust the default settings for their applications and favorite websites. Microsoft understood this all too well when it bundled Internet Explorer (IE) with Windows, making IE a computer's default search engine—even though that can be easily changed. As we'll see in Chapter 5, Facebook has also caused many a ruckus by changing users' default settings.

The Importance of Ratings and Tags

Amazon has spent a great deal of time, money, and effort deploying and customizing its internal applications and systems. The end result for the customer is a seamless experience that makes shopping easy, efficient, and even fun. Consumers who log on to Amazon are unknowingly also interacting with the company's state-of-the-art systems. This technology can instantly access previous sales transactions and recommend other products. But sophisticated technology alone can only do so much. Customers contribute to—and enhance—the Amazon experience in another essential way.

What if you bought John Grisham's book, *Theodore Boone: Kid Lawyer,* on Amazon? Let's say that you hated it, but Amazon kept sending you recommendations for books similar to this one you couldn't even finish. Bezos is too smart to encourage you to opt out of these critical customer touchpoints. Instead, Amazon lets customers easily increase the relevance of their own recommendations. Customers can effectively "teach" the site in several ways. First, they can review products, even if they have not purchased them on Amazon. In this case, you would give *Theodore Boone* a one-star review on the book's Amazon page.[45] Second, customers can read reviews by others with similar viewpoints and answer the following yes/no question: (Was this review helpful to you?)

While it may make you feel better to "vent" your frustrations with *Theodore Boone*, something important is happening behind the scenes that will affect each interaction you have with Amazon in the future. Amazon's systems are storing information on your preferences. This data will allow Amazon to refine its profile on you and your viewing and purchasing habits. In the end, Amazon will recommend fewer books like *Theodore Boone: Kid Lawyer* to you.

But how does Amazon know which books are related? In a word, *tags*. Customer-provided tags or keywords allow Amazon to correlate ostensibly disparate products. Consider Figure 3.2:

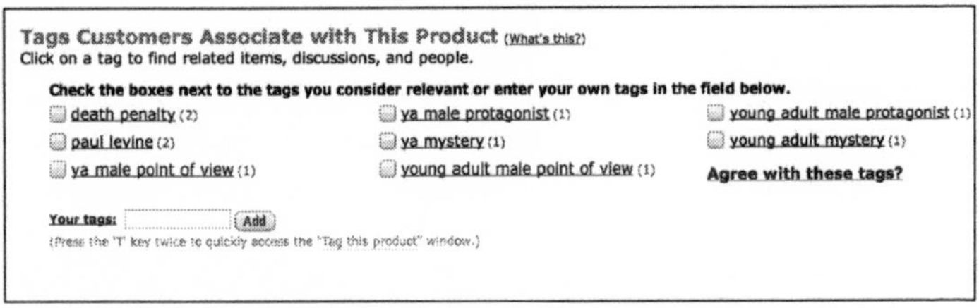

Figure 3.2: Amazon Product Tags for *Theodore Boone: Kid Lawyer*

As Figure 3.2 shows, Amazon's customers presumably have read *Theodore Boone* and can accurately describe the book through keywords. For instance, Grisham's book appears to be suited for people who enjoy legal thrillers with a teen bent. Like-minded customers are more inclined to buy books with these tags—and Amazon can easily find them and automatically recommend books like these.

Finally, it's important to note that Amazon makes it simple to search for products tagged with a particular term. (Bezos understood the power of search early on. He personally funded search startup A9, a site that "helps people find what they want on the world's leading ecommerce sites."[46] It is now a subsidiary of Amazon.) Amazon doesn't want to have to rely exclusively on "pushing" its recommendations onto its customers. Doing so would ignore an equally critical piece of the customer experience—the "pull" aspect. Amazon wants its customers to easily pull or retrieve relevant products—and ignore those that fail to make the cut. More tags, ratings, and reviews mean more sales and, ultimately, more profits and a more robust platform.

> **Technology for the sake of technology is utterly pointless and even counterproductive. Technology is a means, not an end in and of itself. In this case, superior technology allows Amazon to know a great deal about its customers' purchases, likes, dislikes, and habits. No other company knows its customers better than Amazon does, a main reason that its platform is so strong.**

Knowing When to Quit: Getting Out of Auctions

In the late 1990s, auctions were all the rage. eBay was the 800-pound gorilla, making money hand over fist as consumers found great deals on office supplies, furniture, and a whole host of random products. Ecommerce was exploding and companies such as half.com (acquired by eBay in 2000 for roughly $350 million) and overstock.com were changing the playing field. Traditional retailers were scrambling to beef up their online presence, website, and ecommerce strategy.

Amazon realized the power of online auctions and attempted to spread its wings. It launched zShops[47] in September 1999, as well as a partnership with storied auction house Sotheby's later that year. Despite these moves, Amazon could never rival eBay in auctions. It soon morphed its auction business into Amazon Marketplace.

> While its venture was ultimately unsuccessful, Amazon should not be criticized for its foray into auctions. On the contrary, it deserves praise. The outcome itself isn't nearly as important as what it represents: Amazon was and is not afraid to move in different directions, even at the risk of failure. Building a platform requires that mentality.

Not every company embraces such an agile and experimental approach. Consider Borders Group, the bookstore chain founded in 1971. On February 16, 2011, the company announced it had filed for Chapter 11 bankruptcy protection. According to a recent Bloomberg article, the company's market value "shrunk by more than $3 billion since 1998" and:

> …racked up losses by failing to adapt to shifts in how consumers shop. *Its first e-commerce site debuted in 2008, more than a decade after Amazon.com revolutionized publishing with online sales.* The world's largest online retailer beat it again by moving into digital books with the Kindle e-reader in 2007, a market Borders entered in July.[48] [Emphasis added.]

Think about that. Borders would have had a tough time competing against Amazon if it had launched a proper online presence in 2002, as the latter would have had an eight-year head start. By waiting until 2008, Borders fell behind 14 years! This is an eternity in business today, especially regarding anything technology-related. The question to me is not why did Borders have to declare bankruptcy in 2011; rather, how did it manage to survive until then?

To build a platform of consequence, a company has to incur some level of risk. Waiting too long for things to play out, as Borders did, does not mitigate that risk. In fact, dillydallying actually maximizes the risk of irrelevance, obsolescence, and death. Amazon illustrates that it's better to experiment and fail (at least to some extent) than to wait until all risk has been eliminated.

Associates, Partners, Acquisitions, and Vendors

It's no understatement to say that many businesses continue to struggle with emerging technologies at a time when so much is happening online. Realizing that it can provide a valuable service and make money in the process, Amazon launched aStore, an associates product that gives businesses and prosumers the power to create professional online stores. The WYSIWYG (what you see is what you get) setup only takes minutes and does not require programming skills. What's more, the aStore can be embedded within—or linked to and from—associate websites.[49]

To be sure, there are many ecommerce sites and tools available these days. Amazon's aStores may not be superior to best-of-breed applications and websites, but that's not the point. Millions of consumers already have mostly positive relationships with Amazon, making them likely to at least try aStore. For Amazon and its affiliates, the strategy seems to be working. aStores has been a success, and the variety of available products is nothing short of astonishing.

Bezos recognized the value of strategic partnerships early on. In his forthcoming book, *One Click: Jeff Bezos and the Rise of Amazon. com*, Richard L. Brandt writes:

> In 1997, Amazon set up partnerships with competing physical bookstores through the Advantage program. Small bookstores were allowed to sell books to customers through links from their Web sites to Amazon. The bookstores got a percentage of sales.
>
> Bezos thinks strategically and imaginatively, and plans ahead. In November 1997, he set up a meeting with executives from a small London-based site for movie buffs, the Internet Movie Database (IMDb). IMDb didn't even sell anything. It just provided information about movies, and relied on donations and a small group of advertisers to stay in business. He bought the

company in April 1998, but kept it as an independent company (most people don't even realize IMDb is owned by Amazon). The reason became clear seven months later, when Amazon began selling movie DVDs. IMDb became a site where Amazon could place ads for its DVD offerings, and could link people to Amazon to buy movies they were interested in. Forty-five days after launch, Amazon was the biggest seller of DVDs on the Internet.

In 1998 he bought Jungle, a shopping comparison site. It would search the Internet for the best deals, even if that sent buyers away from Amazon. But it gave Amazon a reputation as the best place to start searching for products. That also helped Amazon start Amazon Marketplace, allowing retailers at other sites to sell their products through Amazon, using Amazon's sophisticated transaction processing system—giving Amazon a percentage of the sales. Again, that makes people think of Amazon as the first place to search for products. Bezos knew that customers would be able to find deals elsewhere anyway, so he made sure that they would use Amazon to find those deals, and contribute to Amazon's revenues. Amazon became the center of a retailing keiretsu. Marketplace accounted for 35 percent of Amazon's revenue in the 4th quarter of 2010.

Note how Bezos did not just jump into bed with every company that wanted to get on the Amazon bandwagon. Bezos carefully selected his partners based on their employees, business models, technology, and expectations surrounding collaboration. In so doing, he maximized the chance that each plank of the Amazon platform would be strong, capable of handling additional traffic and lines of business.

Hardware: Creating the Market

Despite its relatively recent rise, ebook software traces back to the early 1990s. However, for several reasons, its adoption was miniscule. Most people are not going to read 250-page books leaning forward, chained to their computers. Up until recently, people had no easy way to read electronic books. Enter Amazon.

On November 19, 2007, the company released the Kindle First Generation, priced at $399.[50] In so doing, Amazon essentially created the current-day ebook market. Amazon's Kindle offered the first affordable and viable means to take an ebook with you. Amazon understood that the money it made from the actual hardware would be inconsequential in comparison to what it could make on the sale of individual books. After all, those who buy ereaders are likely to be book aficionados and bibliophiles. In the words of Markus Dohle, chairman and chief executive of Random House, "People with e-readers buy more books."[51]

One can even imagine a day in the not-too-distant future in which Amazon gives away Kindles and other hardware in return for paid subscriptions. In fact, this would hardly be new. For years, many companies have embraced this "give-away-the-razor-sell-the-blades" marketing strategy.[52]

As of this writing, Kindle's share of the ereader market stands at about 47 percent,[53] a number that has dropped considerably with the success of the iPad.

But Amazon is not finished in the hardware space. Buoyed by the success of Apple's iPad and iPad 2, Amazon is releasing Fire, a color tablet computer in November 2011 with much more functionality than its Kindle. As a precursor, on March 22, 2011, Amazon launched its Appstore for Android,[54] a storefront for apps that will compete directly with Google's official Android Market.

Publishing and Disintermediation

As its business continued to prosper and the publishing industry slowly began to embrace ebooks, Amazon made yet another bold move. Consider the company's recent partnership with bestselling author Seth Godin, dubbed *The Domino Project*.[55] By working with the hugely influential Godin, Amazon is now a *de facto* publisher.

In a Mashable article in February 2011, Lauren Indvik quotes Godin: "A book that isn't read doesn't do anyone any good, and too often, the book publishing industry gets in the way of books reaching people who can benefit from them. Amazon knows what to do to help these books get read." Godin has spoken at length about how Amazon possesses intimate and unique knowledge of its customers, much more so than many major publishers and companies. Case in point: Amazon accurately recommends specific books, CDs, movies, and other products to its customers because it knows exactly which ones they have previously purchased. In Indvik's words:

> Godin will leverage Amazon's Kindle Store and extensive media reach—along with his own considerable following—to market books published under his new imprint. But whether Godin is really redefining "what publishing can become" is debatable. Godin and Amazon aren't doing anything new—rather, Amazon is simply expanding its role as a retailer to perform most of the duties of a publisher as well.[56]

In other words, Amazon is growing and strengthening its platform.

Amazon recognizes the sea change that is taking place in the publishing industry right now—and doesn't want to miss out on the opportunities created by this disintermediation. Through its 2005 acquisition of online print-on-demand (POD) company BookSurge, Amazon launched a publishing offering, expanding its platform in the process. Rebranded as CreateSpace, anyone can now self-publish their writings as both physical and electronic books. Although its deals with individual publishers vary, those opting to self-publish through the company's Kindle Direct Service[57] pay Amazon 30 percent of the price of their books. And these sales add up and create "Amazon celebrities." Consider that in March 2011, Amanda Hocking, a young-adult fiction author of paranormal romance ebooks, procured a $2 million, four-book deal with St. Martin's Press.[58] What's so special about Hocking? In a little under a year, the self-publishing superstar had sold more than $2 million worth of books on Amazon.

Amazon's take from Hocking's sales alone equates to approximately $600,000. Although she may be the exception to the rule, consider the thousands of authors who make their books available on Amazon—a trend that will only intensify in the near future. Amazon will continue to make money on its platform from every sale made by prosumers.

Today, it's ridiculous for a business to forgo so much in potential revenue and profits from up-and-coming individuals and partners. Amazon understands this, and refuses to let rising stars like Amanda Hocking slip through its fingers. But how? It's quite simple: Amazon has developed a platform that not only supports partners like Hocking, but lets them thrive. The Hocking–Amazon relationship was extremely beneficial and symbiotic. Each made the other a great deal of money, and as Hocking describes on her blog in March 2011, her reasons for signing a four-book, multi-million-dollar deal with St. Martin's Press had nothing to do with any dissatisfaction with Amazon.[59]

Amazon seems to be ramping up its publishing efforts. The company recently announced the hiring of highly respected 30-year industry veteran Laurence J. Kirshbaum, a literary agent and former publisher. Kirshbaum will lead a new imprint for Amazon.[60]

> Amazon's publishing efforts illustrate a major point with respect to growing platforms: If it's working, keep doing it—but experiment with different directions. Quickly expand offerings. Today, failing to act soon enough is almost always riskier than acting too soon.

Accidental Lines of Business

In order to power its site and company, Amazon invested in technology infrastructure—specifically, cloud computing. Amazon spends a great deal of money making sure that its customers, affiliates, and partners can easily add products and pages. Bezos understood three things:

- ❏ It's better to have too much storage and compute power than not enough.
- ❏ It's impossible to predict how much technology it will need at any given point.
- ❏ The company could sell the excess to companies that needed it.

In March 2006, the company launched an online storage service called Amazon Simple Storage Service (Amazon S3). Later that year, it introduced Amazon Elastic Compute Cloud (Amazon EC2), a virtual site farm that allows its users to run their own web hosting and simulation applications via the Amazon infrastructure. But Amazon hasn't stopped there. It continues to upgrade its third-party offerings, in effect selling what it doesn't need.

Amazon's fulfillment and billing systems are so efficient that other companies want in. Case in point: Kickstarter is a popular "funding platform for artists, designers, filmmakers, musicians, journalists, inventors, and explorers."[61] I am very familiar with Kickstarter, since I used it to raise both funds and awareness for my third book, *The New Small*.[62] If a project is successfully funded, then Kickstarter routes payments through Amazon, a service for which Amazon receives five percent of the amount funded. For instance, my project raised about $5,000, of which $250 went to Amazon for simply processing the payments. On much larger projects, such as the highly publicized Apple Nano Watch Kit that raised more than $940,000,[63] Amazon collected nearly $50,000.

And the offshoots just keep on coming. For years, customers have been able to purchase movies on Amazon—as in VHS tapes and DVDs. Recently, however, customers have been able to watch streaming videos via Amazon. The site becomes a *de facto* DVR as Amazon goes head-to-head with Netflix, the pioneer in on-demand video.

The results have been nothing short of staggering. In 2009, the company generated more than $220 million from EC2.[64] And this is just the tip of the iceberg. In 2011, analysts predict that Amazon Web Services (AWS) revenue will hit about $750 million. In 2014, AWS could net Amazon roughly $2.5 *billion* in revenue.[65] Not bad for an outfit that, a mere 15 years ago, was just an online bookseller with a host of detractors and questionable profits.

MISSTEPS AND CONFLICTS

Amazon has disintermediated—or expedited the eventual disintermediation of—many companies and industries. Those adversely affected by the Amazons of the world have not always been willing partners. Consider the publishing industry. For decades, it has been a price maker, not a price taker. With varying degrees of success, it would try to dictate to bookstores and consumers the price of books, especially new releases. eBook readers like the Kindle began changing all of that. On TechFlash's Amazon blog, an August 2009 post revealed that Random House epitomized many publishers who were still

> …wary about Amazon's Kindle pricing policy, believing it could eat into sales of higher-priced hardcover releases. *The Lost Symbol** was a big test case. It shot to the top of Amazon's bestselling book (list) the day it became available for pre-order in April (of 2009), and has been mostly in the top ten since then. It appears that Random House didn't want to push the matter too far with Amazon, which is still a critical sales channel for hardcover. Random House/Doubleday spokeswoman Suzanne Herz, in an e-mailed statement, said, "all of our security and logistical issues surrounding the e-book of *The Lost Symbol* have been resolved."[66]

As of 2011, many publishers still haven't embraced Amazon's new model. They want to continue to dictate pricing terms for books on the Kindle—and Amazon is hardly indifferent here. The general point is that disintermediation tends to turn friends into enemies, and money is often not the sole cause of the tension.

---

* By Dan Brown, published in September 2009.

Beyond price, traditional publishers have not always endorsed Kindle's nontraditional functionality, such as text-to-speech (TTS), introduced in the Kindle 2. In 2009, Random House began pulling books from the Kindle Store. While the legal arguments aren't worth rehashing here, note that Amazon didn't see a need to seek the publishers' and authors' permission before making some significant changes. Later in this section, we'll see how this is a common theme among today's most powerful platforms.

Like Wal-Mart, Amazon has endured criticism for what it chooses to remove from its virtual shelves. For instance, in April 2009, many lambasted the company for pulling books that it deemed to be pornographic from its sales rankings. Many bloggers and communities protested the move, saying that the books in question were merely gay or lesbian in nature, not "adult." The protesters took their cause to Twitter, using the hashtag *#amazonfail*.[67] We'll see in later chapters how the most popular platforms today invariably face controversy.

Potential Legal Woes

Launched in summer 2011, Amazon's "music in the cloud" service allows people to access their MP3s from wherever they are connected to the Internet—and via any device they like. Amazon was first out of the gate, with Google and Apple quickly following suit. Amazon did not receive prior permission to do this from the RIAA. Whether this results in a lawsuit or legal problems is anyone's guess, but these examples show that moving fast means potentially angering established interests.

> If you build a powerful platform, you had better be ready for some titanic conflicts—especially with the powers-that-be.

Amazon may also find itself in trouble for launching an Appstore. Selling apps is one thing, but using the term Appstore may violate Apple's trademark. Apple recently filed suit against Amazon for this very reason.[68]

THE FUTURE OF THE AMAZON PLATFORM

Faced with significant competition from Apple and Google, Amazon continues to expand and diversify in unexpected ways. Additional challenges are coming in the form of lawmakers upset that Amazon and other ecommerce companies have long skirted paying state sales taxes. Brad Stone of Bloomberg BusinessWeek explains:

> There's a growing sense among state and federal lawmakers that the online sales-tax reprieve, once meant to support and nurture a fledgling industry, constitutes an advantage that Amazon, with 90 million customers and $34 billion in annual sales, no longer needs. Over the past year an escalating war over online sales taxes has spread to Texas, Connecticut, California, and dozens of other states. Later this month the battle will reach Capitol Hill. Senate Majority Whip Dick Durbin (D-Ill.) says he plans to introduce a bill, called the Main Street Fairness Act, mandating that all businesses collect the sales tax in the state where the consumer resides.[69]

For obvious reasons, Amazon and other etailers are lobbying heavily against potential legislation as we speak. Many states are facing unprecedented fiscal crises and, legalities aside, see companies like Amazon as cash cows. In California, Amazon—along with overstock.com—cut ties in late June 2011 with 10,000 of its affiliates because of tax issues.[70] Expect the stakes to rise until some type of deal is struck.

Regardless of when—not if—Amazon is finally forced to pay state sales taxes, its story is an amazing one. Its platform can withstand a few body blows, and Bezos has consistently shown that he's willing to price products at low margins. Once written off as a future dot-com failure, it has become one of the biggest retail companies on the planet—with no signs of stopping soon. Its platform accommodates previously unthinkable products and services with more undoubtedly on the way.

FOUR

Beyond the Computer

On January 3, 1977, Steve Jobs, Steve Wozniak, and Ronald Wayne officially incorporated Apple Computer. The company's ups and downs have been well documented. Perhaps most notably, Jobs resigned as chairman on September 16, 1985, after losing a boardroom battle for control of the company with then-CEO John Sculley. He ultimately returned in 1997, 12 years after his forced departure.

Beginning in the mid-1980s, the Apple intelligentsia began thinking about high-tech devices other than proper computers. The company started development of digital cameras, portable CD audio players, speakers, video consoles, and TV appliances. They introduced the Newton, its ill-fated personal digital assistant (PDA) in the early 1990s. Although the Newton may have been ahead of its time, Apple was moving beyond the computer—and all without Steve Jobs. The magazine *MacAddict* named the period between 1989 and 1991 as the "first golden age" of the Macintosh.

By the early 2000s, two things were certain. First, Jobs was firmly in control of the company. Second, Apple Computer was no longer really just a computer company and had not been for a while, at least in a traditional sense. In 2007, the company made it official. Apple formally changed its legal name, dropping the word *Computer*. The name change was brilliant marketing, always Steve Jobs' strong suit. Apple is much cleaner than *Apple Computer*. (Mark Zuckerberg did the same thing by dropping "*The*" from Facebook.) Marketing aside, however, the name change better reflected Apple's current thinking—and future direction. It was high time the company's name caught up with its ethos. According to a *Forbes* article published after the announcement, the change:

point[s] to a consumer electronics company more than a computer maker. On the same day it announced its name change, the company launched the iPhone, a cellphone/iPod hybrid, along with Apple TV, a device to deliver video content downloaded through Apple's iTunes service to consumers' television sets. On Jan. 17, Apple announced that it had sold 21 million iPods in its fiscal first quarter ending Dec. 30. For Apple, the revenue from iPod and iTunes' sales represented $4 billion of the company's total $7.1 billion in revenues for the same quarter. Sales of Apple's Mac computers, in contrast, accounted for $2.4 billion in revenue. Apple shipped 1.6 million Macs in the quarter, below the 1.75 million some Wall Street analysts were expecting.[71]

In a way, the name change was meaningless. Today, few people associate Apple exclusively with computers per se. Although Apple makes user-friendly and profitable machines and devices, it is much more than a hardware company.

Apple has moved sideways like few other companies in history. It has introduced iconic devices such as the iPhone, iPod, and iPad, and related accessories. Apple has become an incredibly successful content company, selling *billions* of movies, MP3s, books, and apps. In a true testament to Jobs' brilliance, one does not have to buy the hardware to use the software and enjoy the content. In fact, today, millions of people and companies use PCs and other non-Apple devices while consuming Apple stuff.

Of course, making all of this content available for easy purchase and consumption required a great deal of investment and resources. And Apple has not skimped, consistently spending considerable funds on cloud computing and server farms.[72] (We'll see later in this chapter how Apple is by no means finished.)

The numbers behind this content explosion are nothing short of mind-boggling. As of June 2011:

Around 130 million books have been downloaded from the iBookstore and all major publishers are on board, says the company. And 14 billion apps have been downloaded from the App Store in less than three years. There are currently 425,000 apps in the App Store, and 90,000 are just for the iPad. And Apple says that there are now 225 million credit card accounts listed with iTunes.[73]

More than a few books have been written about Jobs' marketing, design, and overall business genius. With respect to the company name change, Jobs brilliantly knew where the world was heading—and where Apple needed to be when it got there. Branding Apple to be at the forefront of the transformation was nothing short of prescient. Do you think it's a coincidence that the Apple brand, worth more than 153 billion,[74] is the most valuable in the world? Not bad for a company that was on life support in 1997 and needed an infusion of $150 million in cash from its archrival, Microsoft,[75] just to stay alive. (Of course, Microsoft had ulterior motives for the investment, such as quelling claims that it was a monopoly.) In fact, many are speculating that Apple may become the first *trillion*-dollar company.[76]

PUSHING THE ENVELOPE

"In journalism, there has always been a tension between getting it first and getting it right."
—Ellen Goodman

Goodman's maxim applies equally well to technology, innovation, and product development. In the case of Apple, its technology has always been cutting edge. That much is part of the company's DNA. In fact, the company has been criticized for sometimes moving too fast. Apple has routinely pushed the envelope. Let's look at an example.

In 1996, Apple Computer released the iMac. The CD-Info blog reports the latest news and updates in the optical media industry and described the iMac in the following terms:

This new desktop was unlike anything ever seen before in the computer industry. Historically, computers were unsightly beige boxes that attached to a monitor with multiple cords and wires. The iMac computer combined the screen and all components into a single teardrop-shaped case made of translucent plastic.

There was more to the iMac than just its unusual appearance. One significant difference about the iMac was its lack of a 3.5" floppy drive. Up until this point in time, a diskette drive had been an essential component of a personal computer. They were used for backing up files, installing programs, and allowed for boot disks to install or repair operating systems.

To not include a floppy diskette drive was unheard of. It was controversial. Apple came under fire from industry pundits and computer magazine columnists. But you know what? Apple's decision was a pivotal point in the computer industry. It pushed people away from magnetic media and towards optical media such as CD-ROM discs, which quickly became the new standard for data storage.[77]

In 1996, Apple neglected to include what was considered to be essential: a floppy drive. The company saw the future, and that future was optical, not magnetic. Apple today is doing the same with DVDs. While MacBook Pro and MacAir continue to ship with DVD drives, Apple sees a future increasingly reliant on cloud computing. It's not hard to envision a Mac in three years without DVD capability.

THE PLANKS: HOW APPLE BUILT ITS PLATFORM

Apple has long understood the need for simplicity, ease of use, and the previously discussed enjoyment factor. These tenets have always made for great products. But today they make for great *platforms*, especially when partners have some skin in the game.

In a *New York Times* piece in January 2011 titled "The Power of the Platform at Apple,"[78] Steve Lohr writes about how network effects (discussed in Chapter 2) fuel the Apple platform. Apple's current momentum produces future momentum. Lohr explains:

> The more people buy iPhones and iPads, the more software developers and media companies want to write applications for them, as various games and digital magazines. And consumers are more likely to buy iPhones and iPads when more entertainment and information applications are available on them.
>
> These days, Apple is a platform player, though it is taking a hybrid approach. It has courted outside partners and suppliers but has fairly strict rules for how applications look and behave in its devices. Apple is offering users not just cool gadgets but also the software that glues together their digital lives—computing, online information gathering, and entertainment. It all works better together, the company says, so a person's second or third Apple product will make the first and second device more useful. The strategy is working so far. Even sales of MacBook notebooks were up 34 percent in the recent quarter [of 2010], far faster growth than in the overall PC industry.

Like its platform counterparts, Apple has realized that it has more to gain with the help of other developers, partners, and suppliers than without them. Apple has learned from the mistakes of companies that took a binary approach to development and innovation. For instance, during its heyday, Microsoft essentially gave its competition two choices: We'll buy you or we'll crush you. Not so at Apple and the rest of the Gang of Four. Here, the whole can be greater than the sum of its parts, especially if the parties collaborate.

Understanding the New Digital Hubs

As mentioned in Chapter 1, we no longer live in a world in which the computer is the end-all be-all for the consumer. Today, we connect to the Internet almost anywhere and at any time, through an increasing number of devices. Who knew this was coming? Steve

Jobs, of course. Consider what Jobs said about the matter more than a decade ago at Macworld 2001:*

> Jobs cited a quote from *Wall Street Journal* writer Walt Mossberg, who Jobs called "one of the smartest journalists in our business," who had recently written that "The PC, which has carried the digital revolution for 24 years, has matured into something boring."
>
> Jobs laid out a path of PC evolution that defined the early 80s as an initial "golden age" of computing based on productivity software, which began to wane in the early 90s. A "second golden age" began in the mid-1990s with the rise of Internet, Jobs said, but it too began to lose its momentum by 2000. Jobs said he believed a third age would focus on a digital lifestyle, driven by an "explosion of digital devices."
>
> "The Mac," Jobs said, "can become the 'digital hub' of our emerging digital lifestyle, adding tremendous value to our other digital devices." Jobs said PCs could be the center of this digital hub because they had the horsepower to run complex applications that other devices lack, and provide large, inexpensive disk storage, can burn discs, and offer big screens and fast networking.[79]

Jobs' words are eerily prescient, although he and Apple were hardly idle bystanders here. To a large extent, Apple *forced* this third golden age by developing its platform—and making it so compelling to use. The computer may still be the center of the consumer's computing universe, but it is no longer the entire universe. Today, the computer is the proverbial sun around which the other (devices) revolve.

---

* Watch Jobs deliver the speech at *http://www.youtube.com/watch?v=9046oXrm7f8*.

Minimalist Design

"My goal wasn't to make a ton of money. It was to build good computers."
—*Steve Wozniak*

In an era rife with feature-creep, it's not uncommon for software and other electronic products to contain functionality that the vast majority of users either simply don't know about or choose to ignore. Lots of PC users have switched to Apple products because of the Wow Factor. Many people believe that Apple products require much less technical sophistication than their Microsoft counterparts. Cool products and ease of use have enabled Apple to grow its share of the U.S. consumer computing market to a respectable 15 percent.[80] Before the turn of the century, Apple's share was all but a rounding error.

At a high level, Apple knows that today, more than ever, impatient users want to create and consume on their new iMacs, iPhones, iPods, and iPads; they don't want to struggle with complicated configuration issues. Apple's intuitive products lack superfluous functionality. While it no longer peppers its ads with the slogan *Think Different*, the company clearly continues to understand that less is more.

Effectively Managing Multidevice Chaos

It's easy to be ambivalent about the second golden age—that era in which the computer was the sole means by which people managed their digital lives. On the one hand, it was extremely limiting. Yes, laptops allowed people to work on the road and away from their "home bases." However, that era was extremely restrictive. To be productive away from our homes, we had to find a quiet space, plug our laptops into an Ethernet connection, and fire them up. We'd frequently have to tell colleagues and clients that we would respond to emails when we were home and in front of our computers.

On the other hand, the limitations of that age weren't entirely bad for the average consumer. One hub made for a simpler experience. Think about what many of us have to manage today. We can easily take our computing experience with us through smartphones, portable MP3 and movie players, tablets, Netbooks, and near-ubiquitous Internet access. We can be productive, reached, and entertained whenever and wherever we want. At the same time, though, we have to manage multiple devices. We now have to worry about synching individual files and version control. We may well need multiple software licenses and installations of our applications.

The question is: How do you reconcile simplicity and ease of use with the potential chaos described above? Here, Apple has done a fantastic job. In the words of CNBC technology correspondent Jon Fortt:

> Steve Jobs himself coined the term *digital hub* more than a decade ago, referring to the PC. In ten years defined by a gadget explosion—digital cameras, iPods, webcams, and more—the PC (or more specifically, the Mac) would be the *platform* that managed them all. Apple's iLife suite was built around that idea: in iTunes, iPhoto, iMovie, iDVD, and GarageBand, Jobs bet on a few key apps that would organize the chaos.[81] [Emphasis added.]

Apple has long recognized the need to make consumer life simple in this multidevice, hyper-connected world. To this end, it is making another big bet on cloud computing. On June 6, 2011, the company announced the launch of its long-anticipated iCloud service, letting "users synchronize and access data on Apple devices and Windows PCs running iTunes."[82]

The iPhone and the App Explosion

After Apple announced the launch of the iPhone2 in 2008, *New York Times* technology columnist David Pogue wrote an article titled "Hello BlackBerry, Meet the iPhone." Pogue clairvoyantly opined:

I can't tell you how huge this is going to be. There will be thousands of iPhone programs, covering every possible interest. The iPhone will be valuable for far more than simple communications tasks; it will be the first widespread pocket desktop computer. You're witnessing the birth of a third major computer platform: Windows, Mac OS X, iPhone.[83]

Skeptics scoffed. They believed the iPhone wouldn't amount to much more than a hill of beans, much less extend Apple's existing platform. In hindsight, however, Pogue and even hardcore Apple evangelizers were probably too conservative. The iPhone 2 exploded, and Apple opened its App Store on July 10, 2008, via an update to iTunes.

Not even Apple could have predicted the tsunami that the App Store would generate. Philip Schiller, the company's senior vice president of Worldwide Product Marketing, remarked that the App Store "has revolutionized how software is created, distributed, discovered and sold. While others try to copy the App Store, it continues to offer developers and customers the most innovative experience on the planet."

Schiller's enthusiasm must be viewed with a jaundiced eye—after all, he works in marketing for Apple. At the same time, though, Apple's brilliance here is tough to understate, especially when you consider that the company keeps 30 percent of each app sale. Do the math. Aside from extending its platform and its overall "stickiness," Apple generates billions of dollars in immediate revenue by working with hundreds of thousands of partners like Jordan Rudess.

Apps Tap into Existing Communities and Ecosystems

Rudess is a renowned classical pianist. For the past 12 years, he has served as the keyboardist for the progressive rock band Dream Theater—one of my favorite groups. Nicknamed "The Wizard," Rudess entered the prestigious Juilliard School of Music *at the ripe old age of nine*. He is quite possibly the most talented musician on the planet. If you gave him an empty soda can and

ı it into a primitive instrument, figure out how to
ın interesting song, and post a rocking video of his
entations on the web. I'm not kidding.

Rudess is a long-time Applephile. He watched as apps began exploding in popularity and decided to try his hand at them. He founded a separate company, Wizdom Music,[84] which launched its first music-oriented app in 2009, MorphWiz.[85] It was a success, and in late June 2011, Wizdom released its follow-up app, SampleWiz.[86] The app "lets sound enthusiasts play around with samples via their iPads and iPhones. Users can play the app musical instrument and record samples from more traditional ones."[87] A picture of the app is shown in Figure 4.1:

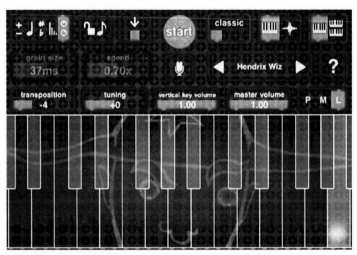

Figure 4.1: SampleWiz Screen Shot

Rudess is active on social media sites, with more than 30,000 followers on Twitter.[88] Dream Theater fans like me are rabid, to say the least. As a result, when Rudess releases an app, people take notice.

But it gets even better—for the Wizard and for Apple. It's a trip watching Rudess play his iPhone, iPad, and apps on stage in front of tens of thousands of people. Fans wonder how he creates these atmospheric sounds from a small electronic device. Since many of Rudess' fans are musicians themselves, he's effectively demonstrating the product at every show to people very likely to buy it. Rudess' energy and passion for all things Apple is palpable, as he explained to me:

> When I first put my hands on a very preliminary piano keyboard app on the iPhone in 2009, I knew things were about to change in the world of music.
>
> It was very soon after that first experience that the Apple app world began to explode. I sat for hours playing any app that generated a sound, fascinated with the possibilities. My wife Danielle said to me, "Why are you not playing your beautiful Steinway grand piano? Why do you just sit and tinker with that iPhone?" I tried to explain to her that I was on to something. After the success of MorphWiz and now SampleWiz, it's a little more accepted at home if I play with my devices.
>
> My relationship with Apple is one of pure inspiration. Both the company's technology and its method of distributing apps work perfectly for me and my lifestyle. Together with my partner in Wizdom Music (Kevin Chartier—the numerical magician), we are passionate about what we do with Apple's iOS. We love having the ability to shake things up a bit in the music world. We offer apps that are not only really fun and sound cool, but actually provide expressive musical control that is not found on any other instruments on the planet![89]

Jordan Rudess' SampleWiz example shows how Apple routinely taps into popular existing platforms and communities, reaping major benefits in the process. Rudess—and people like him—are good for Apple, something of which the company is well aware. Case in point: Apple invited Rudess to speak at its Macworld Expo in January 2011.

Strategic Partnerships and *The Long Tail*

Apple has long understood the importance of what its partners bring to the table. Apple's offerings can only be so successful on their own; their success hinges on incentivized third parties. Remember that iTunes was hardly the first online digital music store or service. In 1997, entrepreneur Michael Robertson started MP3.com.

So why did iTunes win without being first to the dance? As Chris Anderson explains in *The Long Tail*:

> The reason MP3.com's model didn't succeed and the iTunes model—which is less oriented toward independent musicians—did is that iTunes began by making deals with major record labels, which gave it a critical mass of mainstream music. Then it added more and more niche content, as "rights aggregators" shipped it hard drives full of hundreds of thousands of independent musicians. Thus, iTunes customers were able to dive into an already working market where the categories were defined by known commercial acts, which served as a natural leaping-off point for the discovery of niche music.

For years, Apple has embraced a partner-based strategy. It continues to ink new agreements with all types of third parties that add to its catalogs. As of this writing, Apple is negotiating with movie and TV studios to put films and popular programming in its iCloud offering.[90]

But Apple isn't just interested in doing deals with huge studios and record companies. Apple clearly understands the Long Tail very well. As we saw in the last section with Jordan Rudess, Apple wants even relatively small developers to keep churning out new and interesting apps. Anderson's book shows that sales from these small apps add up. Remember that Apple takes a 30 percent cut on all sales. To this end, it encourages third-party development by making its toolkits and application programming interfaces (APIs) freely available.

But not everyone is a developer, and Apple knows this. Many people are simply consumers who enjoy different products. Apple lets nondevelopers monetize their sites by making available a completely different API. From its site:

Search API allows you to place search fields in your website to search for content within the iTunes Store, App Store, iBookstore, and Mac App Store.* You can search for a variety of content; including apps, ebooks, movies, podcasts, music, music videos, audiobooks, and TV shows. You can also call an ID-based lookup request to create mappings between your content library and the digital catalog.[91]

Apple understands that open APIs trump "suggest a feature" links and forms. Consider what happens when users and customers add enhancement requests to already lengthy lists. Overworked teams and committees typically prioritize and review these requests. In the end, it's unlikely that rapid and positive responses will result. Impatient customers become frustrated and look for alternatives.

It is here that open APIs make complete sense. Neither Apple nor any company can conceive of or produce every possible app. It cannot fix every bug or make every tweak. Open APIs democratize and expedite development and innovation. More important from a business perspective, they allow thousands of individual platforms like Rudess' to grow, exponentially extending Apple's own in the process.

> **"It's all about bucks, kid. The rest is conversation."**
> —*Michael Douglas as Gordon Gekko,* Wall Street[92]

Apple's unprecedented success in selling apps cannot be attributed solely to its well-designed products. Apple has done exceptionally well here because it benefits from arguably the world's largest and most vibrant developer ecosystem. Unlike zealous Wikipedians, this is no volunteer community. Apple has paid out more than $2.5 billion to developers building off its iOS platform.[93] (iOS is Apple's mobile operating system.) For its trouble, Apple has generated more than $1 billion in commissions from apps sold in

---

* This is the App Store for Mac computers, not for iPads and iPhones.

its App Store. Like Amazon, Facebook, and Google, Apple has figured out other ways of monetizing its ecosystem beyond selling
its own hardware and software.

Apple embraces partnerships and third-party development perhaps more than any other company in the Gang of Four. Its annual
Worldwide Development Conference (WWDC) is a hot ticket. This
year, more than 5,000 developers "rushed to register before the
$1,599 tickets sold out, flew to San Francisco to be there in person,
and stood in lines that snaked around three city blocks…the conversations that took place in the hallways between sessions were
half the reason to attend."[94] Apple understands that many developers who wanted to attend simply could not. As such, it makes
much of the content and sessions available online for on-demand
streaming.[95]

Porn, Purgatory, and Apple–Partner Tensions

That's not to say every potential Apple partnership has gone
just swimmingly. First, let's consider the obvious. Pornography
has long been one of the most successful lines of business in
the Internet Age. Despite its obvious demand, Apple wants no
part of porn on its App Store and clearly states as much on its
website: "Apps containing pornographic material, defined by
Webster's Dictionary as 'explicit descriptions or displays of sex-
ual organs or activities intended to stimulate erotic rather than
aesthetic or emotional feelings,' will be rejected."[96] Under this
policy, Apple denied the ChatRoulette application in September 2010. ChatRoulette pairs random strangers from around the
world for webcam-based conversations. While arguably not the
intention and vision of its founders, the site quickly became a
hub for scantily clad people doing less than wholesome things.
Brass tacks: On platforms as popular as Apple's, not everyone is
going to be happy.

Beyond those unhappy with Apple's decision to outlaw porn,
some have criticized Apple for its opaque guidelines surrounding

App Store approval. Some companies have spent hundreds of thousands of dollars on time-sensitive marketing campaigns, only to sit in App Store purgatory for months. To minimize frustration and confusion, in September 2010, the company clarified its app approval policy:

> We have over 250,000 apps in the App Store.* We don't need any more Fart apps. If your app doesn't do something useful or provide some form of lasting entertainment, it may not be accepted. If your app is rejected, we have a Review Board that you can appeal to. If you run to the press and trash us, it never helps.
>
> If your App looks like it was cobbled together in a few days, or you're trying to get your first practice App into the store to impress your friends, please brace yourself for rejection. We have lots of serious developers who don't want their quality Apps to be surrounded by amateur hour.[97]

Some are uncomfortable with Apple's ostensible paternalism, although I have no complaints. As a personal aside and by way of disclaimer, I submitted an app for *The New Small* in April 2011. Developed by Arbor Moon and the Whole Brain Group, the relatively simple app dispenses technology tips. About a month later, it was approved.

Because it benefits so much from the apps submitted by third parties, Apple knows it must tread carefully. After all, what's to prevent a popular site such as the *New York Times* from putting its content behind a pay wall, not a proper app? Doing so means that the *Times* would not have to kick 30 percent of app revenue to Apple. In early June 2011, Apple addressed this potentially volatile issue and:

> ...quietly changed its guidelines on the pricing of In-App Subscriptions on the App Store. There are no longer any requirements

---

* As of June 2011 that number exceeded 400,000.

that a subscription be the "same price or less than it is offered outside the app." There are no longer any guidelines about price at all. Apple also removed the requirement that external subscriptions must be also offered as an in-app purchase.[98]

Apple understands that its platform isn't the only one. Wars with content providers over pricing are probably not worth fighting. They can always pull their apps from the App Store altogether.

This doesn't mean Apple is afraid of conflict. Case in point: In early 2010, the company irritated many users and developers by refusing to support Adobe Flash. (Perhaps Jobs and Gates weren't so different after all.) As a result, users soon discovered that many videos would no longer play on their iPads and iPhones. But beyond that, many developers who used Adobe as an application development platform now found themselves stuck in a quandary. Chapter 11 will have more to say about Adobe as a platform and plank.

Apple's current approach to partnerships is arguably the most restrictive of the Gang of Four. As a general rule, in the Age of the Platform, companies are better off erring on the side of openness, not restriction and bureaucracy. This encourages development and doesn't punish the many for the sins of the few. Yes, all companies have to make choices about what they will and will not support. But virtual product recalls are much easier than their real-world equivalents. Inappropriate or controversial apps or content that violates a company's terms of usage can quickly be disabled and removed from the store with a few clicks or changes of code.

The Power of Tags and Recommendations

With so many songs, apps, movies, and books in its catalog, the natural questions become:

❏ How will Apple know which products to recommend?
❏ How will customers actually find the products that interest them?

Yes, customers are very social these days. They post their opinions and reviews all over the web. Still, they need a user-friendly means of associating different songs, movies, TV shows, books, and apps with one another. It's not terribly efficient to keep bugging your friends about what else you should consider watching, reading, or listening to. And this is exactly what Amazon provides.

As we saw in Chapter 3, Amazon uses powerful technology and user-provided tags to recommend products to others based on common interests. It should come as no surprise that the Apple platform operates in a very similar manner. Let's look at the example of the incredibly popular game *Angry Birds*. Apple suggests games related to *Angry Birds*, as depicted in Figure 4.2:

Customers Also Bought

Mini Touch Golf	The Karate Kid	Air Hockey Gold	Parcel Panic - Post...	Guess 'em
Games	Games	Games	Games	Games
View in iTunes ▶	View in iTunes ▶	View in iTunes ▶	View in iTunes ▶	View in iTunes ▶

Figure 4.2: Apple Recommendations for *Angry Birds*

Apple also uses predictive technologies based partially on user tags in iTunes. In version 8 of the software, Apple introduced the Genius feature (see Figure 4.3), which automates the creation of playlists based on genre, ratings, and collaborative filtering.* Although not perfect, Genius is quite good at helping users decide which songs to queue up in their existing libraries—and *which ones might be worth buying.* By embracing the power of crowdsourcing and the masses, Apple's recommendations are far more relevant than relying on the few.

Note how Apple asks for permission to send personal user information from an individual iTunes library to Apple. We'll see in the

---

* Collaborative filtering (CF) is the process of filtering for information or patterns using techniques involving collaboration among multiple agents, viewpoints, data sources, etc. Applications of collaborative filtering typically involve very large data sets. See *http://en.wikipedia.org/wiki/Collaborative_filtering*.

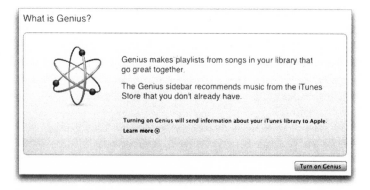

Figure 4.3: Genius User Prompt

next section how Apple has made iTunes and its overall platform more social.

GETTING (MORE) SOCIAL

Google is hardly the only one in the Gang of Four to struggle with social. In this key area, Apple is no Facebook. To its credit, however, Apple saw the need for vast improvement here. Recent enhancements to iTunes allow fans of the same artists and groups to easily connect with one another and share recommendations. Apple is making music more *social* in a few different ways. Without leaving iTunes, you can easily comment on your favorite artists' updates and like photos and songs. Figure 4.4 shows the most recent activity for English pop and jazz-pop singer-songwriter Jamie Cullum.

Then there's Ping, a relatively new iTunes functionality that allows you to easily "join the conversation, and follow your favorite artists and find out what your friends are listening to."[99] The Gang of Four—and Apple, in this case—understands that group discussions about bands, songs, tours, and events ultimately lead to sales. Why not develop planks that keep users on its platform? Figure 4.5 shows the artist page for the Canadian power trio Rush (my favorite band).

Figure 4.4: Apple iTunes Sidebar with Social Functionality for Jamie Cullum

Note iTunes' rich content and increasing social functionality. Artist profiles, such as that for Rush (pictured in Figure 4.5), are almost like micro-sites. They contain photos, reviews, and comments from fans. I can easily learn about the band, its members, and its history. I can follow or subscribe to band updates, buy music (obviously), and even find tickets to future shows—all from one page. It's almost as if iTunes concurrently aggregates:

❏ The social nature of Facebook
❏ The ecommerce functionality of Amazon
❏ The search capability of Google

Consider the simple design and ease of use of iTunes and the App Store. Coupled with the massive popularity of its hardware, Apple has become the choice of many for *legal* music. Look for Apple to continue improving its platform with enhancements to iTunes, the App Store, and its other planks.

MISSTEPS AND DETRACTORS

Apple certainly has its detractors. Perhaps because of his personal success and outspoken nature, Jobs in particular was a frequent target of attacks. Count rocker Jon Bon Jovi among Jobs' critics.

Figure 4.5: iTunes Artist Profile for Rush

Bon Jovi recently remarked that Jobs was "personally responsible for killing the music business" with iTunes.[100]

No one is saying that Apple is perfect. However, it's hard to agree with Bon Jovi here—and not just because he wore acid washed jeans in the 1980s. Don't think for a minute that companies like AOL and Microsoft aren't envious of Apple. Their forays into music weren't nearly as successful as Apple's iTunes. In fact, one could argue that Apple and iTunes actually saved the music industry, or at least prolonged its existence. It's equally silly to "blame" Craigslist for killing newspaper ads. If Craig Newmark's company hadn't done it, surely another would have.

Others scoff at Apple's prices and fat margins. Again, it's not Dell Computer. It doesn't compete on cost. It offers a premium product at a premium price. Customers have spoken: They are willing to pay.

THE FUTURE OF THE APPLE PLATFORM

The future of the Apple platform and company looks rosy. The former hardware company has transformed itself into the world's most valuable content company. Over the last five years, it "has hit that magical combination of gradually shifting from a product to a platform strategy,"[101] says Michael A. Cusumano, a professor at the M.I.T. Sloan School of Management and author of *Staying Power: Six Enduring Principles for Managing Strategy and Innovation in an Uncertain World*.

Apple will face increased competition from Amazon and Google in several key areas, including online movie and music streaming and storage. As Macs, iPhones, and iPads have become more popular, they have attracted the attention of more and more hackers. Apple will have to spend more resources on both proactively and reactively combating malware, Trojan horses, worms, and phishing attacks. Contrary to popular belief, security and privacy threats are not confined to PCs. The company also finds itself in the middle of a few legal squabbles, including (along with Research in Motion Ltd.) a potentially large patent infringement suit with Kodak over photo previewing technology.[102]

> "Show me a thoroughly satisfied man, and I will show you a failure."
> —*Thomas Alva Edison*

More than most companies, Apple may well be able to withstand these threats. Jobs imbued such a strong culture of innovation, excellence, and design sensibility into the company. Consider a 1994 interview that Jobs gave to *Rolling Stone*. At the time, he was the head of the short-lived NeXT Computer. The window into his philosophy was particularly instructive, and it's not hard to see how he was able to conceive of such revolutionary products:

> What we learned was that the reward can't be one and a half times better or twice as good. That's not enough. The reward has to be like three or four or five times better to take the risk to jump out of the mainstream.

> The problem is, in hardware you can't build a computer that's twice as good as anyone else's anymore. Too many people know how to do it. You're lucky if you can do one that's one and a third times better or one and a half times better. And then it's only six months before everybody else catches up. But you can do it in software. As a matter of fact, I think that the leap that we've made is at least five years ahead of anybody. [103]

It's obvious that Jobs understood the perennial need for innovation, and Apple's tremendous recent success has not quelled its thirst for more. Unlike many faltering companies struggling to survive, Apple is not trying to retrofit different consumer tastes into a dated model or product. It continues to push the envelope, and it's hard to see the Apple juggernaut slowing anytime soon—with one critical caveat.

Because Apple has been so successful, many technology and retail companies covet its senior managers—and some of the company's top brass have accepted lucrative external offers. Apple has lost more than a few talented executives to companies trying to import some of Apple's mojo.

The Day of Reckoning: Life Without Jobs

For years, Jobs' health was a legitimate concern for Apple, its platform, and its stockholders. Apple partners, employees, customers, and the public at large knew for quite a while that the company would have to face life without its iconic leader. That day finally arrived on August 24, 2011. Jobs stunned the business world by announcing that he was stepping down. COO and longtime heir-apparent Tim Cook took over as the company's new chief executive.

Sadly, on October 5, 2011, Jobs passed away at the age of 56.

FIVE

The King of Social

Born in 1984, Mark Zuckerberg is wise beyond his years—and has been for quite some time. As we'll see soon, one could argue that no company has faced greater challenges in building its platform and planks. (Admittedly, some of those challenges result from self-inflicted wounds.) In no way does this minimize the efforts of Amazon, Apple, and Google. Although these three companies also created vibrant ecosystems, Facebook is somehow different. For one, the speed of Facebook's ascent has been unprecedented. It was so successful so soon that, in an era of 24/7 media, it found itself under near-constant scrutiny. In other words, the company lacked the early learning curves afforded to Amazon, Apple, and Google. Those companies had more time to get their chops.

Let's look at Facebook's meteoric rise.

A RAPID ASCENT

Along with Dustin Moskovitz and Chris Hughes, Zuckerberg founded Facebook in 2004. (Moskovitz and Hughes have since moved on.) Without question, however, Zuckerberg is the face of the company. Some have called him arrogant, socially awkward, and unpolished. In this author's opinion, however, no one can legitimately call him myopic. Zuckerberg understood the importance of platforms for Facebook's future from his company's inception. Here, Zuckerberg is nothing short of a sheer visionary.

In his 2011 book, *The Facebook Effect: The Inside Story of the Company That Is Connecting the World*, David Kirkpatrick writes:

Mark Zuckerberg has had a particular obsession since Facebook's early days. On the night that his early collaborator Sean Parker first met Zuckerberg at that trendy Tribeca Chinese restaurant in May 2004, the two got into a curious argument. Zuckerberg, in Parker's opinion, kept derailing the discussion by talking about how he wanted to turn Thefacebook into a platform. What he meant was that he wanted his nascent service to be a place where others could deploy software, much as Microsoft's Windows or the Apple Macintosh were platforms for applications created by others. Parker argued that it was way too early to think about anything like that.

Zuckerberg knew from the get-go that his company benefits as its users spend more and more time on the site. But the site has to do more than offer a raft of features and easily connect users with one another based on common interests, backgrounds, and locations. First and foremost, it has to be stable and actually work—no small challenge given its popularity. Even in his early 20s, Zuckerberg wasn't interested in building a social networking site or even a profitable company. He wanted to build a great platform.

Let's turn to understanding the obstacles that Zuckerberg and Facebook needed to overcome in creating the most popular website and platform in the world (with nearly 800 million global users as of this writing). Doing so requires looking at one of Facebook's predecessors.

LESSONS FROM FRIENDSTER: SCALE, SPEED, AND PARANOIA

> "Friendship is born at that moment when one person says to another, 'What! You too? I thought I was the only one.'"
> —C. S. Lewis

The promise of Friendster is hard to understate. Along with classmates.com, Friendster was a seminal social network. Founded in 2002, it preceded even MySpace. During its apex, Friendster claimed more than 115 million registered users and more than 61 million unique monthly visitors. Today, that number sits at a paltry 8.2 million.[104] Friendster is a case study in supply not being able to meet demand. So what happened with Friendster and what did Zuckerberg learn from it?

Although it ultimately failed, users loved the concept of Friendster. This was not lost on Zuckerberg, then a Harvard freshman with a penchant for hacking and fiddling with technology. Paradoxically, the site's popularity actually killed it. From a technology standpoint, the site's lack of sufficient servers meant that pages often took minutes to load. In the end, users decided that—despite its promise—the site wasn't worth the trouble, and Friendster essentially died on the vine.

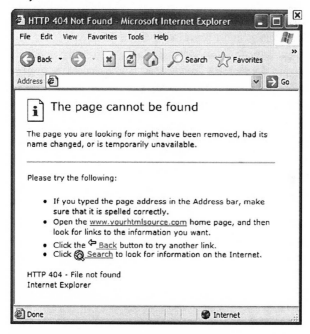

Figure 5.1: A Standard 404 Error in Internet Explorer*

---

* The 404 or Not Found error message is an HTTP standard response code indicating that the client was able to communicate with the server, but the server could not find what was requested.

In the end, the message of Friendster was loud and clear: User demand for a powerful and ubiquitous social site was strong, but not so strong that users would wait three minutes for a page to load. No matter how cool, the frequent 404 errors shown in Figure 5.1 weren't worth the trouble. This lesson was one of Zuckerberg's early obsessions.

Zuckerberg was determined to succeed where Friendster had failed. To this end, he knew that Facebook would have to manage its expansion somewhat cautiously. That is, the Facebook platform would have to concurrently grow *without sacrificing performance*. And this would mean temporarily saying no to thousands of users who wanted it. Yes, schools clamored for Facebook and eager students wanted to know when it was finally coming. But, smartly, Zuckerberg did not take the same "get big fast" approach that Jeff Bezos did with Amazon. (Note that this isn't an apples-to-apples comparison. Early on, Amazon had much more available funds than did Facebook.) Zuckerberg understood the importance of managed growth; he knew that he simply couldn't make everyone happy. Early demand for Facebook exceeded the company's ability to meet it. In this way, Facebook resembled Apple, a company that often has difficulty meeting demand.

Although Facebook today has billions more in backing and revenue than it did in the mid-2000s, Zuckerberg's paranoia about speed and scale has never stopped. Facebook continues to add data centers and make technical tweaks behind the scenes to ensure an optimal (read: fast) user experience.[105] Zuckerberg's actions belie his age. He knows that, if not properly curated, platforms can come and go, a subject discussed in Chapter 9.

THE PLANKS: HOW FACEBOOK BUILT ITS PLATFORM

As prescient as Zuckerberg may have been about creating a platform, he could not add individual planks until he was sure Facebook was strong enough to support a tsunami of users and activity. Once it was out of the woods, Facebook began adding rich features designed to strengthen its platform.

Ads

While a small business can get by on free tools and services, companies the size of Facebook that reach nearly one billion people need cash to build and grow their platforms. Facebook doesn't sell iPads or Kindles—and would surely not have taken off so rapidly if it had charged users even a nominal fee to join the site. Much like Google, it has had to sell ads to fund its operations, infrastructure, and expansion. With so much demographic information on so many users, Facebook is clearly on fire (even though its financials are not publicly available). "Facebook's distinctive form of display advertising is increasingly attracting advertisers. These are mainly smaller companies, and some of them have a strong direct-response focus," says eMarketer principal analyst David Hallerman.[106] As such, Facebook's market share of online display ad sales in 2011 will reach 17.7 percent.

Authenticity

We saw in Chapter 3 how Jeff Bezos and Amazon successfully utilized first-mover advantage (FMA). At times, however, it can actually be a disadvantage. Companies sometimes pave the way for their competitors by making costly mistakes, allowing others to leapfrog their systems, processes, business models, and technologies. Trailblazers had better be circumspect, as they may be providing others with an extremely valuable playbook of what not to do.

Many companies have successfully and deliberately employed copycat strategies. That is, they forgo FMA *on purpose*. Consider United Parcel Service (UPS). It has carefully studied the moves of its chief competitor, FedEx. UPS followed FedEx in the integrated door-to-door shipping business. UPS' über-efficient and precise handling of operations and logistics are well beyond the scope of this book. For now, suffice it to say that many of its moves were taken directly—or slightly modified—from the FedEx playbook.

Sometimes there are major benefits associated with *not being first*. In the words of Colin Hickey, technology executive and serial entrepreneur:

> Very often, it's not who is first to market, but who is first to mass market. One hundred years ago, Sunshine introduced the Hydrox—a cookie with a cream filling sandwiched between two circular chocolate wafers. But it was Nabisco that popularized the treat we now refer to as the Oreo, making it the bestselling cookie of the last century. Fast forward to today. The technology landscape is littered with startups that launch new products but never achieve escape velocity. Larger and more established firms often engage in watchful waiting. They observe the innovation race from the sidelines. They don't jump in themselves until market consolidation begins—platforms, standards, and/ or capabilities coalesce in favor of a certain technology. The ability to graduate from market introduction to volume—and ultimately profitability—often hinges on choosing the right horse not out of the gate, but at the quarter or halfway mark.[107]

Facebook took heed. It avoided core mistakes made by similar social networking companies such as MySpace and Friendster—and not just in terms of ensuring that its technology was strong enough to support massive growth. Yes, those sites utilized deficient technology. More than that, however, they ultimately suffered because they allowed users to pretend to be anyone they wanted. Early in their histories, MySpace and Friendster focused on growing their user bases at all costs—even if those users were unsavory types, spammers, and "poseurs." Quantity trumped quality and authenticity.

Not at Facebook. From its inception, Zuckerberg has taken great pains to authenticate users. While it has not been entirely successful in preventing fraud and identity theft, the vast majority of users are precisely who they say they are. (Note that LinkedIn operates in the same manner.) Consider what happens when I try to open a new Facebook account under the name *Barrack Obama*, as shown in Figure 5.2:

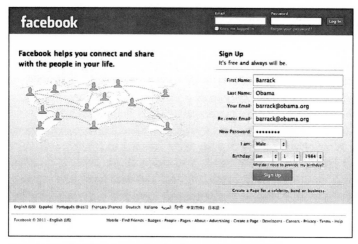

Figure 5.2: Facebook New Account Creation Attempt As Barrack Obama

There may well be other people on the planet with the same name as the current U.S. president. Nonetheless, Facebook is smart enough to know attempts like mine are probably fraudulent or less than savory in nature. After hitting the "Sign Up" button, Facebook presents the following message to me: "Our automated system will not approve this name. If you believe this is an error, please contact us."

And Facebook doesn't just raise a red flag when someone tries to pose as a highly visible politician. Even entering the name of a movie star like *Bruce Willis* will result in the same error message. Facebook does provide potential users with an appeals process in the event that a user shares the same name as a celebrity. The point here is that Facebook takes significant steps to ensure that everyone is being honest while on its platform. Not only is this ethical, but it's good business. Advertisers want to connect with people legitimately interested in their products—and have shown that they'll pay a premium to do so. Businesses don't want to waste time deciphering screen names like *knucklehead1972* or *stoner_deadhead_123*.

Facebook Connect

Without question, Facebook's initial growth resulted in much more growth. This is hardly surprising (see the section "Platforms and Network Effects" in Chapter 2). Although impossible to determine with any degree of precision, much of its growth has stemmed from some remarkably useful innovations. Facebook Connect is perhaps at the very top of this list. It turned out to be a wildly popular service that let users connect to *different* websites via Facebook. In other words, you could access content on sites such as cnn.com and patch.com without ever having to register on them. At a high level, Facebook's footprint is on some of the most popular sites in the world, seamlessly integrating with Facebook. More specifically, from the company's announcement on May 9, 2008, Facebook Connect offers the following features:

❏ **Trusted authentication**. Users will be able to connect their Facebook account with any partner website using a trusted authentication method. Whether at login, or anywhere else a developer would like to add social context, the user will be able to authenticate and connect their account in a trusted environment. The user will have total control of the permissions granted.

❏ **Real identity**. Facebook users represent themselves with their real names and real identities. With Facebook Connect, users can bring their real identity information with them wherever they go on the Web, including: basic profile information, profile picture, name, friends, photos, events, groups, and more.

❏ **Friends' access**. Users count on Facebook to stay connected to their friends and family. With Facebook Connect, users can take their friends with them wherever they go on the Web. Developers will be able to add rich social context to their websites. Developers will even be able to dynamically show which of their Facebook friends already have accounts on their sites.

❏ **Dynamic privacy**. As a user moves around the open Web, their privacy settings will follow, ensuring that users' information and privacy rules are always up-to-date. example, if a user changes their profile picture, or removes a friend connection, this will be automatically updated in the external website.[108]

Three years after its introduction, Facebook Connect remains extremely popular. Many companies and people have implemented it in some very interesting and innovative ways on their sites.*

Games

Facebook is not just about connecting with others. Many people (including yours truly) take much-needed breaks throughout the day by playing one of the site's astonishing array of games. From *Mafia Wars* to *FarmVille* to *Texas Hold'em*, the site's millions of users spend untold hours enjoying themselves or wasting time, depending on your point of view. Without question, games increase Facebook's stickiness factor. In fact, a 2010 Nielsen survey reported that "social networks and online games take up about a third of our Web time. That's up from last year, when the two categories combined to take up about 25 percent of our time."[109]

And games have become big business. Social gaming company Zynga announced on June 28, 2011 its intention to go public.[110] Many estimate that the company will raise more than $1 billion by selling a mere 10 percent of its equity. While Zynga may be the biggest social gaming beneficiary of the Facebook platform,† it certainly isn't the only one.

Credits

Perhaps the ultimate sign of Facebook's rise to prominence is its creation of a *de facto* currency—and how that unit of "money" will fuel its ecosystem. In late June 2011, Facebook made

---

* For some of these, see *http://tinyurl.com/greatplatforms-8.*

† At any point, at least seven of the top 10 Facebook games are from Zynga. See *http://tinyurl.com/facebook-top-games.*

Credits the platform's *universal* currency, with $1 U.S. equating to 10 Credits. As Samuel Axon of Mashable writes, the company will:

> …soon roll Facebook Credits out to even more application developers, so it has publicly announced that it will take 30% of the revenues earned for goods sold via Facebook Credits.
>
> Facebook Credits make up Facebook's virtual currency; the currency became available to some users last spring. Those users could buy gifts with it. Facebook then made a deal that gave users the ability to purchase Facebook Credits with their PayPal accounts and offered Facebook Credits as a currency option to several application developers, including über-huge gamemakers Playfish and Zynga.
>
> Facebook says it's taking the 30% cut so it can invest "heavily in the ecosystem" by educating users and marketing to them about the currency, testing out incentives to get people to try the credits out, and seeding credits to get people comfortable with them.[111]

Without question, some might consider the creation of Facebook Credits as further proof of Zuckerberg's God complex. That may be, but Facebook's insistence upon the use of a standardized unit is actually good business. Thousands of developers have created social games that allow users to purchase virtual goods and services via different "currencies." With Credits now serving as the standard, users can seamlessly make purchases across the entire Facebook platform, even on different games. That is, no longer do users need to hold 10 different currencies to buy 10 different things. Parenthetically, it's interesting to note that Facebook's 30 percent take of the action is equal to that which Amazon and Apple charge for related products. Again, the Gang of Four is often in synch.

Like Button

In April 2010, Facebook introduced the Like button for its own site[112] and soon after allowed for its easy installation and integration with just about any external website. The Like button works exactly as it sounds: Users can indicate that a particular story, photo, blog post, or web page interests them. In turn, that little bit of information cascades to the user's Facebook news feed—allowing that user's friends to view that "like" and potentially view it themselves.

It's natural to ask a few questions at this point. How many "likes" are clicked every day? And how much revenue does this generate for Facebook? Niall Harbison of Simply Zesty, a social media and online PR site, writes:

> Carolyn Everson, Vice President of Global Advertising Sales at Facebook, was talking about her new role when she revealed that 50 million likes are clicked for brands every single day. This is different to the one billion likes that are clicked around the web in general. It's a stunning figure that shows just how much data Facebook is gathering around our likes and interests with each of those likes popping in to databases which advertisers can of course use to help them target us. Everson who is new in the job also revealed that mobile usage was massively on the up and that users accessing Facebook via their mobile device were twice as engaged as users arriving from a computer. On mobile advertising, she said that they didn't have anything in place "yet," with a serious emphasis on the word yet.[113]

Harbison estimates that Facebook makes an unbelievable $9 million *per day* from its Like button alone. It's hard to imagine that number being anywhere near as high if millions of websites did not *voluntarily* install it.

Fan Pages and f-Commerce

We saw in Chapter 4 how Apple is turning iTunes into micro-sites for artists and music groups. Facebook is doing the same thing.

Its launch of Facebook Markup Language (FBML) and eventual replacement (iFrames) are serving as complements—if not substitutes—to traditional websites. Consider the Skittles' Facebook fan page, shown in Figure 5.3, liked by more than 18 million users as of this writing:

Figure 5.3: Facebook Fan Page for Skittles[114]

Through its fan page, Skittles—a division of Mars, Incorporated—has held contests, engaged its customers, and responded to customer feedback. But Skittles is hardly alone. In fact, there are many examples of interesting fan pages—and new ones emerge every day.* Another one of my favorites is Zappos' fan page. It provides "a great call to action that tells visitors exactly what they should be doing the first time they come to the site. They also have a 'Fan of the Week' section where they ask fans to send in pictures of themselves posing with a Zappos box in the photo."[115]

---

* For more examples, see *http://tinyurl.com/greatplatforms-5.*

Lest you think that building a robust Facebook fan page requires a great deal of money and technical skill, look at what only an admittedly modest programmer like me can do with a little time and money. Figure 5.4 shows the fan page I created for my third book, *The New Small*:*

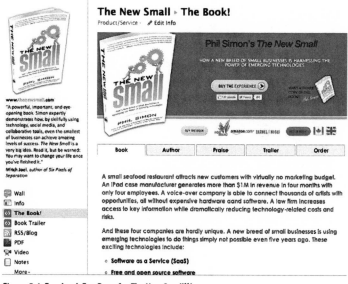

Figure 5.4: Facebook Fan Page for *The New Small* [116]

It isn't terribly difficult to create multitabbed fan pages that encourage interaction, buzz, and even commerce. (The term *f-commerce*, for Facebook commerce, is making the rounds.)

Fan pages are yet another example of Zuckerberg's profound understanding of the importance of platforms. Facebook wants its users to create interesting fan pages. Again, this encourages user participation, interaction, and time spent on the site. And let's not forget that companies with strong Facebook presences are more likely to buy ads. To encourage development, experimentation,

---

* I bought and customized a template from HyperArts, a web design firm.

and creativity, Facebook develops and gives away free tools such as FBML and iFrames. These utilities let developers, partners, and technically inclined individuals create visually compelling and feature-rich micro-sites on the Facebook platform.

In the words of Tim Ware, owner of HyperArts, a San Francisco-based web development firm:

> The fairly recent introduction of iFrame support for page tabs has further expanded these possibilities. It has allowed standard web coding methods previously not available with FBML, the now-deprecated proprietary Facebook coding language. The more time users spend on Facebook, the better for both fan pages and for Facebook.[117]

At a high level, Facebook has created a multitude of mutually beneficial scenarios through its platform. First, by attracting some of the most powerful brands in the world, the company generates considerable advertising revenue. Second, brands benefit as well. Creating visually compelling fan pages means that they can better engage their customers with contests and promotions, sell products, provide tech support, and so on.

News Feed

In September 2006, Facebook introduced two features that made its platform stickier than ever. News Feed and Mini-Feed allowed users to easily see the most recent happenings from their friends, groups, and other assorted interests. From the Facebook blog:

> News Feed highlights what's happening in your social circles on Facebook. It updates a personalized list of news stories throughout the day, so you'll know when Mark adds Britney Spears to his Favorites or when your crush is single again. Now, whenever you log in, you'll get the latest headlines generated by the activity of your friends and social groups.

Facebook makes it easy for a user to see an individual friend's latest updates in chronological order, something that Twitter also does. Alternatively, users could see all updates, and remove those that no longer interest them. Here, Facebook succeeded where MySpace failed. It struck the right balance between standardization and customization. (Chapter 9 will have more to say about MySpace.)

> Mini-Feed is a new part of the profile that shows all the latest stuff someone has added on Facebook.[118]

> Mini-Feed is similar, except that it centers around one person. Each person's Mini-Feed shows what has changed recently in their profile and what content (notes, photos, etc.) they've added. Check out your own Mini-Feed; if there are any stories you don't like, you can remove them from your profile.

Tags

In 2005, Facebook added the ability for users to upload photos of themselves, others, and just about anything else they could imagine. For any social site, photos were becoming a *sine qua non*. While this functionality may not have been terribly imaginative, allowing users to tag photos was pure genius. Through tags, users could easily indicate that a friend of theirs was also in a picture. Related notifications encouraged users to view these photos— and spend more time on the Facebook platform.

Tagging was enormously successful—and continues to be. In the words of Justin Mitchell, a Facebook engineer:

> Every day, people add more than 100 million tags to photos on Facebook. They do it because it's an easy way to share photos and memories. Unlike photos that get forgotten in a camera or an unshared album, tagged photos help you and your friends relive everything from that life-altering skydiving trip to a birthday dinner where the laughter never stopped. Tags make photos one of the most popular features on Facebook.[119]

Tags don't stop with photos, though. Facebook added the ability to tag friends, groups, celebrities, causes, and the like in notes, status updates, and even comments. All of this increases interaction, engagement, and time spent on its platform. Tagging is not only useful, it's flat-out addictive.

Other Planks

Other valuable planks in the Facebook platform include:

- ❏ **Events**. Obviate the need for standalone sites such as Evite.
- ❏ **Games**. Allow friends to easily compete with each other on an integrated platform.
- ❏ **Email messages**. Although no substitute for a fully functional email service, it does the job.
- ❏ **Instant messages (IMs)**. Reduce the need for standalone IM clients.
- ❏ **Groups**. Reduce reliance on standalone emails and allow for creation of simple wikis.
- ❏ **Notes**. Turn Facebook at least partially into a blogging platform like WordPress, TypePad, or Blogger.

And the enhancements keep coming. Facebook is constantly updating its platform and adding useful features designed to improve the overall user experience. A perfect example is the addition of integrated video calling and group chat via Skype, announced on July 6, 2011.[120]

MISSTEPS

> "I started the site when I was 19. I didn't know much about business back then."
> —*Mark Zuckerberg*

Facebook has fumbled the ball on more than one occasion. It's not batting anywhere near 1.000. At the risk of minimizing some pretty significant gaffes, Zuckerberg and company are under a much stronger microscope than just about any other company today. As Sergey Brin and Larry Page know all too well, that's the price to pay for building such a ubiquitous and powerful platform.

Censorship

We've seen in Part II how companies are often placed in the untenable position of having to make extremely difficult calls with respect to their platforms. And Facebook is certainly no exception. For instance, in June 2011, the company effectively censored popular movie critic Roger Ebert. In the words of John Hudson of the *Atlantic Wire*:

> When Facebook temporarily shut down the Facebook page of arguably the most well-known film critic in the world today, it was surprising but not at all uncharacteristic of the social network, which can't seem to find a consistent method of policing its site. Earlier today, the Facebook page of *Chicago Tribune* film critic Roger Ebert was removed for violating the company's "terms of conditions" following a controversial tweet* about Jackass star Ryan Dunn who died Monday in a car crash after posting a photo of himself drinking with friends an hour before the accident.[121]

Some claimed that Ebert was addressing a legitimate issue: drunk driving. Others disagreed, claiming that the tweet was in bad taste. Whether Facebook was justified or not in this (or any other case) isn't very important. A platform the size of Facebook cannot escape controversy. Even an ostensibly neutral stance is inherently political.

Privacy

Facebook has taken a great deal of legitimate criticism over its mishandling of privacy issues. At times, it hasn't seemed terribly concerned with personal and account safety. It also has

---

* Ebert started the controversy on Twitter with an ill-advised tweet, but the brouhaha quickly spilled over to Facebook. Note that Facebook did not take action exclusively because of what Ebert did on a competing site.

automatically opted its users in to certain programs and settings, causing a cauldron of other issues.

Exhibit 1: The company's Beacon program represented an early attempt to monetize its site through user purchase habits. Started in late 2007, the *service* (and I use that term loosely here) automatically publicized user purchases via their news feeds. In hindsight, this ill-conceived idea could only turn out to be a PR disaster, and Facebook killed the program after a little more than two years.

Beacon's immediate outrage and protests actually signified the strength of the Facebook platform. Think about it. If Facebook had been relatively anonymous, then many users may not have cared if information on some of their purchases was shared with others—or at least not have been as offended. To Zuckerberg's credit, however, he recognized two things. First, Facebook had become a powerhouse. Tweaking the design of the home page was one thing. In the future, however, he would not be able to institute these types of wholesale changes without user consent. Public outcries such as Beacon made Zuckerberg realize that he had succeeded in his goal of creating a great platform. Second, if Zuckerberg ignored these types of legitimate user complaints, his company might go the way of MySpace.

Since Beacon, Facebook has taken greater pains to preserve user privacy. The company's chief privacy officer, Chris Kelly, seems to be saying all of the right things. Armed with plenty of cash, Facebook has hired expensive Washington, DC-based lobbyists to ensure that its voice is heard by influential politicians. Although users have quit Facebook in droves (and I certainly can't claim they weren't for completely valid reasons), the company is proving to be extremely resilient to privacy and PR gaffes. Platforms can withstand a few body blows.

Battles

Internecine battles among members of the Gang of Four are quite common, and Facebook is no exception to this rule. For instance, in version 10 of iTunes (discussed in Chapter 4), Apple introduced Ping, a feature designed to make the music application more social. These days, *more social* typically means—at least in part—integration with Facebook Connect.

According to sources familiar with Facebook's platform, the social networking giant essentially denied Apple's Ping access to APIs that would let it search for an iTunes user's friends on Facebook who also had signed up for Ping. Normally, this API access is open and does not require permission.[122] However, Facebook retains the exclusive right to closing it, especially when it doesn't like the specific application or functionality deployed by a partner, developer, or other third party.

Using the Platform—to Fight the Platform

The Facebook platform has been a dynamic one. The company has introduced new features, retired old ones, and altered existing ones. Depending on your point of view, Facebook's platform now may be better or worse. No site or business with hundreds of millions of users is bound to make everyone happy, and Facebook is no exception. As a platform, however, Facebook is exceptional in that its users can rail against it by using Facebook! Users have started groups protesting home page redesigns, privacy changes, and default settings. Some have added hundreds of thousands of members. Groups even start protesting other groups, begging the Facebook powers-that-be to remove those with offensive views.

THE FUTURE OF THE FACEBOOK PLATFORM

Looking to the future, Facebook may find itself at a crossroads, much like Apple and Google (discussed in Chapters 4 and 6, respectively). It is the only one of the Gang of Four not publicly traded, but that may be changing—and not because Zuckerberg necessarily wants his company to go public.[123] In fact, as a few legal experts have pointed out, the Securities and Exchange Commission (SEC) might force Facebook to go public. While this may allow Facebook to raise billions of dollars, it will not come without cost. The company will have to open its books for the world to see, although it certainly will not have to divulge everything. For instance, Amazon chooses not to disclose the number of Kindles sold and is not legally obligated to do so.

Going public may in fact be inevitable, as evinced by a few of the company's recent moves.[124] If it happens in early 2012 as is rumored, then Facebook will no longer be able to operate in such a vacuum. If and when it begins to report publicly available financial results, expect a maelstrom of concern from many privacy advocates who have been chomping at the bit. The irony is considerable: Many people are dying for more internal information about a company that knows so much about us.

An IPO would result in a financial windfall for many of Facebook's troops.[125] While unquestionably great for the employees who've worked so hard for so long, this could present a significant issue for Facebook. Remember that key employee departures or *brain drains* have affected Google and many other startups that went public.

In fact, key Facebook turnover is already taking place. Many long-tenured employees received private shares of company stock that could be sold in secondary markets. That is, they can cash out *before* any Facebook IPO—or they could leave the company knowing that they can do so at any time. And some are doing just that. For instance, former marketing head Jonathan Ehrlich left Facebook in late 2010 to start Copious, a social marketplace for buying from and selling to people—not strangers.

Regardless of whether an IPO is in Facebook's future, the company's platform has proven to be quite resilient. Zuckerberg is preparing for more growth, although he surely understands that his company's torrid rate cannot possibly continue. In fact, it has already showed signs of waning, even as its total users keep climbing.[126] Facebook is still adding new users, but at a slower rate than even a few months ago. Perhaps its user base will reach a billion or so and then level off.

On the mobile front, look for Facebook to up its game. In a recent piece for the *Wall Street Journal*, Geoffrey A. Fowler and Yukari Kane write:

> The social network, which has turned its popular website into a platform for developing games and other add-on programs, so far hasn't wielded the same influence on mobile gadgets like Apple Inc.'s hit iPhone and iPad. But there are signs the company is trying to change that situation.[127]

Bret Taylor, Facebook's CTO, has been understandably tight-lipped about the company's forthcoming products. In the same *WSJ* piece, however, he acknowledged the importance of mobility, saying, "You want to reach as many people in as many places as possible." Translation: Facebook will beef up its mobile presence in innovative ways. It wants to reach more untethered customers and users.

Look for Google and Facebook to continue to collide, especially in the online advertising space. From the eMarketer report mentioned earlier, Google and Facebook are "going after many of the same advertisers to some extent, and this is where one facet of the competition between them will heat up. However, with the vastly different advertising experience each company offers, many marketers will run display ads on both platforms." [128]

In late June 2011, Zuckerberg and Facebook finally rid themselves of the pesky lawsuit from the Winklevoss twins who had claimed that the entire notion for the site was their idea.[129] Zuckerberg publicly dismissed the Winklevoss' claims, which to be sure, was more of a minor annoyance than a serious threat to the company's future. Still, at least Facebook can now put that issue behind it and tackle the other challenges and opportunities associated with its future.

Lessons Learned?

You would think that, as they say, the burnt hand teaches best. At times, it appears as if Facebook has learned from its privacy and security missteps. (At other times, the opposite is true. As this book was going to print, Facebook found itself in the middle of another imbroglio surrounding its decision to introduce facial recognition technology tags in its photos—by opting users in and forcing them to opt out.) While Zuckerberg may only be paying these issues lip service, it does appear as if he is maturing into more of a leader. To that end, as David Kirkpatrick writes in *The Facebook Effect,* at some point in 2010 Zuckerberg began seeing an executive coach to polish his leadership skills.

Moreover, the company realizes that it's better to ask for permission, not forgiveness. As a result, it now takes steps to ensure that third-party apps accessing its API received explicit user permission before connecting, as evident in Figure 5.5:

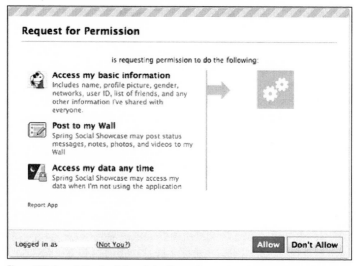

Figure 5.5: Generic Facebook Permission Request

While it does result in an extra click and slows down the overall user experience, asking permission builds trust and reinforces the notion that Facebook cares about user perception.

In the end, a Facebook discussion solely focused on whether it goes public, the amount of money it makes from advertising, and the absolute number of users, misses the point. The company has become a daily and integral part of the lives of hundreds of millions of people. Its platform provides mostly free and extremely useful services—and is responsible for more than enough money to keep adding more while making a profit. To boot, its leader knows full well the importance and responsibilities associated with a great platform. Don't expect Facebook to falter anytime soon.

SIX

From Search to Ubiquity

I routinely roll out of bed at 5 a.m. and wonder if I should move to Europe so I would fit in. I just don't sleep that much, and I wake up way before any of my friends—or most of the United States, for that matter. I turn on my computer to start my day and begin by checking my email messages. Although I have seven different email accounts, Gmail easily handles them all. For millions of people like me, one-stop shopping is the way to go. I couldn't imagine having to log in to seven different web pages.

I then check my favorite blogs—and I follow quite a few. Fortunately, I don't have to go to 100 different sites and manually see if there's anything new. Nor do I have to sift through my inbox. Google Reader handles them all on one page. I can quickly see which of my friends and favorite thought leaders have written a new post or published a new video. I'll also check Google News to see what happened while I "slept."

After making my coffee, I start with the day's writing. Right now, I'm working on this book. Although I use Google Docs on a regular basis, I still use an older version of Microsoft Word for long-form pieces. In doing my research, I often turn to Google Books, a product that acts like my own personal librarian—although Amazon's search inside this book feature is also very useful.

Over the course of the day, I'll use Google Maps to find directions to a few places. I'll search the web in general (as well as specific sites) with Google's core search product. I'll refine my searches with keywords, negative keywords, timeframes, and quotes. But having to *pull* information gets a bit tiresome. Ideally, I would like to be quickly notified when there's news on something important to me—that is, *what I deem to be* relevant would be *pushed* to me. No problem. My customized Google Alerts tell me almost immediately when that happens.

I used to surf the web with Firefox, but switched a few months ago to Chrome, Google's lightning-fast search engine that I've easily customized with different extensions. While away from my computer, I can even search by voice by just talking into my iPhone.

Around lunchtime, I'll call a few friends on Google Voice and maybe even send them instant messages (IMs) from my computer. I won't miss my meetings, though, because Google Calendar will remind me of them via email notification or text message. When scheduling with others, Google will even suggest appointment slots. This minimizes the tedious back-and-forth of finding a commonly acceptable time and date. Perhaps later I'll waste a little time or learn something new by watching a few videos on YouTube. I might even publish one myself. And the options on YouTube abound. As of May 2011, I can watch entire movies there.

At least a few times throughout the day, I'll "cheat" on Google. I'll see what my friends are doing on Facebook and listen to music on GrooveShark. While I could use Orkut and Google Music for largely the same purposes, respectively, they're just not my cup of tea. That is, I'm not completely "loyal" to Google, but it should be obvious now that I'm a really big fan. In total, I'll use at least 10 different Google products within any given day. It's fair to say that I, like tens of millions of other people, spend a great deal of time on the Google *platform*.

If I could only use one platform and I had to be as productive as possible, I wouldn't have to think twice. It would be Google. I have no doubt that millions of other people feel the same way I do. What was once a small search engine company has evolved into arguably the most powerful and far-reaching digital platform the world has ever seen. Let's take a brief look at how.

A BRIEF HISTORY

> "Google is this era's transformational computing platform."
> —Stephen E. Arnold, 2005

In 1995, two graduate students in their early 20s met on the campus of Stanford University. At the time, they were anonymous, even to each other. The two *wunderkinds*, Sergey Brin and Larry Page, did not exactly hit it off. [130] Fast forward a few years to September 1998. Brin and Page officially filed papers of incorporation in California for their company, Google.

At some point in the 2000s, Brin and Page figured out three critical things. First, Google's technology could do a great deal more than scour and index the web, returning the most accurate results in fractions of a second.

Second, although search had been incredibly important and profitable, it has limitations. One person can only do so many searches each day. Even when multiplied by billions of people, this limitation restricts how much money Google can make. On a related note, Google's competitors were already vastly improving their own search offerings in the hope of getting in on the action. As Google continued to profit from its core products, imitators would attempt to catch up.

Third, Google would benefit tremendously if it had more to offer than just search. What if different people could use Google products and services in entirely different ways? In order to make this happen, Google would need to become much more than the place for people to find answers to their questions. It would have to become a platform.

The impact of these three key realizations is hard to overstate. As Google became more powerful, it started to push its limits—and those of established institutions. There are too many examples to list here, but a few are worth mentioning.

The company stunned traditional telecommunications heavy-weights by placing what was believed to be a multibillion-dollar bid in 2007 on wireless spectrum.[131]

And let's not forget Google Books, a particularly instructive event on a number of levels. The project began in late 2004 as a curiosity: Why not make all books available for searching? To that end, the company bought fast, high-tech scanners that would not damage original books. Google then began scanning entire libraries for digital consumption—without ever receiving the permission of publishers and authors. This prompted lawsuits that continue as of this writing.

Google at times has seemed more interested in whether it *could* do something than whether it *should* do it in the first place.

THE PLANKS: HOW GOOGLE BUILT ITS PLATFORM

Google never could have become a platform if search were its only club in the bag. Today, Google's array of products and services is astonishing. Its platform consists of many planks, including:

❏ Geography-based tools
❏ Home and office
❏ Innovation
❏ Media
❏ Mobile
❏ Social
❏ Specialized search
❏ Web

You'll probably recognize many of the icons associated with Google products, presented in Figure 6.1.

And Google keeps adding more products—and improving existing ones.* For instance, through a partnership with Samsung, in June

---

* For a complete and updated list of categories and specific products, see *http://www.google.com/intl/en/about/products/index.html.*

Figure 6.1: Icons for Google Products[132]

2011 Google launched the Chromebook, a light, lightning-fast computer with Chrome serving as its operating system. Although not yet a replacement for the traditional PC or arguably even tablets,[133] the move is an important one for Google, a company attempting to cement its foothold in increasingly competitive markets.

Google is operating here just like Amazon, Apple, and Facebook. Each of these companies realized that it needed to move sideways. In the case of Google, the company recognized the need—and had the financial resources—to offer complementary products and services. Brin and Page know the importance of keeping users on Google's platform. Let's look at the multipronged strategy by which Google has done this.

AdWords

It's safe to say that Google wouldn't be Google today without AdWords. All of Google's experiments, random products, and new directions stem from the money it makes from those little ads seen at the right of its search results. Proving that time flies, AdWords is nearing its 10th anniversary. AdWords' history is quite the interesting story. According to a *Wired* article:

> Engineers at Google took the concept of pay-per-click search results and in 2002 turned it into a smooth-running, money-printing machine called AdWords. The company developed an automated process for advertisers to bid on keywords. It also made the auctions more sophisticated so customers couldn't game the system. Crucially, Google determined ad prominence on a Web page not just by the price advertisers were willing to pay per click—as Overture had done—but also based on how many clickthroughs that ad generated. As a result, Google's system responded quickly to ineffective ads: They disappeared. Google also had a massive database that tracked which ads worked and which didn't, information it could pass on to its customers to help them create better ad campaigns. By the time that Google announced its financial results for the first time in 2004, the cat was out of the bag. Without question, the company had invented one of the great products of the Internet Age.

But AdWords is just one means by which the company has monetized its platform.

AdSense

Google realized long ago that monetizing search had enormous potential. That potential is hardly unlimited. The company could only make so much money on Google-based searches. Surely, Google's technology could be adapted and pushed to the masses?

Much like the Amazon affiliate program mentioned in Chapter 3, Brin and Page figured out that millions of other websites could drive traffic and revenue to Google—or, perhaps more accurately, revenue *through* Google.

In 2003, it purchased the technology behind what would ultimately become AdSense.[134] After some tweaking to the core technology, Google now describes AdSense on its site as a free program that empowers online publishers to earn revenue by displaying relevant ads on a wide variety of online content, including:

❑ **Site search results**. Easily add a custom search engine to your site, and earn from ads on the search results pages.
❑ **Websites**. Display ads on your website that are suited to your audience's interests, and earn from valid clicks or impressions.
❑ **Mobile web pages and apps**. Connect your mobile users with the right ad at the right time as they seek information on the go.
❑ **Feeds**. Display targeted ads in your RSS feeds, wherever they're viewed.[135]

AdSense does a number of important things for Google. First, it spreads and democratizes Google's search technology. By inserting a snippet of code, even the smallest websites become Google partners, making money for both themselves and Google. This reinforces the "win-win" scenario. Much like the rest of the Gang of Four, Google knows that sharing a bigger pie trumps keeping a smaller pie all to itself.

Beyond direct monetization, however, AdSense gives Google a footprint on millions of other websites whose owners also want to monetize their own platforms. This is similar to the Facebook Like button discussed in Chapter 5. And for Google it gets even better. Because of these positive interactions—and the attendant revenue generated—these partners have greater proclivities and incentives to try future Google products.

We know Google has become a platform—and a very powerful one. The natural question is how?

The 20 Percent Rule and Institutionalized Innovation

At many organizations, senior leaders espouse vague and facile platitudes such as "innovation is important." When times are tight, they'll often look first to research and development (R&D) when trimming budgets. Particularly in publicly traded companies, meeting quarterly numbers becomes paramount to long-term growth. Paradoxically, executives at many of these companies then wonder why, at the end of the year, few if any new products or ideas have gained any traction.

Of course, Google is not your average company. To encourage creativity, it has gone as far as just about any company. It has *institutionalized* innovation. In order to create complementary products, management formally allows (insists?) that its software engineers spend up to 20 percent of their time working on products that interest them—and lie outside of their normal responsibilities. At Google, this isn't considered slacking off or goofing around. It's considered wise, innovative, and a *requirement*.

And the policy works. It is responsible for products such as Gmail, Google News, and others. Based on my research, very little is off-limits at the company. The top brass there is smart enough to realize that its lead in search is hardly guaranteed. Look at what happened to Microsoft with Windows and Office. There are legitimate alternatives to each—and that trend won't be abating anytime soon.

Let's look at a few things here. First, Google isn't utopia—nor is any company and its platform, for that matter. It has problems just like any other company. Second, in terms of size, reach, and value, your company isn't anything like Google.

But is your business primarily tied up in one revenue stream? Is this healthy? Can't you adopt some of Google's principles?

One-Stop Shopping

> "I think Google should be like a Swiss Army knife: clean, simple, the tool you want to take everywhere."
> —Marissa Mayer, Google vice president of Location and Local Services

As we saw in Chapter 1, Web 1.0 introduced instant messaging, email, search, Voice over Internet Protocol (VOIP), and other essential building blocks for the contemporary and future web. Years ago, people needed to use a number of disparate and standalone tools to manage their communications. This is no longer the case. Google understands the benefits of one-stop shopping.

Google doesn't want its users to go to another site for anything. By keeping you on its platform, Google collects more information about its users and their friends—where they are, what they like, what they do, and other critical aspects of their lives. More information leads to better, more relevant ads. This leads to more money.

Consider Gmail. Even if it isn't the single "best" email service or application (and it may very well be), it's just easier for people to do everything under one umbrella. These days, not too many people want to log in to eight different sites or launch eight different applications to do eight different things. While in front of their computers, few people manage absolutely everything from a single dashboard. However, tools such as iGoogle allow users to easily add gadgets; chat; access spreadsheets, pictures, and other documents; send and receive email; and do countless other things. Today's consumer demands maximum interoperability, integration, and convenience.

Personalization

We have seen in this section how Amazon, Apple, and Facebook allow users to create personalized experiences for themselves. Amazon's and Apple's product recommendations stem from customer ratings and previous purchases. Apple makes it easy to customize iPads and iPhones with myriad options. Facebook enables simple customization of news feeds, groups, profile pictures, and the like. (Note that Facebook does not allow its users to create highly customized home pages—something MySpace did. As we'll see in Chapter 9, this ultimately turned out to be a mistake, and contributed to the downfall of MySpace.)

Google is no exception to this rule, something of which I am certain despite having no insider's knowledge of its highly protected search algorithm. Google guards its secret formula quite closely, and with good reason. While people use the Google platform, the company and its software constantly learn more and more about user preferences and habits. As far as I can tell, its software never stops learning. More knowledge is always better, allowing Google to return more relevant search results and ads. Places include the right side of Google's search results, at the top of Gmail messages, and wherever else they make sense (to Google, at least).

The bottom line is that your search results and mine are not the same because you and I are not the same. Google has the ability to serve up more relevant search results to people depending on many factors: geography, gender, age, religion, income, ethnicity, previous search history, and whatever else it can deduce about its users. Of course, many users choose not to provide this information to Google—but willingly provide it (and much more) to Facebook. For this reason, Facebook could usurp Google—and soon. This is not lost on Brin and Page.

Attention Is Currency

Google realizes it is ultimately competing for people's time and attention as much as it is for money. If this forces Google to play defense, then so be it.

Let's look at an example. For years now, people have been using their computers to easily make one-to-one phone calls and conference calls over the Internet. Up until recently, however, one could not use Google to do so. Google realized that it was losing the attention of its users who had to go elsewhere—in this case, to Skype. For Google, this was a problem that it had the means to solve.

In 2007, the company acquired Internet-based communications service GrandCentral for $95 million. After making some enhancements, in March 2009, it introduced the rebranded Google Voice, equipped with video chat. Today, Google's offering is not nearly as popular as Skype, a service with nearly 100 million registered users—many of whom only use its free version.[136] Google Voice may never reach Skype's numbers, although the latter's acquisition by Microsoft has rankled many who like Skype just the way it is. The point remains: Google recognized that it was losing the attention of its users—and did something about it. Or, if you like, its platform needed to add a plank.

Embrace Freemium

Google realizes that people today can select from a bevy of free email programs, search engines, online productivity tools, and the like. So, why does Google spend so much time, money, and resources developing products that it plans to just give away?

Google embraces freemium because monetization these days is often indirect. Sure, some users of the free versions of Gmail and the aforementioned Google Voice, Google Docs, and Google Apps will upgrade to paid versions. However, Google realizes that it benefits even when most of its users opt for the free versions of its products. Let's explore why.

At least for basic services, it's tough to charge when legitimate free alternatives exist. Would most people pay $50 for *basic* Gmail when Yahoo! Mail or Hotmail or some other application will do the trick? Probably not, especially when a quick Google search of "free email" returns 44,000,000 results.

The amount of revenue that Google derives from its noncore, ancillary products is not significant, at least in comparison to AdWords, AdSense, and other paid search products. Focusing on that, however, misses the big picture. Each product and service extends the Google platform and makes the company's brand more valuable.

Yes, from the consumer's perspective, products such as Gmail and Google News are certainly useful, and it's hard to argue with their prices (free). However, each product is simply a clever means to a very common end—make more money.

If I use Gmail to send a few messages about playing golf with my friends, then Google is likely to show me ads for discounted clubs or trips to resorts. The more I use Gmail, the more Google will learn about me. (Admittedly, this scares many people who believe that Google employees are reading their emails.) Perhaps Google's software is smart enough to figure out that I like to play early in the morning and that I'm a lefty. As its ads become more specific, I'm more likely to click on them.

Partners

Beyond launching more than 100 products, Google has embraced many different types of partners. Big telecom companies such as Verizon and AT&T sell Google Droids. Much like Apple's ecosystem, thousands of developers submit apps to work on those devices. Google is working with LG on a tablet to compete with the iPad.[137] Institutions of all sorts can license Google Earth Pro.[138] As discussed before, many websites make money via Google AdSense. Or you can sign up to resell Google Apps to enterprises.[139]

MISSTEPS

> "A hero is someone who understands the responsibility that comes with freedom."
> —Bob Dylan

Let's face it: Being Google isn't easy. Launching new products and services, entering new markets—and creating others—and taking on mighty corporations with vested interests in the status quo carries with it enormous risk. Along the way, Google has made its share of mistakes. While hardly a comprehensive list, let's briefly discuss three.

Privacy

As much as people have loved Gmail (particularly its free sticker price), many have objected to what they falsely perceive as Google reading their email messages. Google ads at the top of messages are often a little too relevant, making some question whether their information was being used for nefarious reasons. The word *creepy* has been used more than a few times.[140]

And this general unease doesn't stop with Gmail. In 2007, Google Maps launched a feature called *Street View* that, as its name implies, allows people to view many public—and private—areas and events with astonishing detail.*

In an effort to compete with Twitter, Google announced the launch of Buzz on February 9, 2010. Buzz's tight integration with Gmail proved to be too tight, as users found themselves *automatically* added to lists of *public* networks based on their own email histories. Few users knew about this default setting—and how to change it.[141] A mere two days later, Google tweaked Buzz's

---

* For some extremely entertaining shots taken with Street View, see
http://mashable.com/2007/05/31/top-15-google-street-view-sightings.

settings and "belatedly recognized the backlash over privacy concerns with the new service." [142]

China

After much internal debate, Google entered China in early 2006. The promise of reaching more than one billion people proved too much to ignore, even at the expense of compromising its quixotic corporate goals by censoring its results. Steven Levy devotes a considerable portion of his book, *In The Plex: How Google Thinks, Works, and Shapes Our Lives*, to the China issue. He explains:

> Google had hoped that its decision to create a search engine in the .cn domain—one that followed government rules of censorship—would lead to a level playing field. But even as Google rolled out its .cn web address, there were indications that its compromise would not satisfy the Chinese government. Unexplained outages still occurred. (Meanwhile, Google's competitor Baidu seemed to hum along unscathed.) And not long after Google got its operating license, in December 2005, the Chinese declared that the license was no longer valid, charging that it wasn't clear whether Google's activities made it an Internet service or a news portal. (Foreigners could not operate the latter.) Google then began a year-and-a-half-long negotiation to restore the license.

Things went downhill from there. Malicious and highly sophisticated attacks from Chinese sources, the need for constant "cooperation" with Chinese officials, claims that it was selling out and violating its core mission, and a host of other problems caused Google to pull the plug on its China experiment after a little more than four years. [143] Eric Schmidt was rumored to have considered resigning over the fiasco.

Paternalism and Perceived Arrogance

Many have called Google employees and the company paternalistic and arrogant. [144] Remember that the initial release of Gmail lacked a delete button—by design. Google a bit pompously assumed that people only deleted messages to save space. In reality, there were many other reasons at play beyond the scope of this book. Much like Apple, Google tried to remove features that its users were clearly not ready to forgo. Apple has arguably had more success in this area.

But more than any one feature, product, or statement, the perception by many of Google as arrogant is a function of its utility and its ubiquity. Mark Zuckerberg can certainly relate. He's under an equally powerful microscope. Google has rolled out features and offerings faster than many societal institutions have been able to grasp. At least in the United States, we are simply not ready to address many of the core privacy, security, and legal issues that stem from these amazing innovations. In other words, while certainly not perfect, Google is not inherently evil. Mistakes aside, Google just happens to be the entity responsible for giving us what we want. Blaming it for "the death of privacy" is analogous to blaming Apple for the death of the music industry or Craig Newmark for the death of newspapers. Each argument misses the mark. If Microsoft or IBM had launched the equivalent of Google Maps, people would be screaming at the leaders of those companies instead of Google.

2011: THE STATE OF GOOGLE

Today, Google makes virtually all of its money from two related forms of advertising. As of October 2010, 67 percent of its revenue came from ads on Google websites. Another 30 percent came from Google's ad network (AdWords). What this means is only three percent of its revenue comes from nonadvertising sources.[145] For some time, Google's lack of major alternative revenue streams has been cause for great internal concern.

This concern has intensified since Facebook has come into prominence—and threatens general Google domination and revenue from search. Remember a few key points here. First, you can't use Google to search within Facebook the same way that you can "Google" espn.com, cnn.com, or any number of sites. (This is called Google Site Search.) Zuckerberg and company won't likely ever open that bridge. Second, one minute spent in Facebook's walled garden means one minute less spent on Google. It also means that Google cannot collect a significant amount of very valuable data.

Insiders have noted that Google is scared of Facebook. And this fear is justified. Consider that, in late 2009, users spent three times as long per session on Facebook compared to Google.[146] Chris Anderson, *Wired* editor-in-chief, recently said that number had climbed to more than four times as long.

THE FUTURE OF THE GOOGLE PLATFORM

This chapter has explored the juggernaut that is Google. By embracing the 20 percent rule, allowing for one-stop shopping, recognizing the importance of consumers' attention, embracing freemium, and keeping its products simple, Google has become a highly admired, innovative, respected, and profitable machine.

Ultimately, the future of the Google platform does *not* depend on:

❏ Getting social right, although it may have finally done so. In June 2011, the company launched a small field trial of its latest social networking play, Google+. Reviews have been largely positive, and it has quickly amassed more than 25 million users.[147] Although not a potential rival to Facebook yet, Plus represents Google's most successful foray into the social space.
❏ Fending off Microsoft and Facebook in the battle for search and related advertising dollars.
❏ Making peace with increasingly interested regulators.
❏ Avoiding additional privacy gaffes.
❏ Keeping pace with companies such as Apple.

Yes, these factors are certainly important. However, for Google to remain a great platform, it will have to successfully manage a unique tension between two valid and conflicting internal needs.

For years, many inside the company have been concerned about its lack of revenue diversification. Today, Google remains predominantly an advertising business. On the one hand, at the most senior levels, the company recognizes the limits of search. And it is that awareness that has spurred policies and a culture conducive to innovation (hence the 20 Percent Rule). It is critical for Google to keep expanding and innovating. Beyond capping revenue and profits, the company knows the long-term dangers of being a one-trick pony, even if it's a lucrative trick.

On the other hand, this need to diversify has to coexist with some degree of focus on the here and now. Google can't coast on search, what with Facebook and Microsoft trying to build a better mousetrap. Even ambitious Google executives know that no company can realistically be everything to everybody. And mighty Google is no exception.

Moving too far from traditional areas of expertise can lead to major financial and PR disasters, nasty collisions with governments, and an erosion of the powerful Google brand. For instance, perhaps because the upside did not justify the risk, in June 2011, Google announced the eventual retirement of Google Health. The company's official statement is, "we've observed that Google Health is not having the broad impact that we hoped it would."[148]

> **Looking toward the future, it will be critical for Google to strike the right balance between expansion and focus.**

A Unique Tension: Is Google Between the Wheels?

At this point, it's fair to ask: Is this tension with Google unique? I suspect that the answer is *yes*. Few companies face the same dilemmas that Google does. Given its incredible technology, boatload of cash, and über-smart employees, executives can and do ask themselves, "What world should we conquer next?" Google can then set out to do so. Not many organizations have *ever* had that ability. To boot, consider the company's stated credos:

❏   Organize the world's information.
❏   Don't be evil.

These aren't the goals of your average company. They are much more ambitious and, one could argue, even noble.

Google has certainly accomplished the first. Depending on your point of view, it does a pretty good job at the second. But there's a flip side to the Google coin. Its overarching ethos aside for a moment, doesn't Google really have much more pedestrian objectives? Isn't it just like Facebook—trying to make its users divulge as much information about themselves as possible? Aren't all of its cool and mostly free products and services simply attempts to increase the amount of information it has on its users, customers, and the world at large?

In other words, one can credibly argue that the entire goal of Google's platform has been—and continues to be—to serve up more and more accurate ads. In turn, these ads generate more money for the company. Google has realized that search is but one of the many means of delivering relevant and revenue-producing ads.

Let's say that Google's advertising revenue drops considerably and the company is forced to diminish its lofty ambitions. While important, cool products and an avid user base by themselves cannot replace billions in lost revenue. Monetization ultimately matters. Fortunately for Google, its executives realize that it must generate profits from other lines of business—and soon. Google may not know how it will accomplish this, but understanding the importance of its task is step one. In the words of Malcolm Gladwell, "The key to good decision making is not knowledge. It is understanding."

Will Google remain one of the most dominant platforms around? Because of its ample resources, remarkable leadership, willingness to experiment, and highly intelligent employees, I certainly wouldn't bet against it.

PART III
SYNTHESIS: UNDERSTANDING THE POWER OF THE PLATFORM

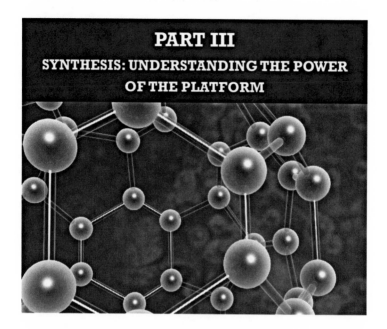

Part III of the book takes a step back. It extrapolates and distills the lessons of the previous four chapters. It looks at the components, characteristics, benefits, and perils of platforms. It concludes by providing lessons for building your own platforms and planks.

Chapter Seven—The DNA: Platform Components and Characteristics

Chapter Eight—Gimme the Prize! The Benefits of Platforms

Chapter Nine—Slings and Arrows: The Perils of Platforms

Chapter Ten—The How: Tips for Building a Platform

SEVEN

The DNA: Platform Components and Characteristics

art II focused on the four most important platforms today. It showed how Amazon, Apple, Facebook, and Google have become increasingly influential, profitable, self-perpetuating, and self-sustaining ecosystems. By working with hundreds of thousands of partners, affiliates, and third-party developers, the Gang of Four extends its platforms in innovative and fascinating ways.

PLATFORMS EVOLVE—AND SO DO THE COMPANIES BEHIND THEM

> "We create monsters and then we can't control them."
> —Joel Coen

First, let's state the obvious. Compared to their early stages, Amazon, Apple, Facebook, and Google are very different companies today. As Part II of this book demonstrated, each is almost unrecognizable from its former self—and not just in terms of exponentially greater revenue and profits. Each offers more, deeper, and better products and services than even just five years ago. Their platforms contain more planks.

With the possible exception of Facebook, the Gang of Four did not begin as a platform. Consider Amazon for a moment. As we saw in Part II, in 1994 it was essentially a one-trick pony, as was Google in 1998. Apple designed cool products, but it was not a true platform in 1997. As each company evolved, so too did its platform. Absent the multiple metamorphoses of these companies, it's hard to imagine that they would have built such powerful platforms today.

THE ABILITY TO SCALE

> **"Temporary solutions often become permanent problems."**
> —*Craig Bruce*

As we saw in Chapter 5, Mark Zuckerberg immediately grasped the importance of scale for Facebook. If he had taken on more schools and users without the bandwidth to handle this expansion, Facebook would have gone the way of Friendster. Google engineers have studied ways to shave *fractions of a second* off of search retrieval times. They understand that even nanoseconds add up—and detract from its platform and user experience. Amazon and Apple don't turn down business because they don't have sufficient room for new customers, vendors, and partners. They look at excess capacity as an asset, not a cost to be minimized. As we saw in Chapter 3, Amazon just sells computer power it doesn't need—to the tune of hundreds of millions of dollars in pure profit.

> Perhaps the single most important attribute of a platform is its ability to easily incorporate more. I use the ambiguous word *more* here intentionally because more may mean users, customers, planks, apps, communities, products, partners, searches, web pages, or ads. It all depends on the platform.

Cloud Computing

These days, companies and technologies can scale much easier than in years past. This is primarily possible through cloud computing. While Amazon, Apple, Facebook, and Google have all invested heavily in data centers, most businesses need not spend millions of dollars to do the same. Doing so would be analogous to producing their own electricity, a point Nicholas Carr makes in his 2009 book, *The Big Switch: Rewiring the World, from Edison to Google*. Reputable cloud computing vendors such as Rackspace offer a bevy of secure, stable hosting products and services.

Regardless of where your compute power comes from, make sure you have enough of it. In the Age of the Platform, companies need the ability to easily scale up if their platforms explode in popularity. The axiom "better to have it and not need it than need it and not have it" comes to mind. It's no coincidence that cloud computing has allowed Amazon, Apple, Facebook, and Google to operate at light speed—and never have to worry about lacking sufficient technology resources.

DYNAMIC STABILITY AND CHANGE-TOLERANT ORGANIZATIONS

McGraw-Hill's *An Illustrated Dictionary of Aviation* defines the term *dynamic stability* as "the characteristics of an aircraft that, when disturbed from an original state of steady flight or motion, allow it to damp the oscillations using its inherent restoring moments and gradually return to its original state."

The Gang of Four maintains and grows its platforms and powerful ecosystems via dynamic stability (see the sidebar on page 136, "Building a Change-Tolerant Business"). Amazon, Apple, Facebook, and Google handle change well because they are concurrently stable and in motion. Consider the following questions in the context of some of the major changes made by these companies:

❏ What if you could only buy songs on iTunes—and not books, movies, TV shows, and apps?

❏ What if Amazon stuck to its original plan? What if it only sold physical books?

❏ Would Google's brand be as valuable if it only made a search engine?

❏ What if Facebook had not added photos, chat, messages, and apps?

❏ Although it is not a true platform, think about Netflix, a Wall Street darling. Would it be as formidable if it dismissed the importance of streaming video, opting instead to only ship DVDs?

I could keep going here, but you get my point. These companies would not be nearly as valuable as they are today—nor their platforms nearly as robust—if they had not quickly and adroitly added important new products and services.

These days, inertia is a death knell. In each case, the Gang of Four would have done far worse than leave money on the table. It's entirely possible they might be shells of their current selves. One could even argue that these companies might have faltered or been acquired if they hadn't continued pushing the envelope, broadening their platforms, and moving sideways.

Building a Change-Tolerant Business

Robert N. Charette, Ph. D., President of ITABHI Corporation

Excerpted with permission from Charette's paper, *"Challenging the Fundamental Notions of Software Development."*[149]

Change tolerance is an organization's ability to continue operating effectively in the face of high market turbulence, where market turbulence is defined as the instability, uncertainty, and lack of control within a firm's market environment. A market with a high degree of turbulence experiences rapid and/or discontinuous changes in its structure, operations, and technology basis. A highly change-tolerant business can both adapt to and cause market turbulence for its own benefit. Businesses able to withstand or create market change possess a change-tolerant business design.

According to innovation expert Adrian Slywotzky, a business design is the summation of how a company does the following:

❑ Defines and differentiates its offerings
❑ Selects its customers
❑ Defines those activities it will perform itself and those it
   will outsource   *(continued)*

❏ Configures its resources
❏ Organizes itself
❏ Goes to the market
❏ Creates value for customers and creates profit[150]

Simply put, it's the entire ecosystem for delivering value to customers and generating profit from the activity.

A change-tolerant business design is one that possesses dynamic stability, to use a term coined by IMD Professor Andrew Boynton and Vanderbilt University Professor Bart Victor.[151] In other words, it's a design that encourages the servicing of a wide range of customers with changing demands (the dynamic element), while continuously building on internal processes that are general-purpose, flexible, and reusable across a range of products and product families (the stable element). This ability to accommodate changes in the marketplace is superior to changing an organization's internal processes in response to every change in the market.

HEAVY RELIANCE ON DATA AND TECHNOLOGY

As we saw in Part II, Amazon, Apple, Facebook, and Google know a tremendous (some would say excessive) amount about their customers and users. Not only is this detailed level of customer knowledge incredibly valuable in and of itself, it allows the Gang of Four to quickly and easily roll out new offerings. By using highly advanced technology and troves of customer information, these companies can do much more than reactively meet customer needs. To increasing extents, they can actually *predict and even drive* what their customers will buy.

Intimate Knowledge of Customers

The powerful technologies deployed and utilized by these companies have allowed them to collect very personal information about their customers and even many of their users. Equipped with this data, the Gang of Four can make individual suggestions based on two dimensions:

- ❏ A customer's own previous purchases
- ❏ Previous purchases made by similar customers, largely enabled by tags or descriptive labels applied to different products

Although they no doubt use different technologies behind the scenes, Amazon, Apple, Facebook, and Google are building and refining individual profiles on each of users. Through these highly valuable profiles, they can easily and specifically target those customers who will be more likely to consider (and ultimately purchase) each product. Examples include the following:

- ❏ Facebook's group or product suggestions on the right side of virtually all of its billions of pages
- ❏ As discussed extensively in Chapter 3, Amazon's email and site recommendations
- ❏ Similar recommendations from Apple's iTunes Store

Contrast this with many organizations' complete dearth of understanding of their customers. Lamentably, many senior executives in large organizations cannot even agree on the definition of the term *customer*. Throw in legacy systems and bad data, and it should be no surprise that many organizations cannot answer simple questions such as:

- ❏ Who are the best customers?
- ❏ Which customers buy which products?
- ❏ Which customers have and have not bought from us in the last month?

THE NEW BLUEPRINT FOR INNOVATION

The traditional executive mentality at most large companies doesn't exactly embrace partnerships, particularly with respect to innovation. Many of these organizations continue to suffer from the "Not Invented Here" syndrome. For a long time, far too many large and successful companies arrogantly acted as if *all* innovation had to come from inside their own walls. They refused to see the value that small and nimble partners could provide. Only recently have many conglomerates recognized the need to change their corporate DNA. These types of profound cultural changes typically take years to accomplish.

Of course there are notable exceptions, but they only serve to prove the general rule. One such outlier is Procter & Gamble (P&G), the storied consumer products company. P&G has been enormously successful but, in the mid-1990s, the company began to struggle with its next big idea. In short, it needed a new blueprint. In 2000, the company launched its Connect+Develop (C+D) program,[152] the brainchild of then-CEO A. G. Lafley. C+D allows *anyone* to browse the company's current product needs and submit innovations. If her ideas are accepted and adopted, she becomes a partner. That is, she shares the upside of her innovations. The goal of the program is to create an innovation *platform* by embracing the outside—and it has been an unqualified success, spawning a number of key innovations. Unfortunately, not too many large corporations act like P&G with respect to seeking outside expertise.

Growing the Pie

By contrast, Amazon, Apple, Facebook, and Google generally exhibit tolerance, openness, and fairness toward potential partners (read: developers, vendors, and other third parties). As we saw in Part II, management at the Gang of Four believes there's plenty of room for others. Although the current pie might be fixed, these companies know that only by working with external parties can the size of the pie grow. Through collaboration, everybody wins. Other developers and startups have a great deal to bring to the table. As discussed previously, the highly sophisticated technology of Amazon, Apple, Facebook, and Google allow them to create, store, and analyze a great deal of customer data. This results in an unprecedented understanding of their customers. As smart as Bezos, Zuckerberg, and the rest of the gang are, they just can't do it all. These days, motivated partners aren't just luxuries—they are necessities.

LOYAL AND VOCAL COMMUNITIES

In Chapter 2, we saw how network effects allowed technologies and platforms to thrive. In a similar vein, Malcolm Gladwell discusses how ideas and products spread organically in his epic 2002 book, *The Tipping Point: How Little Things Can Make a Big Difference*. Other books explain the bottom-up nature of growth and buzz these days, such as Seth Godin's *Purple Cow: Transform Your Business by Being Remarkable, Unleashing the IdeaVirus*, and *Tribes*.

The Gang of Four has created and grown its platforms largely through organic means. For instance, consider Facebook's early days. Back then, the company required its users to have a ".edu" domain to register. For largely technical reasons, Zuckerberg held back Facebook's expansion, prompting frenetic emails and IMs from students in colleges yet to be covered. Google was no different. People used Google *en masse* because it was simple, fast, and just worked. When Google announced the launch of Gmail in 2004[153] by invitation only, demand was so strong that eBay auctions for accounts appeared. Apple operates in the same way. Whether by design or because the company simply cannot keep up with the tremendous demand for its products, Apple customers frequently line up hours before its stores open on the day that the latest iPad or iPhone is released.

In each case, customer and user passion does not stem from traditional marketing—far from it. Up until recently, Google did not advertise. I have never seen a Facebook commercial, newspaper ad, or billboard. (Of course, companies will often tout their Facebook fan pages, but that's an entirely different story.) For its part, Apple generates buzz by saying very little about its products, and this invites intrigue. When people on an airplane or subway see a stranger holding a Kindle, they're likely to stare at it for a while. They might even inquire about whether the person likes it. The answer is almost always yes, and frequently the stranger becomes a friend.

Loyal and vocal communities serve as the street teams for these great brands. Amazon, Apple, Facebook, and Google don't need to rely on conventional marketing, at least not to the same extent as other, more traditional companies. In point of fact, their platforms market their products for them—and quite effectively. Today, which of the following is more likely to make you try a product or service?

❏   Enthusiastic recommendations from your friends and partners, *or*
❏   An expensive and slick ad telling you to do something

This is why attempts by Microsoft to buy its way into the search market are not likely to succeed. Expensive commercials that promote Bing as a "decision engine" are not prone to move the needle. (Nor is Microsoft likely to make "*Bing*" a popular verb. It should have learned from Coca-Cola, a company that failed in the 1980s to convince its customers that New Coke was better than the original.) And so far, Microsoft hasn't made a dent in Google's search lead. The latter still controls more than three-fifths of the search market. As Godin and Gladwell point out in their books, long gone are the days in which large companies can effectively buy market share by spending their competition into the ground. In the Age of the Platform, word of mouth is king.

A DUAL FOCUS: CUSTOMERS AND USERS

If given the choice, would you rather own a popular company or a profitable one? Ideally, you'd like to have your cake and eat it too, right? Without question, some companies fall into both buckets: They make money because people actually purchase their products and services. We call these individuals *customers*— and every business needs them. Unless you're independently wealthy, it's unlikely you'll be able to stay in business for very long unless you figure out how to turn at least some of your users into customers.

At the same time, though, a company cannot build a platform by only focusing on its existing customers. This may seem paradoxical. After all, isn't the customer king?

Well, yes and no. Part II of this book showed that the Gang of Four understands the importance of users and an optimal user experience. Users are *not* free-riders to be ignored or trivialized; they are potential future customers and brand evangelists. Users may not directly drive revenue, but as we saw in the previous section, today they often generate referrals through word of mouth, sometimes via their own platforms.

This is why Amazon frequently gives away ebooks. It also lets users review books—even if they didn't buy those books on amazon.com. For its part, Apple gives away a free song every week on iTunes and makes many apps available for free download. Google and Facebook charge nothing for the vast majority of their services.

In the Age of the Platform, it is not enough to build a respectable business with a few highly profitable customers. Today, success stems from curating many passionate users and encouraging them to participate in innovative ways. Users become paying customers.

SIMPLICITY

Generally speaking, users and customers alike find the Gang of Four's websites, products, and services extremely intuitive. (Remember, each is not the only game in town. Products and services deemed too complex to use quickly wane in popularity.) For instance, one can set up a Facebook account or fan page in a few minutes. As we saw in Chapter 3, Amazon is famous for its "1-Click" button. Google's front page is known for its bare-bones design and eye-catching doodles.[154] Buying songs, movies, TV shows, and apps through Apple requires zero technical sophistication (see Chapter 4). A five-year-old can use an iPod and iPad. It's clear the Gang of Four understands what Matthew E. May calls "the temptation to get too clever." May, the author of *In Pursuit of Elegance* and *The Shibumi Strategy*, continues:

> Many companies fall prey to the bells-and-whistles trap. Too often, they lose sight of what customers and users truly want, need, and require—aka real value. Feature creep sets in, followed by feature fatigue. Finally, you realize that you've built something excessive, wasteful, confusing, hard to use, and ugly. Compare that to the Google homepage, the buttonless iPhone, the Amazon 1-Click. The common element is that burden of enormous complexity is made invisible to the user. They're examples of what Oliver Wendell Holmes meant when he said, "I wouldn't give a fig for simplicity this side of complexity, but I'd give my life for simplicity on the other side of complexity." That's what you're after: simplicity to die for.[155]

Let's extend May's view. Simplicity, elegance, and ease of use all spur the adoption of products and consumer passion. In turn, this drives network effects (see Chapter 2) and the expansion of platforms. Given the pace of change today, is it any wonder these design principles matter so much?

The Gang of Four understands the need for simplicity, at least in terms of its mainstream products and services. These companies' platforms would not have become as popular had their users needed computer science degrees to use them. Of course, to develop new apps and services, one needs more advanced tools, such as software development kits (SDKs). These are entirely different animals that don't concern the average user.

PLATFORMS ARE NOT BUSINESSES

Wikipedia is the incredibly popular, accurate, useful, and editable online encyclopedia. From a legal standpoint, Wikipedia is a nonprofit organization. It supports itself through donations and the countless hours of its core group of volunteers. Although an indispensable resource I use on a daily basis, Wikipedia is not a platform.

> Don't make the mistake of thinking that a company's platform is tantamount to its business. It's not. True platforms allow companies to reach new customers—and sell to existing ones. Platforms support and extend businesses; they do not obviate the need for quality products, competitive pricing, and so on. The two concepts are related but not identical.

EXTENSIVE BORROWING FROM OTHER PLATFORMS

Facebook introduced the Like button, an invention that prompted similar functionality from Amazon, Apple, and Google (with its +1 button).[156] Let's focus for a moment on Apple.

Mimicking Competitors' Functionality Increases Platform Stickiness

Remember the discussion of iTunes with Ping in Chapter 4? Let's not overstate things here. It's not like iTunes now removes the need for me to go to a band's official site.[157] iTunes is not a full-fledged browser, and it's difficult to imagine it evolving into one.

Maybe *mini-browser* is an accurate descriptor. That is, through iTunes, I can do much more than sample music from my favorite band, Rush. Arguably more important from Apple's standpoint, iTunes allows me to easily connect with other fans, view photos, and so on. This makes me more likely to consume content and stay on Apple's platform—and maybe buy a song or video. I don't need to visit the official Rush Facebook page[158] to find other Rush-heads. Nor must I search for Rush music on Amazon, Pandora, GrooveShark, other music sites, communities, and platforms.

The Benefits of Stickinesss

For Apple, stickiness confers another major benefit. The more time users and customers spend on its platforms results in increased knowledge of its customer base—and the same holds true for the rest of the Gang of Four. As a direct result, Apple can tailor special offerings to fans of Rush, Lady Gaga, or any other artist or band in iTunes. Rush-heads often listen to Pink Floyd, Yes, Genesis, and other 70s progressive rock bands. Apple knows what to recommend to different customers and, just as important, what not to recommend. It is unlikely to suggest Metallica's latest album, *Death Magnetic*, to fans of Britney Spears.

And what sticks for one of the Gang of Four is likely to stick for the others. As a result, Amazon, Apple, Facebook, or Google pay very close attention to functionality introduced by one another. And mimicking functionality is not isolated to four companies. Each monitors trends. If features developed by other burgeoning platforms and popular sites (some of which are discussed in Chapter 11) gain traction, the Gang of Four will pounce on them and launch their own equivalents. (This is why Amazon, Facebook, and Google have all recently launched Groupon-like services, although in August 2011 Facebook decided to shut down its Deals program.) It's not quite "monkey see, monkey do," but each company quickly figures out how to integrate popular bells and whistles into its platform.

POWERFUL PLATFORMS OFTEN SPAWN IMITATORS

In early 2011, Goldman Sachs valued Facebook at $50 billion,[159] a number that grew in June 2011 to the staggering sum of more than $70 billion.[160] Its platform—and subsequent reach—is incredibly valuable. And this value attracts copycats. Consider that I can use a service such as Ning[161] to build my own social network. I can hire developers on the cheap to build functionality. I can even play off of Facebook's Achilles' heel: I can adhere to much stricter privacy settings.

It turns out that others have already done this. One such company, Diaspora,[162] is attempting to carve out a niche as a viable alternative to Facebook. The company's value proposition is predicated on increased user choice, privacy, data ownership, control, and transparency. It's trying to preserve what it considers the positive aspects of social networking while concurrently filtering out the bad.

ICONIC AND VISIONARY LEADERS

> "Deliberation is the work of many men. Action, of one alone."
> —*Charles de Gaulle*

Can you imagine Facebook without Mark Zuckerberg? What about Amazon without Jeff Bezos or Google without Larry and Sergey? Probably not. These companies are almost impossible to separate from their visionary leaders. When Steve Jobs (then on medical leave) appeared on stage for the launch of the iPad 2 in March 2011, Apple's stock actually shot up nearly $3.[163]

Platform companies evolve so quickly because they are not very democratic. Everyone doesn't get a vote. They are decidedly unlike their more conservative and more bureaucratic counterparts. In the case of Apple, new CEO Tim Cook may not be able to completely fill the void left by the departure of his company's iconic founder. No one can. However, he will not fundamentally alter Apple's DNA and management structure. Cook understands quite well that, in order for Apple to continue to push the envelope and *think different*, he must try to exhibit the same type of leadership and dynamism as Jobs.

PLATFORMS SYNTHESIZE

Amazon, Apple, Facebook, and Google make it exceptionally easy to move *within* their platforms. It isn't hard to go from plank to plank. For instance, consider Apple's iBooks. Amazingly, a person can start reading a book on her iPhone, "bookmark it," and then continue reading the same book later on her iPad—*from the same page*. Ditto the Kindle. Or consider Facebook. You can effortlessly move within its walls, accessing apps without having to create new accounts or log in again. And Google's products are the very definition of *seamlessly integrated*. The Gang of Four designs its platforms with the user in mind.

SWITCHING PLATFORMS IS DIFFICULT— BY DESIGN

Moving *between* or *among* platforms, however, is a completely different story. Remember that you can't "Google" Facebook. That is, you cannot use Google to query Facebook's content—and you can't use Google Site Search either. Nor can you *easily* export information on your friends or your customers from Facebook and import this data into an external application.* Like the aforementioned features, these restrictions are deliberate.

All of this is just another way of saying that the Gang of Four is, in some ways, no different than your local bank. They don't *want* their users and customers to switch, so they don't exactly make it easy. You can't transfer your Amazon customized product recommendations any easier than you can transfer your Google Voice history *en masse* to Skype.

Of course, from user and customer retention perspectives, the carrot is much more effective than the stick. Amazon, Apple, Facebook, and Google attempt to lure users in and keep them using their platforms by offering compelling products and services. They tend to not penalize people for wanting to stop using a plank—or leave the platform altogether. Google doesn't threaten to publish your naughty searches because it catches you using Bing.

Then there's the time issue. These days, people are often just too busy to go elsewhere once they have found something that works. We just don't have the time to deal with all of the hassles

---

* Some companies claim their apps can do this.

of switching platforms, a point Adrian Ott makes in her award-winning 2010 book, *The 24-Hour Customer*. She explains:

> [S]tress, overwork, and bulging to-do lists often create situations where people resort to sticking with what they know best. Current products and activities usually hold an inertia position for the customer. When given a choice, the status quo will usually prevail unless a Time-Value threshold is exceeded. For example, if you were thinking about switching your account to another bank, you would not only evaluate what the other bank has to offer, but would factor in the time and effort it takes to switch. For many customers, the effort of switching banks is so significant that they opt to stay where they are. In fact, only 11 percent of U.S. customers change banks every year.

Think about the old-fashioned and manual process of managing your money (read: with checkbooks and ledgers). It wasn't exactly fun. But Apple and Google have made even that often mundane process easier and interactive. Apps on iPhones and Droids allow people to more easily track and manage their funds. At the same time, though, nothing is set in stone. Despite the often high costs of switching, it's increasingly rare to see permanent, unfettered loyalty to a company, product, or brand. All of this is just another way of saying that platforms are ephemeral, as we will see in Chapter 9.

PLATFORMS COLLIDE

> **"Of course you realize, this means war."**
> —*Bugs Bunny*

For a long time, many industry observers wondered how Google's then-CEO Eric Schmidt could continue to serve on Apple's board of directors. Apple and Google increasingly found themselves in direct competition with each other, yet Schmidt seemed to be privy to sensitive Apple information by virtue of his role. The situation was odd and untenable, to say the least. In August 2009,

Schmidt finally resigned from Apple's board. In the words of Steve Jobs himself:

> Eric has been an excellent Board member for Apple, investing his valuable time, talent, passion, and wisdom to help make Apple successful. Unfortunately, as Google enters more of Apple's core businesses, with Android and now Chrome OS, Eric's effectiveness as an Apple Board member will be significantly diminished, since he will have to recuse himself from even larger portions of our meetings due to potential conflicts of interest. Therefore, we have mutually decided that now is the right time for Eric to resign his position on Apple's Board.[164]

Translation: Although, Schmidt's advice is extremely valuable, Apple and Google are on a collision course. It was silly to maintain the façade and pretend otherwise. Google and Facebook are also destined to butt heads over many areas, most notably advertising revenue. As expected, Google's new social networking tool (Google+) is designed to usurp Facebook, and talk of a Twitter acquisition isn't going away. Amazon announced its Kindle Fire tablet in September 2011, and rumors persist about a Facebook phone.[165]

Brass tacks: The Gang of Four has shown remarkable agility, skill, and willingness to enter new lines of business. Leaders at each company know that about one another, fueling increased emphasis on speed and innovation. And let's not forget a new war for highly coveted and talented software engineers, developers, and programmers reminiscent of the dot-com boom.[166]

Frenemies and Coopetition

> "The man of knowledge must be able not only to love his enemies but also to hate his friends."
> —*Friedrich Nietzsche*

The tendency for the Gang of Four to collide with one another shouldn't surprise anyone. These battles bring to mind two relatively new terms. The *Merriam-Webster Dictionary* defines a *frenemy* as "one who pretends to be a friend but is actually an enemy."[167] Also, the term *coopetition* has recently entered the business vernacular—a word that describes concurrent *cooperation* and *competition*.

Both labels are completely apropos in understanding the relationships among Amazon, Apple, Facebook, and Google. Like five-year-olds in a sandbox, they sometimes play nicely together, but aren't above knocking over one another's sandcastles. That is, companies that have built powerful platforms and planks do not always see eye-to-eye.

> Platform companies have to walk a fine line. On the one hand, each company wants to steal users and customers from other platforms to switch to theirs. On the other, each doesn't want to be known for being aggressive, greedy, and restrictive.

Let's look at a few examples. Apple allows its customers to read books on their iPhones and iPads via Amazon's Kindle app. Apple does not force its customers to buy the same books again in Apple's iBook format. For its part, Facebook makes it very easy for users to find individual friends with a few clicks, or friends *en masse* via importing Yahoo!, Gmail, and Hotmail email addresses.

But the opposite isn't true. Facebook does not reciprocate with these other services—*unless they are partners*. As Ryan Singel of *Wired* writes, "If you are also a Twitter or Buzz user and want to find out which of your Facebook friends were also using those services, Facebook will not let you."[168]

Perhaps a better metaphor is the game *Risk*, in which players form temporary alliances, only to turn on one another when they have the ability to conquer a continent.

PLATFORMS ARE INHERENTLY POLITICAL

Platforms of consequence cannot duck controversy, especially on today's social web. In fact, they may inadvertently invite it. To varying degrees, Google's decisions to enter and exit China, Apple's approving which apps to put in its App Store, Amazon removing "adult" books, and Facebook revoking Roger Ebert's fan page are all political statements. When hundreds of millions of people routinely use a platform, it is simply impossible for the company behind that platform to maintain a "neutral" stance. Taking any action—and even *not* taking action—is bound to offend a decent percentage of users.

Strangely, controversy can actually *benefit* a platform. When a controversy erupts, people often want to see what all of the hubbub is about. For instance, as we saw in Chapter 5, people flocked to Roger Ebert's Facebook page after his comments about the *Jackass* accident. In a way, this is tantamount to celebrities who understand that all publicity is good publicity. Paris Hilton, Kim Kardashian, and Britney Spears know that even sordid scandals keep people talking about them. Of course, the powerful platforms don't court controversy, and no one would confuse Jeff Bezos with *Jersey Shore* star Snooki.

SUMMARY AND CONCLUSION

This chapter has described the characteristics and components of the platforms from Part II. We have seen that the business models of Amazon, Apple, Facebook, and Google have a great deal in common. Even though these companies cannot be considered startups anymore, they continue to act like them—and in a good way. In building such powerful platforms, they have pivoted extremely well. (Pivoting is "the idea of reinventing or refocusing your business on the fly."[169])

The next chapter explains the specific benefits of building these vibrant ecosystems.

EIGHT

....

Gimme the Prize!
The Benefits of Platforms

From business and technology perspectives, platforms have never been more important than they are today. We saw this in Part II. When companies build platforms, they simultaneously create extremely valuable networks. They also reach a bevy of customers, users, vendors, partners, and even employees. They are more likely to lead to "accidental" lines of businesses, sources of revenue, and innovations. Platforms mitigate risk and enable diversification, build and extend brands, and create virtual barriers to entry to real and would-be competitors. Finally, they receive a great deal of creative input from partners eager to cash in themselves.

RISK MITIGATION AND INCREASED DIVERSIFICATION

Think for a minute about most traditional businesses. In any given day, I might talk to my accountant, visit the grocery store, or go to the dentist's office. I might fill my car up with gas and get my tennis racket restrung. In each case, the business models have nothing to do with platforms. I could never fulfill all of these needs in one place, unless I went to the Mall of America in Minneapolis. In other words, these businesses—and many others—are built on individual and disconnected offerings.

For many companies, the very idea of a platform is downright scary. Platforms unify. They integrate. They force people out of their comfort zones. Platforms require a degree of internal coordination and cohesion that, put bluntly, many companies are in no position to attempt.

Why bother with building a platform? Why mess around with different planks? Isn't it dangerous for companies to muck with their business models—especially when they seem to be working?

At first glance, the skeptics may actually have a point. Those who doubt the importance of platforms are quick to point out that the devil you know is better than the devil you don't. Platforms and diversification run counter to what we are taught and what many of the most famous management gurus espouse. They'll ask questions such as: Ever hear the phrase *stick to your knitting*? Aren't we supposed to focus on what we're good at doing? Well, yes and no.

Rejection of the General Electric Model

On the one hand, companies such as General Electric (GE) are widely renown for their ability to be number one or two in a market—and exit that market if that isn't the case. Under former CEO and management legend Jack Welch, GE simply followed a "dominate or leave" strategy. Not coincidentally, Welch is lauded as perhaps the greatest chief executive in recent American business history.

Even today, this strategy isn't entirely wrong. Diversification for the sake of diversification is the acme of foolishness. It's downright silly for the owner of a boutique management consultancy to launch a completely separate line of business such as delivering groceries or selling tennis apparel.

This isn't diversification. This is stupidity.

On the other hand, let's not get too hung up on the GE model for two reasons. First, in all likelihood, your company isn't remotely similar to GE in terms of size and "the fear factor." In fact, your company is much more likely to be like mine: A single-person limited liability corporation (LLC) with relatively modest revenue. After all, according to the U.S. Census, there are nearly 28 million small businesses in this country.[170] Companies like Wal-Mart and IBM are the exceptions that prove the rule.

Second, if you're really honest with yourself, you'll admit that nothing can stop someone from setting up shop right across the street from you—or in a faraway land—to do exactly what you do. Are you immune from competition? Are you so big that no one would dare try to steal your market share? Even behemoths such as GE with *billions* of dollars to spend cannot keep the competition at bay. (Remember from Chapter 2 that virtual barriers to entry aren't nearly as high as their physical counterparts.)

Many companies have eschewed the GE model and are diversifying more than ever. Peering into the future, many will attempt to derive increasing portions of their revenue from different streams and newer lines of business. They understand that we are now a flat world, as mentioned in Part I. Here, platforms enable this diversification. They are part and parcel of the new blueprint.

> Aided by technology and motivated by necessity, progressive companies are realizing they may not be able to survive if they rely solely on one line of business, even if they're a market leader. To be sure, no business can do everything and be everything to everyone. At the same time, though, more and more businesses are realizing the limitations of being true specialists. Generalists are making a comeback in a big way.

Let's say you run a successful web design firm. Why not expand your services? Don't your same clients have other needs? Can't you teach them how to effectively blog and use social media? Shouldn't they be creating their own platforms—with your help? Do they know how to use the planks discussed in this book? Wouldn't a happy client consider using your company's other services, especially since they're so related?

BRAND BUILDING AND EXTENSION

Platforms can dramatically increase brand value. They can also extend and develop brands. Let's look at Apple as a case in point. As we saw in Chapter 4, Apple's brand is the most valuable in the world.[171] But what if Apple never dropped the word *Computer* from its company name and remained primarily a computer manufacturer? Would Apple's brand be as valuable today (north of $150 billion)? In other words, what if Apple had become a highly efficient maker of low-cost devices? What if Apple had decided to follow the business model of Dell?

Apple shareholders are happy the company did not make that mistake. Over the past 10 years, Apple and Dell stocks have been a study in contrasts. If you bought the latter in lieu of the former, you're kicking yourself. But it doesn't stop with stock price. The Dell brand was recently valued at under $10 billion,[172] a mere fraction of Apple's.

This isn't all about business models, though. Dell has been plagued lately by an accounting scandal. But even a scandal-free company that only manufactures computers is unlikely to build a true platform.

Or consider Google's brand. For four years, it was at the top of the *BusinessWeek* rankings before Apple recently overtook it. Even today, the Google brand sits at $111.5 billion.[173] Would it be as valuable if Google just did search? It's not coincidental the Gang of Four has built great platforms and great brands—but that's not the whole story. Each company's partners, users, customers, and vendors have done just as much—if not more—in building these brands. That is, Amazon, Apple, Facebook, and Google do not operate in top-down, traditionally "corporate" ways. Their processes are much more bottom-up, organic, and user-driven. What's more, as we have seen, key groups within their ecosystems build their platforms for them—which in turn grow their brands. By effectively utilizing this new blueprint, symbiotic relationships naturally develop among a company, its brand, its community, and its platform.

Verb Branding

Strong platforms also lend themselves to *verb branding*, defined as "a state in which many people use a company's name as a verb."

Verb branding wasn't always considered a positive, much less the marketing Holy Grail that it is today. As Rebecca Tushnet—an expert on trademark law at Georgetown University—explains:

> The risk of becoming generic is so low, and the benefits of being on the top of someone's mind are so high. In the past, Xerox ran a very expensive campaign in places like *Editor & Publisher* that said don't use *xerox* as a verb. What people know from marketing experience now and what people now understand as a practical matter is [this] is *very* good.[174] [Emphasis added.]

Although not an entirely new phenomenon, the power of verb branding has arguably never been higher, as consumers have more choices than ever. I can use any number of services to send my package across the country, but most people will just *FedEx* it.

Google attained the vaunted *verb branding* status in two ways. First and most important, it built a better mousetrap. Remember that, during the late 1990s, Internet search engines were terribly inconsistent and inaccurate. Back then, best-of-breed sites such as Lycos, AltaVista, and AskJeeves usually returned questionable results. Then along came Google. The contrast between Google and its competition was beyond stark. In fact, the word *competition* didn't really apply. There was Google and there was everyone else. Google's vastly superior search functionality, clean and simple interface, and powerful enhancements made it incredibly popular.

Second, and as a direct result of its utility, word of mouth grew. Around 2000, people started to use *Google* as a verb. If you didn't know the answer to a question or how to find the nearest restaurant, you would just *Google* it. The term became so useful and ubiquitous that the American Dialect Society chose it as the "most useful word of 2002."[175] It was only a matter of time before it became official. In what can only be described as a major coup, the *Oxford English Dictionary* formally recognized Google as a verb on June 15, 2006. Today, the *Merriam-Webster Dictionary* defines Google as "us[ing] the Google search engine to obtain information…on the World Wide Web."[176]

Google itself didn't try to artificially propagate the use of Google as a verb. Back then, Google didn't advertise. By using Google as a verb, Google's users were being hip. Although there are exceptions, such as Wendy's "Where's the Beef?" campaign, most slogans from multimillion-dollar ad campaigns by billion-dollar corporations are unlikely to enter the vernacular.

While impossible to quantify, the eponymous verb has significantly increased the value of the Google brand. And the same thing has happened with Facebook. New acquaintances will frequently tell each other to "Facebook me"—shorthand for one person adding the other as a friend on the social networking site. In fact, today many people are shocked when you tell them you're *not* on Facebook. The question becomes, "Why not?" When you reach this point, you know that you have built a powerful platform.

THE CREATION OF VIRTUAL BARRIERS TO ENTRY

As mentioned in Chapter 2, the days of physical barriers to entry have largely disappeared. Most businesses today are at least partially virtual, and many are entirely virtual. Virtual supply chains, just-in-time inventory, and enhanced global communications mean that costs can be minimized by routing even physical goods throughout the globe. Transferring and exporting knowledge has never been easier.

Against this backdrop, it is still possible to erect barriers to entry, but these days they are not physical. Platforms allow for the creation of very high virtual barriers to entry. For instance, today I could start a new social network, search engine, or online bookstore. However, it's unlikely to usurp Facebook, Google, or Amazon, respectively. Great platforms absorb body blows from the competition. David can still conquer Goliath, but it sure ain't easy.

Let's delve a bit more into this notion of creating virtual barriers to entry.

Barriers Still Exist: "The Best" Platforms Don't Always Win

Isn't the Internet supposed to be the great equalizer and a massively democratizing force? Doesn't the web page on Amazon for this book take up the same "space" as a bestselling nonfiction book by Chris Anderson or Malcolm Gladwell?

Yes, but that doesn't mean that "the best" platforms (on some objective level) always win. Even in a niche market, there's quite a bit to be said for erecting virtual barriers to entry. For example, let's say that you own a discount wine retailer. You have been a little late to the whole Internet thing and aren't exactly social media savvy. You figure it's about time to launch a website, start a platform, and grow your community. You shouldn't have too much trouble in quickly becoming a major player in this niche, right?

Wrong. Really wrong.

Even in something as ostensibly esoteric as discount wine retailing, you're facing a tremendously uphill battle. Someone has already beaten you to the punch. And that someone is Gary Vaynerchuk.

Vaynerchuk started his online Wine Library[177] in 2006 and has been steadily building his online presence since then. There's a good chance you've already heard of him because he has become quite the celebrity. In 2011, he published his second bestselling book, *The Thank You Economy*. "Gary Vee" frequently keynotes conferences and appears on television to talk about social media.

So, if you're intent on being the biggest and most popular platform for discounted wine (much less anything more mainstream), don't hold your breath. It doesn't matter if your site is better designed than Gary's or you have more content. Many wine aficionados already know about Gary and his company—and have for quite some time.

GREASING THE WHEELS: INCREASED INNOVATION

> "Technology is like a fish. The longer it stays on the shelf, the less desirable it becomes."
> —*Andrew Heller*

Compared to traditional, inwardly focused business models, platforms require new partnerships—and this ultimately breeds innovation. Because of their enormous budgets, ample internal resources, and historically successful track records, many stalwarts arrogantly believe they just don't need help from anyone. These types of organizations shun new ideas, models, and partnerships—and struggle as a result. Today, these inwardly focused companies just cannot innovate as quickly or as well as great platforms can. As we saw in Part II of the book, the Gang of Four drives both external and internal innovation.

External Innovation

By embracing literally thousands of partners, the Gang of Four partially outsources innovation. Developers and partners create new apps, products, and services that seamlessly integrate with core Amazon, Apple, Facebook, and Google products. But developing a cool app or service is only half of the battle; time-crunched consumers and users need to find out about it. And here's where the magic happens. In many instances, these developers and partners already have loyal followings.

As we saw in Chapter 4, Jordan Rudess created SampleWiz for the iPad and iPhone. Consider another example. Let's say I enjoy playing *Angry Birds* by Rovio on my iPhone or Droid. This makes me likely to consider buying other Rovio games. Maybe I'll like *Gem Drop* or *Wolf Moon*.[178] Plus, I probably opted in to the Rovio mailing list and will read emails that mention the company's new games. Coupled with its ratings systems, the Gang of Four makes it easy for its partners' new offerings to spread. Call this *external* or *partner-driven innovation*.

"Platform partners" like Rudess and Rovio are heavily incentivized to innovate, launch products, and spread a platform's gospel. As a result, platform companies are more likely to spawn highly successful products like the Kindle and the iPad. And platform partners need not be massive. Even nascent startups can extend the core reach, functionality, and stickiness of existing platforms. In the words of Todd Hamilton, co-founder of Bubbalon,[179] a sentiment feedback technology company based in Montclair, New Jersey:

> Today, even the smallest of developers have much to offer great platforms. Startups are providing many of the "raw materials" used to build and enhance platforms' existing products and services. For instance, Rain Alert Late[180] is a free app that alerts you when rain is coming and the closest place where you can buy an umbrella. Because great platforms work with so many partners, they can expand in many directions at once.

> Small startups benefit as well—and working with great platforms just makes sense. Without access to these ecosystems, success for startups almost always used to require the attention of millions of people. This is no longer the case. Right now, there are profitable and relatively anonymous companies that work behind the scenes. They provide access to structured data like weather forecasts, business reviews, and even retail product inventories—almost no one knows that they exist. They make broad swaths of data available to users and platforms through application programming interface (API) technology.[181]

As Hamilton explains, myriad startups are developing exciting new planks and innovations for these platforms. The bigger the platform, the greater the incentive for it to attract more—and better—partners.

Internal Innovation

Let's not overstate matters here. We shouldn't make the mistake of characterizing *all* innovation from Amazon, Apple, Facebook, and Google as external or partner-driven. It's not. These companies are not outsourcing all of their research and development (R&D). Bezos isn't crowdsourcing Amazon's core business strategies and visions for the future. Zuckerberg clearly listens to Facebook's users, but it's obvious that his company *independently* makes decisions about things like its privacy policy or the latest home page redesign. After all, each user may have a wholly different idea about what constitutes a cleaner or better user experience.

As we have repeatedly seen, Zuckerberg doesn't fear angering a few (hundred) thousand users. Google routinely tweaks its ultra-secret algorithm to provide users with *what it believes* are better, more relevant results. Of course, not everyone agrees. Its tweaks irritate those whose pages and sites mysteriously disappear from the first page of Google search results—extremely valuable placement, to be sure. Amazon introduced 1-Click to simplify the shopping experience, not because of some customer poll or contest. Apple spent untold millions of dollars developing the iPad, the iPod, iTunes, and the iPhone. Apple led; it did not follow.

The Kindle and iPad are particularly instructive examples of successful innovations. But why are they so successful? Sure, they are useful, but many extremely useful products fail to reach critical mass, let alone enter the zeitgeist. For instance, think about much less successful MP3 players such as Microsoft's Zune, launched around the same time as Apple's iPod. What was so special about Gmail, Kindle, Facebook, and the iPad? It's not as if Gmail was the first web-based email service. People didn't truly *need* to buy new digital devices for reading books and playing games. As we saw in Chapter 5, Facebook wasn't the first social network. So, why did these companies succeed where others did not?

In a word, *platforms*. Apple and Amazon customers already enjoyed using these companies' products. As such, many were willing to buy these new devices *and change their habits*. Without diminishing the quality of these products and services in any way, these companies' platforms increased the chances that their new offerings would be adopted—and successful.

Consumers, Platforms, and Innovation

Although important, admittedly innovation is not some sort of Holy Grail. Not all innovation is created equal. Innovation for the sake of innovation is of limited value. What's more, as Scott Berkun points out in his bestselling 2007 book *The Myths of Innovation*, some innovations arguably do as much or more harm than good. Consider Table 8.1:

Innovation	Good Effects	Bad Effects
DDT	Controlled malaria, elevated living conditions in third-world nations, inspired professional wrestling move	Disturbed ecology, collateral species impact, DDT-resistant mosquitoes evolved
Automobile	Personalized transportation, empowered individuals, boosted commerce and urban development	Responsible for half of pollution in urban areas, 40,000 annual U.S. fatalities, and traffic; prompted urban sprawl
Personal Computers	Individual empowerment, communication, learning, the Internet	Rate of upgrades creates landfill, production creates hazardous materials
Cell Phones	Wireless communication, mobile access, convenience, portable emergency and safety system	Public annoyance, bad drivers become unguided missiles, that annoying person next to you in a restaurant

Table 8.1: The Two Sides of Innovation*

---

* Figure used with permission from *The Myths of Innovation* by Scott Berkun.

Now, I am no Luddite, nor is Berkun. Innovation is a net positive, and it is essential for companies to continue to grow. All else being equal, more innovation is better than less. And this is where great platforms separate themselves from the pack.

Today, as a general rule, an innovation must be popular in order for it to be successful and profitable.* This is especially true in the consumer realm. And this is precisely why platforms are so important. Consumers tend to look at innovations from the Gang of Four as intriguing extensions of current platforms. While the Kindle, iPad, and their ilk may technically be separate products, customers don't think of them that way, at least in the traditional sense. These new offerings are viewed as part of the overall Amazon, Apple, Facebook, and Google experiences.

The consumer mind-set is key here because it allows innovations to spread virally throughout great platforms. This increases the chances that a new offering is popular and profitable.

It also means that the companies behind these platforms will realize unexpected streams of revenue, covered next.

ACCIDENTAL LINES OF BUSINESS

"The heart and soul of the company is creativity and innovation."
—*Robert Iger*

In Chapter 3, we saw how Amazon outsources its billing systems to companies such as Kickstarter. But that pales in comparison to its cloud services. Amazon now makes *hundreds of millions of dollars* by selling excess compute power. Apple's early understanding of digital hubs and the future of computing allowed it to make billions from apps, music, and movie sales. Who knows what types

---

* I am well aware that Boeing may launch a new high-margin airplane engine, but these days the number of big product launches is tiny in comparison to the number of digital products released.

of products and services Facebook and Google will continue to launch with so much detailed consumer information. Some will surely be free, but others will be worth paying for.

Innovation Begets More Innovation

There's an extremely important corollary to this notion that platforms encourage innovation. Let's look for a moment at Amazon. Consider four events in its storied history:

- ❏ 1994: Amazon sold only books via its website.
- ❏ 2007: Amazon launched the Kindle, allowing its readers to instantly buy books—and read them electronically.
- ❏ 2010: Amazon started publishing books to read on its Kindle via the Domino Project.
- ❏ 2010: Amazon created Kindle apps for other devices like the iPad, Droid, and iPhone.

Amazon followed similar processes with music and movies. The company sold CDs and DVDs, but it didn't stop there. Amazon quickly realized that it could sell device-agnostic services. Its customers could listen to their favorite songs and watch movies while on an iPod, Droid, or non-Amazon platform. In each case, Amazon innovations begot future innovations. Bezos and company may not have *needed* to launch the Kindle in order to start a publishing line of business, but it certainly didn't hurt. In the process, Amazon no doubt learned a great deal about publishing. Buoyed by some degree of success, Bezos felt confident enough to enter the arena. So he did.

It's hard to imagine Jeff Bezos conceiving of the Kindle in 1994. But, as Amazon gained momentum and ironed out its early distribution and fulfillment kinks, Bezos obviously thought about other ways to make a buck. The Kindle may have been a pipe dream in 1996, but not in 2006. And the same holds true for the rest of the Gang of Four. For instance, because of its sheer size, Facebook can do things now that it simply couldn't do back in 2005. As platforms grow, previously impossible ideas become possible and easier to implement.

REACHING THE OVERWHELMED CONSUMER

Let's not forget the overwhelmed consumer factor. Many new and potentially useful sites and companies struggle to acquire new users and customers. To attempt to combat this, many offer the ability to sign in with Twitter or to connect via Facebook. Users often distrust new sites' privacy policies or never get around to confirming their new accounts via email.

As we saw in Chapter 1, today people are so deluged with information and new technologies that they often don't want to learn a new application or user interface. Even if they sign up for a promising site, will they continue to use it? Visiting a separate site requires more mental resources—if not effort—than just clicking on an iPhone app or opening a Facebook page; we have to remember to use a new tool or site. For the most part, this is not the case with great platforms. We already use the platforms of Amazon, Apple, Facebook, and Google to do myriad things, often on a daily basis. What's one more?

> Standalone sites, apps, and companies face uphill battles competing against platforms—even if the former offer superior experiences or products. Platforms will often win by offering comparable products or services with similar but lesser functionality. Consumers have spoken. They want one-stop shopping, even at the expense of missing out on "the best" app or service. They like platforms; they don't want to manage 100 different devices, sites, and services.

SUPERIOR UNDERSTANDING OF CUSTOMER AND USER BASES

Customers and users are also quite clear: By and large they will voluntarily provide a great deal of information to Amazon, Apple, Facebook, and Google. Beyond any particular technology or product, perhaps this asset is the Gang of Four's strongest. Think about it. Despite the advent of sophisticated customer relationship management (CRM) applications, many organizations still don't know who their best users and customers are! They struggle trying to determine who buys what, and many organizations cannot even agree internally on the definition of the word *customer*.

Great platforms do not have this problem. Amazon knows exactly which customers buy each of its products. Facebook knows who's active, who's not, and who influences others. Ditto Google and Apple. A profound level of understanding does a great deal more than simply produce interesting reports for executives in corner offices. Through data-mining technology and business intelligence, the Gang of Four can make more relevant recommendations to its customers and users. This means more sales.

INCREASED ORGANIZATIONAL AGILITY

Organizations that build—and actively maintain—platforms can innovate, adapt, evolve, expand, and launch new offerings much quicker than those lacking these powerful ecosystems. While it never hurts to be right, companies that effectively use platforms need not predict the future, a topic discussed more in Chapter 12.

To continue their astronomical levels of success, Amazon, Apple, Facebook, and Google don't need a crystal ball. Nor do they have to double-down on massive, once-in-a-decade multibillion-dollar bets. Their platforms have put them in far superior positions to respond to unforeseen trends, events, and changes in the marketplace. These organizations are more agile than their more traditional, top-down, and bureaucratic counterparts.

PREEMPTIVE STRIKES

If the previous arguments about the benefits of platforms have not swayed you, then consider this: It's quite possible—and maybe even probable—that your competition already gets it. They may well have already established their own platforms. Maybe they're working on them now. Perhaps your primary competitors now have average platforms but are making them better as you read this.

While platforms tremendously benefit their companies, they are no silver bullet. Platforms have their limitations, as we'll see in the next chapter. But let's say you don't believe platforms currently apply to your line of work. Maybe you own a dental practice, a car wash, or a local convenience store. No one in your industry has got platform religion. Why bother with them? Several reasons.

First, as we saw in Chapter 1, the world is changing faster than ever. What's true today may well not be true in six months or a year. Second, think about contingency planning. Isn't it better to build a platform and not need it than need one and not have one—especially when platforms aren't terribly expensive to build and maintain? Third, are you *really* sure that your business doesn't need a platform today—and won't tomorrow?

Perhaps you understand the massive expenses that Amazon, Apple, Facebook, and Google incurred in building their companies and platforms. I'll bet that your company doesn't have anywhere near those kinds of resources. Plus, you're not a techie like Bezos, Zuckerberg, Brin, and Page. Fret not. In Chapter 10, we'll cover specific ways to build your platform, many of which are extremely affordable, easy to implement, and require little to no technical sophistication.

SUMMARY AND CONCLUSION

This chapter has listed and explained the major benefits of building platforms. Although no guarantee of future success, platforms allow organizations to thrive and reach new customers at faster speeds. In the next chapter, we'll discover that platforms aren't all sunshine and lollipops.

NINE

···

Slings and Arrows:
The Perils of Platforms

I t's important to note that many promising platforms never materialize. Others reach a certain level of prominence, only to burn out or fade away, to paraphrase Neil Young. In any event, platforms do not last forever, nor are they immune from disintermediation, changing consumer tastes, and ill-advised merger and acquisition activity. This chapter looks at some of the problems associated with platforms. It also provides examples of declining or failed platforms—as well as missed opportunities.

Let's see which fleas come with the dog. After that, we will move on to recommendations for creating your own platform and adding planks (Chapter 10).

THE LIMITATIONS OF PLATFORMS

Platforms can only do so much—even great ones. They face several important restrictions.

Platforms and Beepers

On the popular and Emmy Award-winning show *30 Rock*, Tina Fey plays Liz Lemon, the head writer of a sketch comedy show. Her less than intelligent ex-boyfriend, Dennis Duffy (played by Dean Winters), sells beepers. No, the show is not set in the early 1990s. He idiotically and hysterically believes that "technology is cyclical." If Duffy built a platform today, he would not sell a ton of pagers because nobody buys them anymore. Platforms cannot:

❑ Save dying businesses and technologies.
❑ Resurrect declining sales of poorly designed, dated, and overly expensive products.
❑ Guarantee successful execution or the proper execution of key strategies.

In other words, building a platform today is almost always a necessary but insufficient condition for growing businesses and reaching new customers. Trying to build a platform for an antiquated product is a waste of time and money.

The Cardinal Importance of Customers and Users

Nor should the fundamental purpose of a platform be misconstrued. Put simply, a platform is a means to an end—it is not the end itself. In *The Thank You Economy*, social media expert Gary Vaynerchuk writes, "When businesses realize that they need to focus on investing in customers, not platforms, they will see amazing returns on investment."

Vaynerchuk hits the nail on the head. Let's return to Amazon. Yes, it has built a powerful platform, but the power of its platform would be diminished if the comapny did not treat its customers well. As we saw in Chapter 3, its sophisticated technology only recommends related products: It doesn't *force* customers to make purchases or automatically make purchases for them. Bezos and his brethren understand that platforms mean very little without customers and users. Later in this chapter, we'll see what happens to platforms whose companies fail to appreciate this important tenet. (Spoiler: It's not pretty.)

PLATFORM ABUSE, SCAMS, AND MISCONDUCT

Bank robber Willie Sutton is infamous for answering one simple question. When a reporter asked Sutton why he robbed banks, Sutton curtly replied, "Because that's where the money is." Although he died in 1980, Sutton's words continue to ring true in the Internet Age. Building a powerful platform invites many different types of theft, scams, abuse, and general misconduct. Let's review two examples.

Click Fraud

First up, there's click fraud. This occurs in the world of pay-per-click online advertising. At its core, click fraud represents an attempt by a third party to run up a company's online advertising expenses. Under a simple type of click fraud, a person, automated script, or computer program (typically from a competitor) imitates a potential customer and clicks on an ad. This click charges the company or person sponsoring the ad, although the "clicker" never had any actual interest in the product referenced in the ad/link. Click fraud is a major problem and the subject of increasing litigation. While publicly eschewing click fraud, advertising networks nonetheless make a great deal of money because of it.

In 2006, Google paid $90 million to settle a click fraud lawsuit.[182] And there's no point in singling out the company here. In 2007, Yahoo! agreed to a $5 million settlement for "not doing enough" to prevent click fraud.[183]

Illegal Advertising

Let's look at another Google example. As we saw in Chapter 6, many companies use AdWords to reach their prospective customers. This makes Google billions of dollars—in fact, the vast majority of its revenue. Against that backdrop, it's fair to ask if Google has turned a blind eye to illegal—yet highly profitable—advertising. In a recent Mashable piece, Jolie O'Dell writes that "Google may have continued to serve ads for illegal drug companies even after being warned by several groups that the ads and the online pharmacies they promoted violated the law."[184]

Justifiably concerned about a potential $500 million fine from the U.S. Department of Justice, Google fired a preemptive strike.

In September 2010, the company announced that it was "suing online pharmacy advertisers for breaking the search engine's terms of service and violating U.S. federal laws by using the Google ad network to sell prescription medication without a prescription."[185]

Beyond click fraud and illegal advertising, each member of the Gang of Four has faced different forms of abuse by less savory individuals and businesses. This problem is not isolated to Amazon, Apple, Facebook, and Google. Craigslist, eBay, and other popular Internet-based businesses have all had similar problems. As a result, on their websites they warn users and customers about common scams.

INCREASED GOVERNMENT SCRUTINY

> "Government, even in its best state, is but a necessary evil; in its worst state, an intolerable one."
> —*Thomas Paine*

In the cases above, who knows if Google knowingly or inadvertently violated any laws? These are issues for the courts to decide. The point is that once a company builds a massive ecosystem, incentives exist for others to exploit it—and for that company's management to look the other way. Beyond deliberate indifference or neglect, there's also the legitimate problem of effectively policing platforms and identifying every conceivable type of abuse. Bigger ecosystems mean more users, more customers, more vendors, and more potential abuses.

Of course, U.S. and international regulatory agencies know that untoward individuals and companies can exploit massive platforms. As such, they tend to devote more time to scrutinizing the Facebooks of the world. Then there's the resource issue. Particularly in a tight economy, government agencies just don't have the time and funds to spend on small potatoes. Consider the huge backlog of cases currently at the U.S. Equal Employment Opportunity

Commission (EEOC). It just can't respond to all of the complaints filed. Agencies have to choose their battles prudently. As a general rule, they have kept relatively close eyes on highly visible and profitable companies (read: the Gang of Four).

The decline in general public sector resources does not mean that Amazon, Apple, Facebook, and Google can completely ignore regulatory threats. To this end, on June 25, 2011, Bloomberg Businessweek reported that the "U.S. Federal Trade Commission has begun what's likely to be a broad antitrust investigation with a review of the business practices of the world's most popular search engine."[186] While clearly not happy with the investigation and its scope, Google is cooperating with government officials.

KEEPING SECRETS

Historically, as shown in Chapter 2, some platforms have become dangerous, anti-competitive, and even omnipotent. Given the right circumstances (a lack of government oversight, few competitors, and concentrated power), certain platforms became monopolies.

In the same chapter, we saw that Bezos, Jobs, Zuckerberg, Brin, and Page have not built *de facto* monopolies. To paraphrase the classic song by The Who, the new bosses are not the same as the old bosses. Still, each of the Gang of Four has created a powerful ecosystem. By definition, this invites scrutiny—and not just from government agencies. At least from a public relations point of view, Bezos *et al* are the Rockefellers and Carnegies of their day. They are constantly being watched. In today's 24/7 news cycle, they are finding it tough to keep their companies' secrets. The robber barons didn't have to worry about Twitter.

For Apple, the iPhone 2 was a case in point.[187] Prior to its release, an employee unscrupulously—and perhaps illegally—obtained a prototype and leaked its specifications to the world. In fact, entire sites such as MacRumors[188] exist for the sole purpose of trying to break the latest news from Cupertino, California. Ditto the other three members of the Gang of Four.

It's interesting to note that Apple has brilliantly maximized the buzz factor by saying *less* about its products before their official releases. Of course, that has not stopped others from trying to beat Apple to the punch.

The *Dilbert* Debacle

Even individuals with popular platforms can easily invite great scrutiny, especially when they are:

- ❏ Extremely visible
- ❏ Extremely opinionated
- ❏ Seen as having violated many unwritten rules on the web

For instance, consider Scott Adams, the creator of the enormously popular *Dilbert* comic. Amidst a maelstrom of controversy on his site and different discussion boards about his views, in April 2011, Adams finally came clean. He confessed he had long been using a variety of aliases to "anonymously" toot his own horn. He was outed not only as being his own biggest fan,[189] but also for criticizing others who didn't share his right-wing proclivities.

By using artificial means to attack those with the temerity to disagree with him, Adams severely damaged his brand and platform. Although he won't be wanting for money anytime soon, Adams and Apple manifest an important point about platforms.

> Because of their size, popularity, and sphere of influence, powerful platforms cannot operate in isolation, act duplicitously, and keep unfavorable news quiet. In the Age of the Platform, ascension almost always means at least a modicum of controversy—and that invites web-savvy and nosy trolls, critics, skeptics, and other naysayers.

ANGERING OTHERS

> "When anger rises, think of the consequences."
> —Confucius

We know that competition these days is as intense as ever. Forget for a moment the battles waged among Amazon, Apple, Facebook, and Google, although some have been downright bloody. As online sites such as GrooveShark and Pandora show, Apple isn't the only music game in town. And it doesn't stop there. Apple also faces *legal* competition from Hulu, Netflix, and others—and illegal competition from myriad BitTorrent sites. Google is hardly the only search engine, Facebook is one of many social networks, and Amazon isn't the only online bookstore. Moving quickly and pounding on virtual land grabs often means incurring the wrath of others.

The Establishment

Part II of this book showed how the Gang of Four has ruffled a few feathers. For instance, Amazon irked traditional publishers by pushing the pricing and functionality envelopes with its Kindle. Apple's previously chilly relationship with the RIAA has certainly improved over the years. However, despite years of work, only in November 2010 did Apple acquire the rights to place the Beatles' catalog in iTunes.[190] While Google Books is extremely useful, the company has been sued by publishers, authors, and even photographers for copyright infringement. Many companies view Amazon's 1-Click patent as wholly unfair and anti-competitive—and have gone to court to prove it. Microsoft is hauling Google into court over the dominance of the latter's search engine.

The Gang of Four moves much faster than traditional book publishers, movie studios, record companies, and other established industries and businesses. By and large, Amazon, Apple, Facebook, and Google have acted in manners best described as "first asking for forgiveness, not for permission." In some cases, building a platform means taking the good with the bad.

Existing Customers and Users

On several occasions, Facebook has quietly made what turned out to be ill-advised changes to its features, settings, privacy agreement, and user interface. Many users despised these changes—and ironically even started or joined Facebook protest groups in support of their causes. In the eyes of many privacy advocates, Mark Zuckerberg's *mea culpas* over his company's, at times, spectacular privacy gaffes have been a day late and a dollar short.

Although not excusing furtive changes to privacy policies and default opt-ins, Facebook would never have built a strong and vibrant platform if it had to *crowdsource* everything—that is, consistently put major policy and design decisions up for democratic vote. Platforms are anathema to pleasing everyone. You're almost always guaranteed to offend thousands or millions of people—and lose customers and users who preferred the old way of doing things.

> Building and maintaining a platform means being willing to move quickly and decisively, even at the risk of angering existing different powers-that-be, customers, and users.

INCREASED COMPETITION

By revolutionizing search and making billions in the process, Google has spawned more than its fair share of imitators. Yes, it remains the dominant search engine, but many others are trying to horn in on the action. Buoyed by Apple's success with the iPad and iPad 2, computer manufacturers released dozens of tablets in 2011.

As we have seen, the notion of a *platform* is hardly new. What's more, platforms offer less in the way of protection. Emerging technologies mean that platforms today may not hold those positions in the future. No lead is permanent. Change and disruption can and do come quickly. Creating a search engine or social network or ecommerce site is fundamentally easier than building a dominant railroad or oil company. (Of course, easier doesn't mean easy.)

PLANKS BEWARE: FROM PARTNER TO RIVAL

As mentioned before, building a platform does not guarantee permanent profits or even continued relevance. The same holds true for individual planks.

Imagine for a moment you are Geesung Choi, the vice chairman and CEO of Samsung Electronics. Along with companies such as NVIDIA, Qualcomm, Sprint Nextel, and T-Mobile, you have bet heavily on open standards—and Android in particular. You are reasonably happy with Google, one of your key partners. Then, on August 16, 2011, you awake to hear the news that Google has made an acquisition that throws your world into disarray. On that day, your partner paid:

> ...$12.5 billion for Motorola Mobility, purchasing more than 17,000 patents it can use to defend against allegations of infringement as competition accelerates in the $206.6 billion mobile-phone market.

> The rival handset manufacturers, which have been building devices with Google's Android software since 2008, may have a harder time cranking out bestselling devices because Motorola Mobility may get earlier access to the newest Android technology, said Michael Gartenberg, an analyst at research firm Gartner Inc. The acquisition gives Google an incentive to favor Motorola Mobility, and association with the Internet company will give Motorola handsets a leg up in competing for consumers.

> "This is their nightmare scenario," said Gartenberg, whose firm is based in Stamford, Connecticut. "Google has gone from partner to competitor."[191]

And Samsung is not alone here. As a result of Google's purchase of Motorola, other smaller handset makers now risk losing their cachet—and becoming less relevant. The same thing can happen if Facebook suspends your fan page, Amazon bans your product, or Apple rejects your app.

> In the Age of the Platform, a partner may suddenly find itself on the outside of a particular ecosystem—or made irrelevant by another plank. There is no such thing as a permanent shelf life for a partner or plank. Relationships among partners are extremely fluid.

WHEN THE MIGHTY FALL: THE EPHEMERAL NATURE OF PLATFORMS

> "Action expresses priorities."
> —Mohandas Gandhi

By this point, it should be evident that the Age of the Platform is not some type of utopia for users, customers, partners, and the companies behind the platforms. Each platform has many detractors—and platforms do not last forever. This section examines a few erstwhile platforms and reveals why each has declined, become largely irrelevant, or perished.

Note that the intent in this section is not to demonize companies that have fallen from grace. I have endeavored to provide high-level synopses of why certain companies now find themselves in their current predicaments, surpassed by companies that were formerly a fraction of their size.

Microsoft

Not that long ago, Microsoft seemed insurmountable. In December 1999, its market capitalization exceeded $600 billion,[192] and

Bill Gates alone was worth more than $100 billion. The company's duopoly of Windows (its operating system) and Office (its productivity suite) dominated the computing landscape.

Perhaps the beginning of the end of Microsoft's hegemony occurred in the mid-1990s. A small company named Netscape released its game-changing web browser: Netscape Navigator. After initially underestimating the importance of the Internet, Microsoft controversially bundled its own browser (Internet Explorer) with Windows, effectively killing Netscape. Although the move worked, it raised many red flags in both the public and private sectors. Many influential people believed that Microsoft had become a *de facto* monopoly—and needed to be broken up.

How times have changed. Despite its size, today Microsoft is in danger of becoming an also-ran in the critical consumer space. (It remains firmly entrenched in the enterprise world.) The company's stock has underperformed over the last decade, trailing not only the Dow Jones Industrial Average (DJIA), but fellow tech titans IBM and Oracle as well.[193]

Although Microsoft's issues won't be solved easily or anytime soon, some believe that the company is in dire need of new leadership. Perhaps first up is David Einhorn, a prominent shareholder activist and founder of hedge fund Greenlight Capital. At an Ira Sohn Investment Research Conference on May 26, 2011, he reiterated his desire for current CEO Steve Ballmer to step down. According to CNBC, Einhorn said that Ballmer's "continued presence is the biggest overhang on Microsoft's stock."[194] Ouch.

Without question, today Microsoft still qualifies as a powerful company, but it is not a platform on par with Amazon, Apple, Facebook, and Google. Despite its public assurances of a solid strategy, Microsoft appears to be reeling. Case in point: Microsoft is desperately—and some would say hypocritically—playing the legal card against its biggest competitor. Microsoft lawyers are pressing for legal action against Google. They claim Google is anti-competitive because its search engine accounts for more than two-thirds of all queries. Microsoft's heavily marketed Bing has been unable to steal market share. Some reports put Microsoft's "Bing ratio" at 3:1. That is, it costs the company $3 for every dollar that it makes on search. Even for mighty Microsoft, those numbers aren't sustainable. In fact, rumors persist that Microsoft may sell Bing.[195]

In a way, this is sad and more than a little ironic. Ten years ago, Microsoft was the target of anti-trust hearings because it had bundled Internet Explorer with its Windows operating system. At the time, Microsoft advocated a *laissez faire* position that trumpeted the merits of the free market. Of course, its stance jibed quite nicely with its relative dominance. Now, ostensibly left with no other options, it has flip-flopped, contending that Google's monopoly in search harms competition. The argument smacks of desperation and is entirely misplaced. Changing operating systems is orders of magnitude more difficult and time consuming than using another search engine.

Why is Microsoft struggling? Why have other platforms eclipsed the Redmond giant?

Paying for Past Sins?

Let's look at how Microsoft has historically comported itself, particularly with respect to potential partners. During its heyday, Microsoft played rough with its suppliers, customers, and vendors—and made many enemies in the process. As a growth strategy, it preferred to acquire companies with interesting technologies, as opposed to fostering collaborative relationships with them. Along with chip maker Intel, Microsoft attempted to conquer the world—and, in large part, it succeeded. It wanted to control *everything*: operating systems, Internet browsing, productivity applications, databases, enterprise software, and so forth. It did not embrace third-party collaboration or the very notion of *partnerships*. Today it is paying the price.

In terms of understanding platforms, Microsoft is instructive on a number of levels. First, it shows the perils of refusing to collaborate with others. For years its ecosystem was entirely too closed. (Admittedly, this is a tightrope that, as discussed in Chapter 4, Apple seems to be walking for the time being.) In the short-term, extremely dominant companies can force their partners and customers to adhere to arguably onerous terms because alternatives may not exist—for now. Microsoft proves that bullies increase the risk of government intervention, lawsuits, increased competition, and customer disaffection.

Over the long-term, a platform will have a hard time surviving if it doesn't provide sufficient incentives to potential collaborators. Here, carrots are more effective than sticks. Platforms are vibrant ecosystems that need the active participation of others to thrive. (We'll see in Chapter 11 how emerging platforms like Twitter and Foursquare completely understand this concept.) Tough competition is par for the course, but there has to be adequate room for cooperation and active, *properly incentivized* communities.

Lastly and arguably most importantly, Microsoft has never been able to brand itself as a hip consumer company such as Google. This is imperative today to build a true platform. (See "The Consumerization of IT" in Chapter 1.) The Zune, Microsoft's response to Apple's über-successful iPod, never gained much traction—and the company mercifully announced its death in May 2011.[196] Yes, Microsoft has attempted to branch out, at least in consumer circles. Despite its efforts, however, the company remains known primarily for Office and Windows, franchises that most people consider business-related (read: not consumer-oriented, and certainly not fun).

> To be sure, acquisitions can expedite the building and extension of a platform. Microsoft proves that you can't buy a platform. Plus, you have to play nice with partners if you want their help.

America Online

By the late 1990s, America Online (AOL) was nothing less than dominant. Its dial-up service was the *de facto* standard by which people connected to the Internet. Millions of people new to the web used AOL's user-friendly browser and email application. At one point, the company boasted a client base of more than 30 million users.[197] Around the same time, the company's stock exceeded $100.

AOL was making a killing by giving away compact discs with its software and selling monthly dial-up subscriptions. The company seemed perfectly content signing up new users, losing about as many, and selling banner ads. Of course, this was back when people believed eyesores at the top of web pages would actually convert new customers.[198]

Demise

At a high level, AOL thought that it would benefit by trying to keep everyone within its walls—via dial-up speeds, no less. It was wrong. Most people wanted to get out and explore the entire Internet, not stay on any one site—something that Google was making very easy to do. Accessing great content over the entire web ultimately trumped staying within an AOL browser with "preferred" sites and search results.

Then there's the elephant in the room. In hindsight, the Time Warner merger announced in January 2000 may have only hastened AOL's inevitable fall from grace. The rise of companies such as Yahoo! and Google may have put a fork in AOL even if the latter hadn't pulled off one of the worst moves in the history of U.S. business.

Fast forward to today's AOL. New CEO Tim Armstrong joined the company after a stint at Google in 2009. He came aboard preaching a mantra of content. To say that he has a tall order in front of him is a gross understatement. As Emily Bell explains in *The Guardian*, Armstrong

> has to try to destroy the memory of AOL's two most infamous mergers—first with Time Warner in 2000 and then with social

networking platform Bebo in 2008. If there were a comp̸
for worst media mergers in history, these could happily e̶x̶p̶
to place one and two without any serious competition.[199]

Today, AOL falls miles short of platform status; it is the very definition of *irrelevant*. Its stock hovers around $12 as of this writing. The
company acquired the *Huffington Post* for $315 million in 2010, an
extension of its hyper-local content strategy. Neither HuffPo nor
Armstrong is likely to return AOL to anywhere near its prior position as a premier media property. More than a few in the know
believe AOL's recent moves will merely postpone its eventual
demise. In March 2011, the company announced that it was laying
off 20 percent of its staff. [200]

> AOL proves that a large user base does not guarantee the long-term
> success of a platform. Meaningful development and planks keep peo-
> ple interested and engaged.

Yahoo!

Yahoo! was founded in 1994 by David Filo and Jerry Yang as a direc-
tory of websites. By the late 1990s and early 2000s, without question Yahoo! was a more popular and desirable web destination
than pure search plays such as Lycos, AllTheWeb, and AltaVista.*
In fact, Yahoo! was arguably the Google of its day. In late 1999, the
company's stock hovered around $100.[201] More important, there
was buzz about Yahoo!

Whether functionality, reach, and speed of Yahoo! search exceeded that of other search engines is a matter of debate. One
could spend years arguing about the merits of different technology and whether "the best" technology always wins. I think that
"best" and "most popular" are often two entirely separate things,
and not just in the technology world. Worth a conversation over
beers sometime.

---

* For a fascinating read on the history of search, check out
http://www.searchenginehistory.com.

The Wrong Bets?

During the early 2000s, Yahoo! placed heavy bets on content, directories, and portals. At the time, these seemed like good bets to make. However, in its quest to aggregate existing content, Yahoo! missed the boat on search, development, and building its platform. Ultimately, these moves minimized the company's importance—and attendant profits.

Yahoo! and Search

For many years, Yahoo! outsourced its internal search service to other companies. Yahoo! could have purchased—or, technically, merged with—Google for $5 billion in 2002.[202] Then-CEO Terry Semel was willing to go to $3 billion but told his team to nix the deal, a decision he would later publicly regret.[203]

By that point, Yang had finally seen the light on search. After the Google deal fell apart, Yahoo! began aggressively acquiring search companies such as Inktomi and Overture, aggregating their technologies into a new search engine. Convinced it had built a better mousetrap, Yahoo! dumped Google in favor of its own internal technology on February 17, 2004.[204]

One can only imagine Yahoo! today had it done a deal with Google. Instead, the company's stock is a fraction of its former value—$13.50 as of this writing. In February 2008, Microsoft made an unsolicited bid to acquire the company for $44.6 billion! The deal fell apart over a few dollars per share; soon after, co-founder Jerry Yang stepped aside.

A New Yahoo!?

To its credit, the company appears to now understand the importance of platforms and planks. Over the past few years, it released a number of development tools designed to encourage creative folks to take Yahoo! in different directions.[205]

Without question, Yahoo! remains one of the most popular web destinations, sporting an impressive Alexa ranking of four as of this writing. It certainly has not fallen as far from grace as AOL, and it's not remotely accurate to describe the company as *irrelevant*. Still, it no longer is considered a tech bellwether and a hip place to work. It's a far cry from 1998, and today no one would mistake Yahoo! for Amazon or Google. These days, the hottest software developers and engineers mull offers from Facebook, Google, Foursquare, and social network game developer Zynga.[206] As this happens, the once-mighty Yahoo! is a shell of its former self, a victim of missteps and big bets gone bad.

> Yahoo! shows that content aggregation—without much else—is unlikely to create a vibrant ecosystem or platform. People need something to do on a platform beyond just consuming content from sites.

MySpace

At one point, MySpace was huge and could have evolved into a true platform. It sure had the numbers. In 2006, the site registered its 100 millionth user. What could have been a massive platform has, a mere five years later, become the punch line to a joke.

That's not to say that MySpace didn't have its proponents back in its day. Many drank the Kool-Aid and applauded when old media company News Corp bought Intermix Media, Inc., in July 2005 for $580 million.[207] (Intermix owned MySpace.com and other popular social networking-themed websites.)

As seen earlier with AOL, true platforms don't result when old media companies buy tech-savvy startups. In fact, it's hard to think of two more disparate company cultures and mind-sets than News Corp and MySpace.

In a way, MySpace never had a chance of becoming a real platform. Consider the organic growth of the Gang of Four and its visionary leaders. Zuckerberg, Bezos, and the others have not run their companies like hired guns and short-term-obsessed CEOs. They have very personal relationships with their companies. They could have cashed out years ago for billions, yet they continue to build their platforms. To them, at a core level, it really is not about the money. Could one ever say the same about News Corp head and media mogul Rupert Murdoch with respect to MySpace? Murdoch treated MySpace like just another acquisition.

In her 2009 book, *Stealing MySpace: The Battle to Control the Most Popular Website in America*, Julia Angwin details the meteoric rise of the company. More germane to this book, she also demonstrates how MySpace and its founders dropped the ball. They were unable to recognize and meet the technological requirements necessary to sustain its explosive growth—and ultimately build a real platform. Perhaps this failure stemmed from not having a tech-savvy leader at the helm. No one would confuse Rupert Murdoch for Mark Zuckerberg.

Design Issues

And then there's the design issue. MySpace allowed and even encouraged its users to extensively customize their home pages. It certainly seemed like a good idea at the time. After all, who wouldn't want to personalize their MySpace home page with "skins," custom colors, fonts, photos, and even streaming songs? Remember, customized portals were all the rage in the mid-2000s.

Unfortunately, this lack of a standardized user interface made it very difficult for users to find basic information on one another. Just about every individual page was an adventure; MySpace was little more than a messy collection of personalized statements. Person A might put links for his friends in the upper right-hand corner of his page in a yellow font. Person B might have put that same section in the lower left-hand corner—or not include it at all.

Many people found the default music setting annoying. They did not want to hear booming tunes upon going to a particular page, especially as they increasingly streamed *their own* music over their computers. In October 2010, MySpace considerably simplified its user interface,[208] but by then it was too late. Facebook had cleaned its clock, becoming *the* place to be in social media.

Beyond a clunky, overly busy, and inconsistent frontend, MySpace suffered from a more fundamental business problem: It did not have a clear path toward monetization. A raft of executives could not crack that nut. The company faced additional problems related to accessibility, reliability, security, and safety. Despite its early promise and significant lead over Facebook, no one would ever call MySpace a powerful and successful platform today.

MySpace may in fact die a quiet death. In late June 2011, Specific Media purchased the once-vaunted site for a paltry sum, rumored to be $35 million in stock, not cash.[209]

> **MySpace proves that platforms have to offer real features and benefits. Building a powerful platform is not just about providing a means for people to connect with one another.**

eBay

In his wonderful 2003 book, *The Perfect Store: Inside eBay*, Adam Cohen explains the prodigious rise of one of the Internet's most enduring companies. Once a crazy idea and curiosity named *AuctionWeb*, founder Pierre Omidyar thought he might be on to something big when, in 1995, his site sold a broken laser pointer for $14.83. The sale has become legendary.

Throughout the 1990s, eBay grew to unprecedented heights and became an auction powerhouse. The company went public more than a decade ago. Since that time, its stock has performed reasonably well. Reflecting on that era, I'm hard-pressed to think of a more successful Web 1.0 company.

At the height of the dot-com craze, it seemed as if auctions would supplant fixed prices, fundamentally altering the way that many, if not most, products were sold. That just hasn't happened; online auctions are, as James Surowiecki explains in a June 2011 *Wired* piece, "a niche service."[210]

To its credit, eBay long ago hedged its bets. It saw the need to diversify and move beyond auctions. In this vein, it has been successful. Today, auctions account for a mere 31 percent of eBay's sales.[211] As of this writing, the company had done 34 deals over the course of its history. At a high level, each was supposed to enhance eBay's offerings, functionality, or reach. Some have been unqualified successes, such as its purchase of PayPal for $1.5 billion in 2002. StubHub and half.com also generate considerable revenue for the company. Other purchases, however, have been only modest successes.

And then there's Skype.

Getting Sidetracked: The Skype Acquisition

In September 2005, eBay bought Internet telephony company Skype for the staggering sum of $2.6 billion.[212] At the time, John Blau of IDG News wrote:

> …in addition to its current transaction-based fees, eBay could allow charge for deals through a pay-per-call basis using Skype. And, for its part, Skype could make it much easier for customers to pay for its fee-based services through PayPal, the online payment service owned by eBay.

Numerous integration attempts failed. To make a long story short, Skype didn't work out for eBay. In 2009, eBay finally had to admit defeat and sell Skype for approximately the same amount that it had paid.[213] eBay president and CEO John Donahoe attempted to spin the sale, but no company spends close to $3 billion—and untold millions on related changes, reorganizations, and severance packages—just to get its money back four years later.

eBay Today: Opportunities Squandered

The inclusion of eBay in this section may seem odd. After all, it has certainly pivoted much better than MySpace, AOL, and Yahoo! Today, eBay is alive and well. But the question of consequence is *not* whether it has been successful and profitable. The answer is clearly *yes*. And eBay is a great story. On a personal level, I like eBay and use it frequently. I'll also give former CEO Meg Whitman and the company's top brass credit for trying to grow and diversify its core business.

Nor is eBay completely behind the technological times. On its website, it offers free apps for all mainstream mobile devices,[214] including Android, BlackBerry, iPad, iPhone, and the like. People and companies are developing applications and extensions of eBay as we speak.[215] The company also maintains an official Twitter account[216] and other social media presences.

But if eBay's ultimate aim was to build a platform, it cannot be considered a success on par with Amazon, Apple, Facebook, and Google. At the risk of overemphasizing the importance of one move, in hindsight, the company should not have bought Skype. Although its numbers belie the reality, the widespread perception of eBay remains: It is still the same company it was a decade ago—a popular auction site. Today, when one thinks of the hot technology companies and brands, few in the know would place eBay at the top of any short list. Amazon and eBay may have been contemporaries a decade ago, but it's clear that the former has built a robust and dynamic platform while the latter has not.

Although no one is throwing a pity party for eBay, think about what the company could have become if it had built and integrated more planks à la Amazon. What if it had done a better job of branding itself as something other than an auction company? At least to the same extent as the Gang of Four, eBay has failed to create a powerful platform and ecosystem.

> eBay illustrates the importance of both branding and perception for a platform. What people think your platform does is just as—if not more—important as what it actually does.

Enron

Although more of an energy than technology company, Enron warrants a brief mention here. The company's Internet trading platform (Enron Online, or EOL) was nothing short of revolutionary, prompting Fortune to name Enron "America's Most Innovative Company" for six consecutive years. Of course, this was all smoke and mirrors, as Bethany McLean and Peter Elkind demonstrate in their detailed account of the company and its spectacular collapse, *The Smartest Guys in the Room: The Amazing Rise and Scandalous Fall of Enron*. Enron's highly publicized implosion reminds us that once-mighty platforms can quickly end with a big bang.

SUMMARY AND CONCLUSION

Platforms cut both ways. As we saw in Chapter 8, platforms mean more affiliates, partners, customers, and users. This can and often does result in more profits, revenue, opportunities, innovations, exposure, and fandom. At the same time, however, all of that means more baggage, controversies, headaches, uncertainty, lawsuits, competition, and potential problems. What's more, a powerful platform does not last forever, nor does it inoculate a company against fickle consumers, questionable mergers, bad management, and the like.

In the end, building a platform is worth doing—its pros outweigh its cons. Ask executives at former giants AOL, Yahoo!, and MySpace if they'd like to have the "problems" of Amazon, Apple, Facebook, and Google.

So, how does one build a vibrant platform and integrate different planks? That is the subject of the next chapter.

TEN

....

The How:
Tips for Building a Platform

Now that we have analyzed the ins and outs of platforms, let's move on to how your business can adopt them. This chapter provides specific advice for building an effective platform. It answers the question, "What can my business learn from Amazon, Apple, Facebook, and Google?" It also profiles several smaller companies that have successfully built their own platforms. These interesting stories will clarify and personalize the advice given in this chapter.

What follows does not serve as a checklist for building a powerful platform and integrating planks. Even if you follow all of this chapter's advice, it's very unlikely that your company will become the next Google. Rather, this chapter provides some high-level and tactical guidance for individuals and organizations seeking to build and grow their own ecosystems.

> In the Age of the Platform, every business stands to benefit from creating its own ecosystem—and engaging in others. All else being equal, companies that have embraced platforms and planks will fare far better than those that have not.

ACT SMALL

In his 2011 book, *In The Plex: How Google Thinks, Works, and Shapes Our Lives*, Steven Levy writes about the company's challenge to remain small. Levy explains, "Google had become a big company by thinking like a small company." Levy also tells the story of Larry Page ripping into an executive with very "deliberate" plans to expand global positioning systems (GPSs) country-by-country. At Google, acting like "a big company guy is a cardinal sin."

Now, acting small in a big company is much easier said than done, a topic discussed at length in my previous book, *The New Small*. In fact, as many close to Google have noted, staying small represents arguably its fundamental challenge for the foreseeable future. "Bigness" and all of its attendant problems—bureaucracy, politics, infighting, and the like—put platforms at risk. The trick is to effectively juggle the benefits of being both big and small. That is, exploit the fruits and accoutrements of bigness (financial resources, scale, and a cauldron of smart employees most readily come to mind) while concurrently remaining as agile and proactive as smaller companies.

Limit Bureaucracy at All Costs

While differences exist among Amazon, Apple, Facebook, and Google, observers of these companies have euphemistically noted that they aren't particularly democratic. Apple was Steve Jobs' company—at least until he completely removed himself from the fray. Zuckerberg and Facebook are virtually impossible to separate, and it's hard to imagine Amazon without Bezos. (Google was briefly a triumvirate until Eric Schmidt stepped down as CEO. As of this writing, he serves as executive chairman of the company as well as an advisor to Sergey Brin and Larry Page.)

It's silly to label any of the Gang of Four as a dictatorship, despite the online carping of a few disgruntled employees. The sheer size of each company means that its leaders cannot possibly be involved in every decision. At the same time, though, it's evident that these companies do not follow more traditional (read: bureaucratic) management structures and principles. They want to avoid becoming stiff, inflexible, and overly political environments—and will shake things up when that appears to be happening. Case in point: After assuming the title of Google CEO on April 4, 2011, Page reorganized the company's entire senior team and reporting structure. According to *Wired*, the purpose of the move "was to create clear lines of responsibility by streamlining the product and engineering process."[217] Page knows that speed kills—and that bureaucracy and excessive democracy kill speed.

BE OPEN AND COLLABORATIVE

> "Contemplation often makes life miserable. We should act more, think less, and stop watching ourselves live."
> —*Chamfort*

Generally speaking, platform companies are open to all sorts of new ventures, partnerships, and offerings. We saw in Part II how the Gang of Four almost always makes its application programming interfaces (APIs) freely available to developers, partners, and consumers. That is, by default, new uses, applications, and extensions are approved—unless they violate the company's terms of usage. By allowing third parties to easily integrate new offerings into their own platforms, the Gang of Four creates mutually beneficial outcomes. For instance, Amazon and Apple customers become affiliates and send traffic their way. Facebook and Google developers can access key software code and functionality, creating exciting new games and apps in the process. In each case, this is symbiosis at work.

It's the Community, Stupid

William Hurley, co-founder of Chaotic Moon Studios, a mobile app development outfit says:

Often people don't understand the importance of open APIs. They think that it's just a technical thing, but this is only part of the story. Yes, APIs speed up the development and integration of disparate applications. Often overlooked is one obvious and invaluable fact: It's not about the code. It's about the community.

> Open APIs do much more than solve technical issues. They bring together like-minded individuals who often share surprisingly similar goals. Together these individuals make up the most powerful component of any open project: the community.

Hurley is absolutely right. The importance of openness and collaboration should not be mistaken for a technical requirement or "spec."* These essential concepts are not limited to only APIs for different web-based products and services. Yes, websites and technology matter. However, cool technology and technical sophistication will only get a business so far.

An overall mind-set based on openness and third-party collaboration is absolutely essential in building a true platform. That mentality is much more important than any individual API or technology.

SEEK INTELLIGENT ACQUISITIONS, EXTENSIONS, AND DIRECTIONS

The Gang of Four routinely considers and makes strategic acquisitions to enhance its platforms, both in terms of depth and breadth. Consider some examples:

- ❏ Amazon has bought or invested in many companies in its history, including print-on-demand (POD) company Book Surge (since renamed CreateSpace), online shoe retailer Zappos, and a host of others. [218]
- ❏ Just over the past five years, Apple has spent billions acquiring companies with complementary technologies[219] and has taken significant stakes in others.
- ❏ Facebook did 10 deals in 2010 alone.[220]
- ❏ Google paid an estimated $50 million for the Android mobile platform in 2005 and more than $3.1 billion for DoubleClick's display ad technology in 2007.[221]

---

* Shorthand for *specification*.

Size Doesn't Matter: How HubSpot Built Its Platform

Kristen Knipp, Director of Product Marketing, HubSpot

HubSpot's vision is to provide a killer marketing platform and great marketing advice. This will enable business of all sizes to:

- ❏ Leverage the Internet
- ❏ Increase the number of visitors to their websites
- ❏ Convert more of those visitors to leads and customers

Used by more than 5,000 customers, our platform includes applications for website management, blogging, search engine optimization (SEO), social media monitoring, landing pages, email marketing, lead intelligence, and marketing analytics.

Why Platforms Matter

In many industries, the days of isolated and standalone tools and processes are over—or are quickly dying. Consumers and businesses have spoken: They want systems and apps that make their lives easier. Increasingly, they are gravitating toward a "one-stop shopping" experience. For the user, it's more efficient to use all apps on a single iPhone or access all reports and activities from a single marketing dashboard. Each piece makes customers less likely to want to leave.

Making closed systems part of more open platforms is risky, but the rewards more than justify the risks. First among them is increased innovation. Platforms by definition foster rapid innovation. One smallish player can build an app designed to make many consumers happy and give many businesses a foothold for success. As more people use a platform, more developers create valuable and complementary tools and extensions. This virtuous network effect benefits our customers and us.

(continued)

Leveraging Existing Platforms

HubSpot has used many platforms to build its own. For instance, we utilize Amazon's cloud infrastructure. This has let HubSpot reduce IT costs and allowed our own people to quickly develop valuable marketing applications. Leveraging robust platforms has made it that much easier for us to build and expand our own platform.

In the marketing arena, HubSpot helps businesses grow faster through smart and efficient inbound marketing. While the scale is amazing, every company has its limitations. We certainly can't build *everything* for everyone as fast as the market dictates. Enter HubSpot's own platform: the Application and Services Marketplace and HubSpot APIs (HAPI). Recognizing demand for advanced or niche functionality, HubSpot opened up a few APIs to allow developers to consume data and integrate with other tools.

We quickly saw demand for mashups of existing data or extensions baked right into the product. We have since formed an internal team dedicated to helping more developers build a bevy of marketing applications. We call this the *HubSpot Application and Services Marketplace (HSASM)*. We like to think of it as the iTunes equivalent for marketing apps. HSASM houses thousands of marketing services and applications. One of the prime objectives of HSASM is to help other businesses and developers build their own successful apps on top of HubSpot. This will benefit our clients—and ultimately us. Increasing the amount of content and number of apps available to our family of marketers creates tremendous value for the members of our entire ecosystem.

Interestingly and somewhat unknowingly, we have also built an educational platform for marketers. We originally created Inbound Marketing University (IMU) as a thought leadership and educational vehicle with tight ties to HubSpot. It has received such acclaim that users are taking the content and

(continued)

creating their own mashups. IMU now sports university curricula, training programs for small- and medium-sized businesses, and more based on HubSpot content. Our content reuse policy encourages derivative works, as long as developers provide attribution to HubSpot. Moreover, it truly empowers others to build on top of HubSpot's starting point. Call it a mini-content platform if you will.

As the marketing discipline grows more sophisticated, we will keep improving our core features. However, we fully expect that amazing innovations will take place outside the walls of our business—driven by customers, partners, and third-party developers. And we couldn't be more excited!

The Gang of Four knows it has the resources to build just about anything it wants. For instance, Amazon surely could have launched a Zappos-like competitor. But doing so just didn't make sense. Amazon had plenty of money and the Zappos brand could not be easily replicated. So Amazon just wrote a check. The lesson here: Sometimes it's simply easier to acquire a company outright because of its existing technology, employees, products, and customers.

MAKE LITTLE BETS: ENCOURAGE EXPERIMENTATION

> "If we do not find anything pleasant, at least we shall find something new."
> —*Voltaire*

At least in theory, the great financial promise of social media is that it gives companies of all sizes the ability to "target members by their own self-proclaimed interests and demographics."[222] Throughout its early days, Facebook relied on relatively small investments, starting with $500,000 from PayPal co-founder Peter Thiel in June 2004.[223]

No matter how alluring, however, the potential of Facebook meant very little without a clear and relatively quick path toward monetization, if not a current and sustained stream of revenue. Finding your friends from high school is all fine and dandy, but at some point Facebook needed to figure out a way to make money from its colossal user base. It wasn't Wikipedia. It wasn't going to rely on donations and the benevolence of others.

By virtue of its sheer size, reach, and detailed *user-provided* data, arguably no company has ever had a greater potential to serve up relevant ads than Facebook. Despite this incredibly valuable asset, for years Mark Zuckerberg didn't want to advertise. In particular, he stubbornly resisted the placement of tacky banner ads, as he felt that it would detract from the user experience—and he knew they didn't work anyway.

Eventually, Zuckerberg had to reconsider his quixotic stance. He realized that, in order to sustain his company's torrid level of growth and build its platform, he would need lots of revenue— and fast. To that end, Facebook went down the advertising path. In October 2007, Facebook quietly launched Facebook Flyers. While not banner ads *per se*, these Facebook-controlled advertising widgets appeared in the sidebars of users' pages. They allowed for relevant ads to appear based on user interests and searches. Conceptually (if not in terms of revenue), some compared Flyers to Google AdWords.[224] Ultimately, Flyers didn't bring in much money. Facebook abandoned this experiment in lieu of other advertising mechanisms. The point remains: Facebook wasn't then—and isn't now—afraid of experimentation. As mentioned before, building a platform depends on it.

In a similar vein, Chapter 6 showed how Google employees spend a great deal of time and money on products and services that ultimately go nowhere. And it turns out that here the Gang of Four is hardly alone. In *Little Bets: How Breakthrough Ideas Emerge from Small Discoveries,* Peter Sims writes about the need for companies to make, well, little bets. Long gone are days in which companies can risk their futures on the next product launch. While still possible, "big bang" single discoveries and eureka moments are unlikely to occur. For instance, Merck & Co. should not bet the farm on the success of its next big blockbuster drug.

Today, and for the foreseeable future, organizations will need to take on many different small projects and develop many ideas. To be sure, a majority will fail, but others may blossom into profitable offerings and lines of business. Sims contends—and I agree—that most successful product launches will likely emanate from these small ideas and side projects. Even big companies will have to make many small bets, as companies such as P&G and Starbucks have discovered.

Balance Change with Maintaining Successful Lines of Business

> **"Things do not change, we change."**
> —Henry David Thoreau

Larry Page and Sergey Brin are two of the most intelligent and dynamic business leaders around. As discussed in Chapter 6, for several reasons, they're not moving Google *completely* away from search and advertising. Google is making both better and has been for quite awhile. Over the years, Google has made many significant improvements and innovations to its core products. Recent additions include real-time search, data-specific search options, and auto-complete. Note that Google has introduced these enhancements while maintaining the minimalist appearance of its core product. Google is well aware that feature-creep and excess clutter detract from the overall experience—and has avoided these at all costs.

Making little bets does not mean neglecting the core of your business.

A Note on Scale

Note that, to the Gang of Four, a little bet is still pretty big in absolute terms. A $10 million gambit for Apple is nothing. For a company with 500 employees and $50 million in revenue, however, that same $10 million bet probably determines the company's future. And $10 million is nothing to sneeze at. It may represent much more than your company's annual revenues.

Don't get hung up on the numbers. Think percentages and scale, not absolute dollars. That same 500-person company probably has $50,000 to throw at a promising idea—or $1 million to throw at 20 ideas. Should it fail, those relatively conservative investments probably won't make or break the company. Should one hit, however, it could result in massive revenue and profits. Think of it as putting 20 $10 chips on a few different numbers on a roulette table. You'll probably survive if you lose $200. If one hits, though, your net payoff is $3,400.* You can probably do something substantial with that money.

Of course, there are limitations to little bets. As Amazon, Apple, Facebook, and Google have shown, sometimes you have to bet big. Building a platform—and the individual planks—means knowing how to balance little and big bets.

FAIL FORWARD AND EMBRACE UNCERTAINTY

If you make a bunch of little bets, you're going to fail much if not most of the time. Management at the Gang of Four knows there's absolutely nothing wrong with failing. This is especially true when they minimize the costs of failure and learn something from it. Intelligent people and companies understand this.

Amazon could have failed with its forays into publishing and hardware. Ditto Apple with iPhones, iPads, and apps. These big bets eventually worked out very well and led to other lines of business.

---

* Roulette wheels in U.S. casinos typically consist of 38 numbered slots: numbers 1 to 36, a zero, and a double zero. The house typically pays out at 36-1 on individual numbers.

Let's continue with the roulette analogy from before. If number 23 hits, you can't have 20 vice presidents screaming at each other for not picking 23. Forget the fact that senseless bickering doesn't change the spin of the wheel. The consequences are much more pronounced. Managers and employees will be less likely to take risks—and ultimately innovate—because they fear being reprimanded for things outside of their control. To build a platform, you have to be willing to take chances.

The Myth of Perfection

Perhaps my favorite Apple story took place in 1983. Racing against a deadline to release the latest version of the Macintosh computer, Jobs' team frantically worked against the clock, fixing bugs at lightning speed and forgoing sleep for days. Andy Hertzfeld (Apple employee number 435) was faced with the unenviable task of telling Jobs that Apple would be unable to ship a bug-free version of the software.* To make a long story short, Jobs refused to postpone the product's release. And perhaps he then uttered his three most famous words: "Real artists ship." Remember Voltaire's quote earlier about perfection.

Google, Facebook, and Amazon also adhere to this philosophy, personified by Leonardo da Vinci's quote, "Art is never finished, only abandoned." Insisting on perfection hurts much more than it helps. This is not to say that security and usability don't matter. However, today fixes on digital products can be easily disseminated over the web.

OVERSHOOT

In the consumer technology world, experts will tell you that you should always buy more computer than you need. For instance, let's say that you go out today and buy a computer with a relatively small hard drive, perhaps 200 megabytes. You load up your

---

* For more on this story, check out *http://tinyurl.com/greatplatforms-10*.

computer with a ton of music, pictures, and movies. Within a few months, you have only a small amount of free disk space—and that causes memory and performance problems with your computer. What to do?

Can you buy a larger internal hard drive and have the old one swapped out? Of course. If you're inclined, you can even do that yourself. You can also move some of your data to the cloud. These are all viable options now that you've run out of space. But aren't you wishing that you had just bought a bigger hard drive to begin with?

On a much grander scale, the same principle applies to organizations building their own platforms and planks. Consider Mark Zuckerberg's insistence on having sufficient technology *before* taking Facebook to schools clamoring for it in 2007. The same principle is in effect. By design, Google and Amazon have access to much more compute power than either currently needs—and each keeps adding more. Doesn't this run counter to what we are taught in business classes? Isn't excess inefficient?

No, not in the Age of the Platform. Spikes in traffic and system problems may necessitate extra capacity at an unexpected period of time. At least from a technology perspective, redundancy and excess are very good things, particularly when new users are trying out your platform or plank. It's better to have too much than not enough.

> It's better to overshoot than undershoot. Too much bandwidth is better than not enough. Performance issues will wound and can kill a popular and burgeoning platform headed toward greatness.

KNOW WHEN TO PUNT

Let's say you question the value of a platform. At present, your business operates without one. Furthermore, it is making decent money doing what it's currently doing. Is this likely to continue when—not if—others enter your market? Of course, many businesses cannot scale and build true platforms. But what should you do when your business has already reached its limit—and is in danger of being obliterated?

Let me give you a few examples of the steps that two of my entrepreneurial friends took in response to that very question.

Timing Is Everything

Walter White* has started a number of successful businesses over the past 15 years. Soon after graduating from college, he founded an Internet professional services firm that designed and built large-scale Internet systems. With more than 50 employees, White sold his profitable company to a large Internet conglomerate in 1999. White had taken his company as far as it could realistically go. He knew that his company wasn't going to compete with then-Andersen Consulting or even boutique firms, so he sold it.

A few years later, after getting his MBA, White quickly recognized the popularity of online photo sharing. In 2006, he started a next-generation personal media service that let users send videos and photos directly from their mobile phones to any website.

While that seems passé now, five years ago it was avant-garde. White knew that 800-pound gorilla Flickr would soon make his outfit irrelevant. Flickr itself may fall to integrated social media sites such as Facebook. Peering into the future, White sold his company to a large multimedia company in 2007.

In each case, White got out ahead of time. Today, White has his eyes on the next planks and platforms.

---

* This is a pseudonym. My friend requested anonymity so I picked the name of the main character in AMC's extremely addictive show *Breaking Bad*.

Private Video Platforms

Jay Miletsky has co-founded and run several marketing agencies over the past 10 years. Along with his partner, he currently runs Mango! Marketing,[225] a hybrid agency that combines digital, print, and traditional marketing with social media.

Miletsky has achieved levels of success that are anything but typical. With his last two companies, he has landed some very high-profile clients, including Hershey's and the National Basketball Association (NBA). Yet, at least for him, sticking with traditional marketing—with a dash of social media—is kind of old hat. There's certainly nothing wrong with running a small marketing agency, but Miletsky knows it doesn't typically scale.

In early 2010, he sensed that many companies (and some of his current clients) wanted to build their own platforms—or at least maintain them. Miletsky saw a bright future in private video platforms. He spotted this niche, moved quickly, and formed MyPod Studios.[226] MyPod allows organizations to create their own private channels without the typical IT headaches. Companies need not worry about hosting their own videos and becoming technology experts. MyPod takes care of all of that. Sign up, and within a week your company can be up and running with its own private video pod.

There are many social media agencies and marketing firms out there. Some are better than others. But, right now, how many companies are doing what MyPod is doing? How many are building scalable platforms for themselves? How many can do the same for their clients?

When forming MyPod, Miletsky knew the answers to these questions. He understands the importance of platforms and first-mover advantage (FMA), discussed in Chapter 3. (As an aside, if MyPod isn't successful, will he forget how to run a marketing agency?)

Many people and businesses stubbornly and mistakenly refuse to adapt to new economics, business realities, and technologies. No one wants to leave a great deal of money on the table, but what if you stay six months or a year too long? Isn't this penny-wise and pound-foolish? What else could you be doing with your time and money?

BREADTH TRUMPS DEPTH

Perhaps you've heard of the popular expression "jack of all trades, master of none." It means someone who can do just about anything (within reason) with a certain level of competence but is hardly an expert at any one thing. For instance, it's not that the best Italian chefs do not know how to make burritos. They can read recipes as well as anyone. But an Italian burrito won't resemble anything you'll find at an authentic Mexican restaurant. Many highly skilled and motivated people fall into this bucket.

Now, there's nothing inherently wrong with having significant depth in one niche area. In fact, many people and companies continue to do very well by being very good at one thing. However, this is a much riskier strategy these days compared to years past. We no longer live in a bits-based world. If you compete on the basis of cost, any edge that you hold over your rivals is fleeting.

True platforms are multifaceted. They do not merely do or enable one thing, no matter how big that one thing is—or how well the company does it. As we saw in Chapter 6, Google isn't remotely satisfied with being what it is now, essentially an advertising company. Robust platforms like Google evolve. When it was "only" the world's best search engine (without the planks it has today), Google was by no means a powerful platform. It only became one after it added a bevy of products, including Android, Chrome, News, Reader, Docs, Apps, Voice, Maps, and Gmail. Collectively, these tools have allowed its existing users and customers to operate entirely in and on the Google platform. In the process, it has attracted millions of new users and customers.

Or consider Apple. As we saw in Chapter 4, Apple Computer formally changed its name to *Apple* in 2007. Steve Jobs realized that, despite the company's tremendous success, its name was actually limiting its brand, platform, and expansion. In addition, its name was not terribly descriptive anymore. Apple was no longer merely a computer company.

EMBRACE RISK AND UNCERTAINTY

Somewhere along the line, paranoia got a bad rap. There's really nothing wrong with being paranoid. In fact, especially today, I'll take paranoia over complacency any day of the week and twice on Sunday. There is such a thing as *healthy paranoia*—and building a platform requires it.

Sure, people generally felt safe working for companies such as IBM or AT&T in the 1960s when terms like *lifetime employment* were taken seriously. While hardly true across the board, pharmaceutical companies are still relatively stable environments based in large part on patent protection. However, even those stalwarts and their employees cannot consider their digs to be nearly as secure as they have been in years past. Increased competition from generic drugs and the shadow of rising health care costs (and subsequent reform) are keeping many "Big Pharma" execs up at night. *And they should be losing sleep.*

These days, most businesses, employees, and solopreneurs ought to be paranoid. Let's say that a large part of a company's revenue comes from a single product, service, or client. More than ever, this type of specialization means that the company is taking on an inordinate amount of risk. Companies further maximize risk when they compete solely on the basis of cost. When their offerings are essentially commodities, they are rolling the dice—even if they can continue to "milk it" for a few more years. These days, doing one thing very cheaply is just about the most dangerous thing you can do.

Safe Is the New Risky

> "The desire for safety stands against every great and noble enterprise."
> —*Tacitus*

To build a platform, a company cannot act safe. In fact, *safe* is my least favorite word these days. Consider the conventional wisdom vis-à-vis safety:

❏ It's safe for movie studios to green light big screen versions of moribund franchises such as *The Green Hornet* and *Get Smart*.

❏ It's safe for the head of PR for a cash-laden Fortune 50 company to turn down out-of-the-box marketing ideas under the aegis of lack of funds.

❏ It's safe for large companies to hire highly recognizable consulting firms such as McKinsey and Accenture over boutique firms. The maxim "no one ever got fired for hiring IBM" still rings true at many large organizations.

❏ It's safe for companies to hire only candidates with a boatload of previous experience in their fields.

❏ It's safe to avoid "risky" projects.

But today, businesses that play it safe face major problems because safe is boring. Safe is predictable. Safe is limiting. Safe can only offer marginal improvements. And safe isn't sustainable. The bottom line is that safe often isn't really safe.

From Facebook's early days, Mark Zuckerberg was obsessed with building a true platform; he was not terribly worried about playing it safe and taking moderate risks. (Maybe he should have been more concerned about user privacy, but that's an entirely different discussion.) The same holds true for Steve Jobs, Jeff Bezos, Larry Page, and Sergey Brin. Great inventors such as Thomas Edison and artists such as Jackson Pollock didn't achieve greatness by being anodyne.

MOVE QUICKLY AND DECISIVELY WHEN SPOTTING A NICHE

When building a new platform, it's wise to exhibit patience and temper expectations. But don't confuse patience with inertia. Waiting too long means that an opportunity may disappear *permanently*—or someone else may beat you to the punch. In the words of Mae West, "He who hesitates is a damned fool."

Let's revisit Amazon for a moment. As discussed in Chapter 3, Jeff Bezos endured many scathing insults and calls for his job while he spent enormous sums of money in the 1990s. Few people saw what he did: the need for massive investments in technology infrastructure. Wasn't this overkill? Many thought Bezos mad, recklessly spending millions of dollars on things the company didn't need now—and for the foreseeable future.

Who's laughing now?

Bezos understood then—and understands now—two critical things. First, it's important to place little bets on individual planks. At the same time, though, you just can't get a little bit pregnant if you want to build a powerful platform. You have to balance little and big bets. Second, the importance of FMA cannot be overstated. If he so chose, Jeff Bezos could probably give his detractors the biggest "I told you so" in the history of capitalism.

USE EXISTING PLANKS

> "Man is a tool-using animal. Without tools he is nothing, with tools he is all."
> —*Thomas Carlyle*

Building a new platform from scratch can be accomplished without creating new planks. (Chapter 12 will examine exceptions to this rule.) Consider Jay Baer, a speaker, social media expert, and the co-author of *The Now Revolution*. Baer argues that one need not build entirely new planks. Existing ones can work quite nicely in creating personal ecosystems. Baer says:

> I view content creation, social media, personal branding, and business development as one unified ecosystem. What I do on Twitter and Facebook (and to a somewhat lesser degree, LinkedIn) drives traffic to my blog. That blog traffic drives speaking engagements (approximately 100 per year between live and virtual events). Speaking engagements drive new consulting clients. And the cycle repeats itself. The key is to understand how the various digital incarnations of your business interrelate. You don't want to build a bunch of freestanding empires, because you can't pay enough attention to all of them. Every business needs a "home base" or platform in which businesses interact with its users, readers, employees, customers, and partners. For me, my home base is my blog.[227]

Baer is absolutely right on two levels. First, every business needs a platform. Second, it's time consuming, expensive, and simply unnecessary for every company to create its own tools from scratch. Rather, they should use existing platforms as planks in their own platforms.

Planks and Outposts

Today, businesses of all sizes can take advantages of many low-cost methods, tools, and planks to build platforms. Some of my favorites include the following:

❏ Content-laden and well-designed websites (WordPress—discussed at length in Chapter 11—is my preferred content management system)
❏ Email newsletters
❏ Discussion forums
❏ Blogs
❏ Presences on social sites (public or private) such as Twitter, Facebook, and the like
❏ Online and offline communities

❏   Applications (mobile and traditional)
❏   Software development kits (SDKs) and other proprietary
    and open source tools

For additional examples of emerging platforms just about every business should consider using today, see Chapter 11.

When used effectively, these planks allow businesses to build and extend their reach and platforms. Social media guru and author Chris Brogan has spoken and written about the need for companies of all sizes to embrace what he calls *outposts*, defined as "those touchpoints away from your main online presence where you connect with others in some way."[228] This can be represented visually, as shown in Figure 10.1:

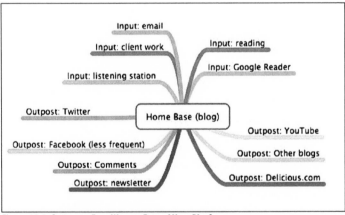

Figure 10.1: Outposts: Easy Ways to Extend Your Platform

As Figure 10.1 shows, outposts represent means for individuals and businesses of all types to do the following:

❏   Consume interesting content
❏   Engage in conversations
❏   Discover a previously unknown source of information
❏   Possibly even purchase goods and services

By using outposts, businesses increase serendipity and exposure. Foolish is the company that attempts to contain everything on its main website, no matter how visually appealing its site may be. These days, prospective customers can discover your company or product in myriad ways, including:

- ❏ Serendipitously on Twitter
- ❏ By searching for recommendations on social review sites such as Angie's List or Yelp
- ❏ Through a Facebook "Like"
- ❏ Via a LinkedIn recommendation
- ❏ Through a random blog post
- ❏ And many, many more

The Importance of Crosspollination

The point is that today conversations can happen anywhere, so companies need to be everywhere—or at least visible on the major platforms. Crosspollination is key, even on competitors' sites and ecosystems. Examples abound. Consider that Google maintains its own Facebook page,[229] as well as many individual product pages. Facebook communicates with others via its official YouTube channel,[230] as does Amazon[231] (see Figure 10.2). Google

Figure 10.2: Amazon YouTube Channel

blasts company messages via its official Twitter account, and it has established separate Twitter accounts[232] for many of its products, including Google Offers—its new Groupon clone (see Figure 10.3). Apple finally started tweeting in July 2010,[233] and Facebook wasn't far behind.[234]

Figure 10.3: Google Offers Twitter Page

Although the Gang of Four hardly needs additional exposure, executives at these companies realize the importance of maintaining presences on different platforms—not just their own. They know that they would be remiss not to participate in conversations, regardless of where they are taking place. Why wouldn't Google want to turn Facebook users on to Chrome? Why wouldn't Amazon want to tell others about its new cloud music offering on YouTube? Platforms are extremely inexpensive, easy, and effective ways of connecting with others—even for companies that have already built great platforms!

This isn't just about websites and software. Let's not forget hardware. Apple wants Kindle fans to read Kindle books on iPads and iPhones—and developed an app to support doing so. Facebook apps exist for the iPhone and Droid.

Then, of course, are the unsanctioned ways of using one platform to access another. In July 2009, Apple understandably pulled Google Voice and other third-party Google Voice applications from the App Store, [235] a move that did not sit well with everyone. A number of Google fans were able to "jailbreak" iPhones so they could continue to use Google Voice while on the Apple platform. (*Jailbreaking* is the process of removing limitations imposed by Apple on its devices. Apple doesn't condone this, but that hasn't stopped people from doing it anyway.)

Consumers and users have spoken loud and clear. When they are using one platform, they don't want to be restricted from using another. While it may not be feasible for platforms to be completely open, err on the side of openness when building your platform. It is unlikely that platforms perceived to be too closed, difficult, and restrictive will reach critical mass.

Add Planks As Needed

Let's return to Google for a moment and its purchase of GrandCentral to compete with Skype. Google used GrandCentral technology to launch Google Voice. Prior to that launch, you would have to leave the Google platform to make a phone call. With Google Voice, that was no longer the case.

Do many of your customers wish that your company offered a particular product or service? You probably don't have $100 million to spend on an acquisition. But what about $500,000? How about $5,000? What about partnerships? Today's most powerful platforms figure out ways to quickly add missing planks.

Branding and Marketing Across Platforms

Ivana Taylor, Publisher of DIYMarketers.com

In the Age of the Platform, defining your brand is no longer a choice. It's an imperative. The question becomes, how do you pull this off? If you want customers to choose your company, it needs to be found across many platforms. To be found, it needs to be visible on each platform. To be visible, it needs a platform-based branding strategy. In the same way that flags or posts mark a territory, the following will define your brand across different platforms:

Own your name. Owning your name as a URL begins the staking of your brand territory. Use this space as a map of your brand presence across different platforms—and the web in general.

Own and protect your brand. Buy a URL that describes your promise or your brand. If you've written a book, own the name of that book as a URL. Be sure to own your brand name across the most important platforms, including Facebook, Twitter, and LinkedIn. Think of your brand as digital real estate and put a virtual fence around it. If you can copyright, trademark, or patent anything around your brand, do it. Do your homework and invest in protecting and using your brand name.

Automate and integrate. Share relevant brand information across different platforms and planks. When you consistently reference and link across the web, you will build links, credibility, and ultimately a larger audience for your brands.

Leverage relationships to build your brand. Today, every major platform has a social component. Leverage your relationships across platforms and use them to enhance your brand presence and relevance. Work with thought leaders, partners, and other brands that complement your brand. Cross-promote where appropriate.

(continued)

> Specific communication platforms come and go, but there is one constant: Develop a strategy for your brand that continually seeks relevant destinations. Begin this process now. The Age of the Platform demands it.

TEMPER EXPECTATIONS

Despite maintaining proper websites, these days most companies have yet to establish their own platforms. Websites are important planks, but they are not platforms in and of themselves. As mentioned in the previous section, many companies spend generously on search engine optimization (SEO), PR firms, and social media marketing campaigns. They hire experts with established platforms, paying them to host webinars, retweet their posts, and help them create their own platforms. How do I know this? This is exactly how some of my clients engage me.

Yet, because they have been late to the game, their efforts typically result in very little *immediate* traction. They forget that building an effective platform takes time. Executives may quickly become frustrated and dismiss platforms, social media, and the web in general as a colossal waste of time. They don't see an immediate return on investment (ROI) for all of the expenses associated with building their company's platform.

These people are short-sighted. They routinely fail to grasp that the world is not waiting for their platform (see "Attention Is Currency" in Chapter 6). So, against this backdrop, you have to be both patient and impetuous. Let me explain.

Balance Patience and Impetuousness

> **"Endurance is patience concentrated."**
> —*Thomas Carlyle*

Never before have so many inexpensive, powerful, and user-friendly tools and technologies been so widely available. Again, in a relatively short period of time and without a terribly large budget, just about anyone can build anything. But *can* and *should* are two entirely different things.

To be sure, today it's remarkably easy to build a platform—especially when you use existing platforms and tools. However, it takes a great deal of time, effort, and resources to build a great and popular one. As we saw in Part II with the Gang of Four, there is no shortcut.

Consider a small business in the process of launching a new website and blog. A bevy of tools allows even a technology-challenged individual to do this in a very short period of time. Many Web 2.0 services and applications allow for the creation of sites that pass the "Mom test"—that is, it's so easy even your mother can do it. The same applies to creating a Twitter account and a Facebook fan page. Neither is difficult nor time consuming to do.

But launching a simple website, blog, and different social media accounts do not a true platform make. Even sites with cool videos, interesting blog posts, stimulating podcasts, and the like typically take a great deal of time to reach a substantial audience. What's more, many sites never make that leap.

Does Quality Even Matter?

It's foolish to expect your platform to immediately eclipse current ones in your niche, even if yours is somehow objectively "better." Perhaps you have created a slicker website. Maybe you publish

> Today, there are tens of millions of blogs and nearly 12 billion pages on the Internet.[236] While some are clearly better than others, businesses that are late to the game face a steep curve in trying to build loyal audiences and followings. In all likelihood, the world—or even a very small part of it—is not anxiously waiting for these companies to build their platforms.
>
> Unless your name is Charlie Sheen, setting up a Twitter account is not going to result in four million followers in a few months. Even if your business focuses on a niche (say, mommy bloggers in Michigan), others have most likely beaten you to the punch.
>
> Launching a cool website, podcast, blog, mobile app, Facebook fan page, or other plank is unlikely to produce immediate results. Building a platform takes time.

more videos or you write more effectively than the Big Kahuna in your space.

Ultimately, this means very little, if anything at all. I don't want you to be discouraged, but it's time for some tough love. The world is not waiting for you or your company to start a platform. Think about it. Are you really wanting for content? Let's say you enjoy reading about progressive rock or professional wrestling or small businesses or Australian rules football. Odds are you struggle to keep up with everything you want to read and watch. You don't have time for more. So, don't expect everyone to flock to your new platform.

The point is that it's crowded in every niche. But don't let that stop you. Today, building a platform is not terribly difficult, but building a popular and powerful one takes time.

SUMMARY AND CONCLUSION

In the Introduction of this book, I mentioned that Roger Federer for years was considered the best tennis player in the world—and quite possibly the greatest of all time. Few people can match his majestic strokes and balletic movements on the court, but that doesn't stop other professionals from playing the game, earning comfortable livings, and winning tournaments. Occasionally, they'll even take a match from him.

Yes, the world's top tennis players make enormous personal sacrifices. Every day, they step onto the court and pick up their rackets. Few athletes train harder, even at early ages. But it all starts with the racket. While having "the best" tennis racket hardly guarantees success, no one can win a match without one. Owning one doesn't mean that you will win Wimbledon.

And the same thing holds true with platforms. Today, they are becoming table stakes. Without a platform, your business is probably invisible to the world at large. Most companies lacking professional and content-laden websites and platforms are not taken seriously. Businesses with primitive sites cost themselves credibility and ultimately customers. Now more than ever, platforms are imperative. This chapter listed a number of rules for building effective platforms. The next chapter looks at emerging platforms.

PART IV
LOOKING FORWARD

Part IV looks at the most promising platforms of the future, provides a brief synopsis of the book, and boldly offers a few predictions.

Chapter Eleven—The Candidates: Today's Emerging Platforms

Chapter Twelve—Coda: A Glimpse of What's Beyond

ELEVEN

The Candidates:
Today's Emerging Platforms

I n Chapter 9, we dicovered that platforms are ephemeral in nature. In the late 1990s and early 2000s, AOL, Yahoo!, Microsoft, MySpace, and other former heavyweights seemed insurmountable. Each has fallen from grace and, in their place, Amazon, Apple, Facebook, and Google have emerged as the new powerhouses.

Looking into the future, the Gang of Four will continue to pay close attention to one another. These companies have never operated in a vacuum; they monitor each other's platforms and lines of business. But it's just plain foolish to think that each will focus *exclusively* on the other three. The people running these companies are far too smart for that. Senior leaders at Amazon, Apple, Facebook, and Google know that many up-and-coming companies are quite eager to diminish them or make them obsolete. These hungry startups may not be nipping at their heels just yet, but complacency could quickly and easily result in their eventual ruins. Don't think for a minute that The Innovator's Dilemma* is lost on any of the Gang of Four—and its leaders.

WHO KNEW?

> **"To the victor belong the spoils."**
> —*William Learned Marcy*

---

* Originally published in 1997, Clayton Christensen's classic business text is about how the same forces that result in success cause companies to become complacent. Paradoxically, organizations need to cannibalize the same business models that made them successful.

Without question, hindsight might explain why each company has risen to such staggering heights and incredible valuations. But only a clairvoyant could have predicted the unprecedented ascensions of Amazon, Apple, Facebook, and Google. Go back for a minute to 2006. Back then no one could possibly have predicted that:

❏ Amazon would be a book publisher, hardware manufacturer, and reseller of excess compute power.
❏ Apple would be the world's greatest content company.
❏ A Harvard dropout would found a company whose services are used by nearly 800 million people throughout the globe.[237]
❏ Google would become the world's most valuable advertising company—with its sights set on conquering just about every other market.

As discussed before, we are experiencing the most rapid technological change in history. To that end, it's reasonable to ask a simple question: Who will be the next victors of the Age of the Platform?

In this chapter, we look at the most promising candidates. We'll see that they have a great deal in common with the Gang of Four—as well as with one another. By and large, they seek to promote the same types of symbiotic relationships with their partners. They are also following very similar blueprints.

FOURSQUARE

As discussed in Chapter 1, mobility is taking off before our very eyes. Few companies seem better positioned to take advantage of it than Foursquare. According to its website, the company is

> a location-based mobile platform that makes cities easier to use and more interesting to explore. By "checking in" via a smartphone app or SMS, users share their location with friends while collecting points and virtual badges. Foursquare guides

real-world experiences by allowing users to bookmark information about venues that they want to visit and surfacing relevant suggestions about nearby venues. Merchants and brands leverage the foursquare platform by utilizing a wide set of tools to obtain, engage, and retain customers and audiences.[238]

As of April 2011, Foursquare laid claim to more than 8 million worldwide users, adding approximately 35,000 new users every day. These users checked in more than 2.5 million times per day, with over half a billion check-ins in 2010. Not bad for a company founded in 2009.

Clearly, some very smart cookies believe that the future of Foursquare is bright indeed. In June 2010, the company received venture capital funding of more than $20 million.[239] A year later, it procured another $50 million, valuing the company at about $600 million.[240]

It's evident that Foursquare's management, led by CEO Dennis Crowley, understands the whole platform concept. First, the company's app and software allows for easy integration with other social media sites, such as Twitter and Facebook, letting users announce to their friends and followers that they're in the local Starbucks. Management at the 60-person company recognizes that it ought to cooperate with complementary sites and companies, not try to take them out.

Second, Foursquare *wants* developers to take its technology in different directions. Like other platforms, Foursquare freely makes its Application Programming Interface (API) available on its developer site.[241]

At its simplest level, an API lets different software programs and services easily communicate with each other. In this way, APIs encourage external development and innovation, making platforms and planks possible.

By making its API open to the world, developers from around the globe can build applications that easily interact with and extend the Foursquare platform. Doing this allows for a great deal more innovation—at a quicker rate—than a "normal" company with fewer than 100 employees could reasonably expect. In addition, the open API sends an unmistakably collaborative message to the company's potential partners: We know that you can figure out extremely innovative ways to use Foursquare as well. We're not the only ones with good ideas. Help us make Foursquare better!

Third, Foursquare knows that the check-in is a two-way street. It may start with the customer, but businesses have to permit it. To this end, the company's Merchant Platform offers friendly terms to businesses of all sizes—hence its remarkable list of customers. The company signed up more than 250,000 businesses using this free set of tools, which help businesses extend their brands, attract new customers, and make their best customers more likely to return. Insisting on onerous terms only deterred prospective business customers—or sent them scurrying to potential competitors such as Gowalla.[242] Foursquare is also working on additional "partner-friendly" features, such as allowing businesses to create their own brand pages through a simple online tool.

TWITTER

Founded in 2006, Twitter has taken a number of critical steps over its short history to ensure its long-term viability—and possible ascension of its platform. Starting in early 2008, the company began experiencing more than its fair share of growing pains on the technical side. It was becoming a victim of its own success. Many users experienced frequent errors for one simple reason: Its users had exponentially increased over the previous six months. Unfortunately, the Ruby on Rails (RoR) infrastructure (an open source web application framework) couldn't support Twitter's current growth, much less its expected future expansion.

Note that Twitter's challenges were hardly unique. We saw in Chapter 5 how performance issues killed Friendster, something of which Mark Zuckerberg was acutely aware—and was determined to avoid for Facebook. Also, eBay's growth expanded beyond the capacity of its hardware in the late 1990s. As a result, the site experienced more than a few system outages.

A Crossroads

Like many successful startups, Twitter seemed to have outgrown its initial technological infrastructure. The company found itself at a crossroads, and management needed to decide what it wanted to be when it grew up. The options:

❏ Remain a standalone company and significantly upgrade its technology
❏ Sell itself to a company that would fix its technical problems

At some point in early 2008, Twitter opted for the former, at least for the time being. In May 2008, the company announced its intentions to move away from RoR.[243] Much like the Gang of Four, Twitter's management moved quickly. In April 2009, Twitter announced that it had successfully migrated much of its internal infrastructure from RoR to Scala,[244] a new, relatively obscure, and powerful programming language capable of

> efficiently handl[ing] concurrent processing—that is, separate instructions that need to use the system's resources at the same time. This is useful when messages from millions of people need to be sent out instantly to different devices all over the world.[245]

Note that Twitter's significant changes and technology investments were invisible to the vast majority of its users. Your average tweeter had no idea about the specifics behind the scenes—and wouldn't care anyway. And that's the point. Users just wanted Twitter to work, regardless of how.

While there have been some bumps along the way, the upgrade to Scala has been very successful. Today, Twitter's technology is more stable and capable of supporting continued growth.

Clearly, the company's current management believes that it can become a platform, as evinced by its recent moves. In May 2011, Twitter acquired the popular desktop client TweetDeck for a reported $40 to $50 million.[246]

Like Foursquare, Twitter makes its API available for developers.[247] This has spawned many interesting Twitter offshoots and byproducts, such as:

❏ **Twapper Keeper**[248]**:** Lets users archive their own tweets for future use.
❏ **TweetDeck,**[249] **Hootsuite,**[250] **and Tweet Grid**[251]**:** Each lets users create their own customized dashboards to better manage what can be a massive stream of tweets.
❏ **Tweet Adder**[252]**:** Lets users find other users via location.
❏ **Sign in with Twitter:** This resembles Facebook Connect, discussed in Chapter 5. When enabled, users can link their Twitter accounts to any participating website, further extending Twitter's platform and reach.

And there are many more creative uses for Twitter, all of which bode well for the company. Now that it has crossed its technological Rubicon, don't be surprised if Twitter takes its platform to the next level.

WORDPRESS

As discussed in Chapter 1, the Internet was starting to mature in 2003. Professional websites were no longer the exclusive purview of large companies and pure techies. At the same time, a phenomenon called *journaling* was increasing in popularity, allowing individuals to easily post their thoughts and feelings on the web for all to see and read.

Against this backdrop, software developers Matt Mullenweg and Mike Little forked an early blogging program called *b2*. (Developers create project forks by legally taking a copy of source code from one software package and starting independent development on it, creating a distinct piece of software in the process.) Mullenweg and Little began a small open source software project, initially called *cafelog,* designed to facilitate the creation of user-generated content. Eventually renamed WordPress, this free content management system (CMS) would allow individuals and companies to easily create web logs or "blogs," and ultimately, powerful and full-blown websites.

Today, WordPress is an extremely popular blogging and publishing platform. As of this writing, more than 14 percent of the 1 million biggest websites use WordPress, as do more than 2 percent of the 10,000 biggest websites in the world.[253] More than 20 million websites worldwide are powered by wordpress.com, including TechCrunch, TED, CNN, the NFL, and others.[254]

I am an unapologetic WordPress evangelist. It powers all of my sites, including www.*theageoftheplatform.com*, the one for the book you are currently reading.*

The Community

Beyond the numbers, the story of WordPress' ascent is fascinating. It has evolved a great deal from its early days, in the process winning plenty of awards and spawning many software development businesses and individual careers.

WordPress is no longer merely a website or software application. It has become a vibrant community with thousands of developers strewn across the globe. Every year, enthusiasts—as well as those generally curious about the platform's new developments and future directions—flock to WordCamp conferences to meet fellow bloggers and developers.

As is par for the course with emerging platforms, WordPress makes its APIs available to everyone.[255] Limited solely by their creativity, developers have built very useful and interesting extensions or

---

* For some other neat WordPress sites, check out *http://wordpress.org/showcase.*

plug-ins that, according to its site, "extend WordPress to do almost anything you can imagine."[256] Plug-ins have been developed to do the following:

- ❏ Create and embed forums within sites
- ❏ Support a raft of ecommerce options
- ❏ Integrate with major social media sites
- ❏ Count down days and hours until a specific event
- ❏ Allow for easy search engine optimization (SEO)
- ❏ Facilitate subscription-based sites

And these represent just the tip of the iceberg.

While WordPress may have initially been the conception of a small cadre of developers, it is now far bigger than even they could have possibly imagined. It has become a massive platform.

GROUPON

Launched in November 2008, Groupon features a daily deal on the best stuff to do, see, eat, and buy in more than 500 markets and 44 countries. According to its website[257] and as of this writing, Groupon employs roughly 1,500 people in its Chicago head-quarters and many more throughout the world. The extremely successful and profitable company aggregates local buyers in "hyper-local" markets through its wildly popular daily emails.

Examples of my recent daily deals include:

- ❏ $35 for a Mani-Pedi ($75 Value) or $85 for a Microderm-abrasion Facial ($170 Value) at Sahana Spa in Montclair, NJ. (I had no interest in this one.)
- ❏ $40 for $100 Worth of Framing Services at Picture Framing Outlet in Whippany, NJ. (I jumped on this one.)

Of course, I received these offers because at the time I lived in northern New Jersey. If I had lived in Las Vegas (as I do now), I would no doubt have received very different deals at 6 a.m. each morning.

The company's success has not gone unnoticed, attracting strong interest from mighty Google. In late 2010, Groupon rejected Google's rumored $6 billion bid for the company.[258] What's more, Groupon has spawned its fair share of imitators, including Living-Social, Facebook Deals, Google Offers,[259] and others.

From a community and partnership standpoint, Groupon clearly gets it, making its API available with registration via its website.[260] The company wants developers and partners to extend and enhance its applications. Consider the text on its site: "Now, you can put all those great ideas for Groupon improvements, extensions, and multiple-platform interfaces to work. We're excited to see what you come up with!"

Talk about inviting others to the party! One has to wonder if Microsoft would be in decline today had it embraced that mindset 10 years ago.

Going Public

With this type of mentality, an innovative business model, and a massive user base, Groupon may be on its way to becoming one of the next great platforms, especially since it announced its plans to go public on June 2, 2011 (since delayed). Buoyed by the results of the recent LinkedIn initial public offering (IPO), Groupon intends to raise $750 million.[261] Analysts expect the company to use these funds to make some fairly large acquisitions in 2011 and beyond that extend the company's platform and offerings.

ADOBE

Adobe Systems is perhaps best known for its two flagship products: Reader and Flash. The former allows people to view PDFs; the latter has been a very popular means of viewing videos. But Adobe is actually much more. According to the company's website, it aims to help its customers create, deliver, and optimize compelling content and applications—improving the impact of their communications, enhancing their brands and productivity, and ultimately bringing them greater business success. Together, we're turning ordinary interactions into more valuable digital experiences every day, across media and devices, anywhere, anytime. [262]

Adobe's Creative Suite (CS) is a best-of-breed set of tools that enables users to create visually compelling and feature-rich websites, apps, documents, and videos.* With its latest release of CS (version 5.5), Adobe has embraced the rental or software-as-a-service (SaaS) model. Its customers and Wall Street have responded favorably. [263] Developers can effectively rent CS for a monthly fee—and even take months off. This should spur adoption of CS, as its admittedly high price tag deterred many independent artists who sought cheaper—and less robust—alternatives.

Adobe also released Flex, a free software development kit (SDK) to create rich Internet applications based on the Adobe Flash platform. Other Adobe tools allow developers to create powerful mobile applications.

But Adobe is not content in the consumer space. Many large companies are finally realizing the benefits of developing web-based and mobile applications. To that end, in June 2011, the company announced the release of Adobe Digital Enterprise Platform (ADEP). ADEP consolidates Adobe creative solutions and "allows enterprises to manage and deliver their digital content across various channels from one place, aiming to make life easier for both IT departments and marketing creatives." [264]

The Apple Problem

Adobe has long been a favorite of developers and creatives. It's hard to think of a more popular development platform and;

---

* At the risk of being immodest, check out *www.thenewsmall.com/book-trailer* for an example of a very cool and graphic-rich video created by Ember Studios.

quite frankly, some of the work that I've seen with Adobe tools is mind-blowing.

Standing in Adobe's way is the mighty Apple. Steve Jobs was not a fan of Adobe Flash, the video-playing software he believed saps device battery life and causes system crashes. (Whether he was ultimately right or not is irrelevant. Apple is under no legal obligation to support any given technology.) As such, he effectively banned Adobe apps and videos from running on iPads and iPhones. For its part, Google does not share the same view, and Android fully supports Flash. Jobs stood pat in his opposition to Flash, much to the dismay of many users unable to watch videos on their new Apple toys. Many developers aren't happy either. While several Flash workarounds exist, Adobe must solve the Apple problem one way or another in order for its platform to flourish.

SALESFORCE.COM AND FORCE.COM

"What if there was an eBay of applications, where companies could buy and sell software, running on our platform? What if there was an iTunes Music Store of online applications?"
—*Marc Benioff, CEO of Salesforce.com*

Few people espouse the benefits of cloud computing more than Marc Benioff, founder of Salesforce.com. The brilliant, extremely opinionated, and controversial Benioff angers many established technology companies by trumpeting the death of software. He believes that just about every company ought to get out of the IT and software development businesses, allowing specialists such as Salesforce.com to handle the often-messy development and backend issues that have traditionally hindered them. From the company's website:

> Enterprise application development with traditional software has always been too complex, too slow, and too expensive. A new model called cloud computing has emerged over the last

decade to address these problems. Applications that run in the "cloud" are delivered as a service so companies don't have to buy and maintain hardware and software to run them—or huge IT teams to manage and maintain complicated deployments.[265]

Benioff's company has been tremendously successful and has ambitious plans for the future. Salesforce.com was previously known for its flagship CRM solution. While vital to a company's operations, Benioff understands that CRM alone does not equate to a true platform. To that end, it has opened up its infrastructure for custom application development. Through its Force.com cloud platform, businesses of any size can build any application they like and run it on the Salesforce.com servers. The company has been trying to brand Force.com as *development as a service*, although it has yet to catch on. Other vendors use the phrase *platform as a service* (PaaS).

Salesforce.com offers quite a few tools to facilitate and expedite development of new applications.[266] To boot, the company's AppExchange[267] offers more than 1,000 apps (as of this writing) in many languages for many industries. Many of these are free. The impressive list of categories includes:

- ❏ Analytics
- ❏ Collaboration
- ❏ Dashboards & Reports
- ❏ Finance & Administration
- ❏ Human Resources & Recruiting
- ❏ Integration & Data Management
- ❏ IT Management
- ❏ Marketing
- ❏ Mobile
- ❏ Partner Relationship Management
- ❏ Sales
- ❏ Sample App Templates
- ❏ Service & Support

Such robust development would not take place without the consent—nay, the encouragement—of Salesforce.com. In his 2009 book, *Behind the Cloud* (co-authored by Carlye Adler), Benioff writes about how the company routinely promotes innovation and collaboration with its partners. It has launched initiatives such as "the Power of Us, a program that invites our partners to provide donated or discounted services or to develop new functionality for the nonprofit sector. The goal is to make it easy for [partners] to get involved and for us to harness the potential power of our ecosystem."

With the increasing usage of cloud computing, look for Force.com to continue fueling the growth of the Salesforce.com platform. According to SeekingAlpha, "the number of paying Salesforce.com subscribers increased from about 230,000 in 2004 to 1.7 million by the end of 2009,"[268] a number that no doubt has grown since then. Plus, in January 2011, the company completed its $31 million acquisition of DimDim. The chief prize: its Chatter collaboration software. Add it all up, and it's clear that Force.com is well on its way to becoming an increasingly powerful platform. If you have any doubt, reread the questions Benioff asks at the beginning of this section.

LINKEDIN

Now with more than 100 million registered users all across the globe,[269] LinkedIn continues to expand. As we saw with MySpace in Chapter 9, oodles of users without any revenue means nothing. LinkedIn has figured out a path toward monetization, generating significant revenue from job postings and displacing traditional heavyweights like monster.com in the process. The basic premise here is that (right or wrong) people who already have jobs are somehow better and more qualified than those looking for jobs.

Fortune reports that LinkedIn's "average member is a college-educated 43-year-old making $107,000. More than a quarter [of them] are senior executives. Every *Fortune* 500 company is represented. That's why recruiters rely on the site to find even the highest-caliber executives."[270] Because of the nearly comprehensive and extremely accurate database *maintained by the users themselves,* recruiters can easily determine who works where and target the most desirable candidates—that is, those who are already employed, highly qualified, and passive in their job searches. Case in point: In 2008, LinkedIn generated quite a bit of buzz when Oracle sourced its new CFO, Jeff Epstein, by using the professional social networking site. Since then, other successes have followed.*

Going Public

In January 2011, the company announced it would be going public.[271] Shares exploded on May 19, 2011, the first day of trading. Although well beyond the scope of this book, many Wall Street analysts believe we are seeing a second technology bubble, as the market is overvaluing social networking companies.

While not nearly on the same scale as WordPress (mentioned earlier), LinkedIn's developer network[272] has taken the company's core technology in some different and interesting directions. LinkedIn APIs[273] are freely available on the company's site.

QUORA

Quora touts itself as "a continually improving collection of questions and answers created, edited, and organized by everyone who uses it."[274] Founded in mid-2009, the company has received a good deal of publicity recently.

As of this writing, Quora doesn't seem to embrace the platform model and the idea of symbiotic partnerships, as evinced by the fact that it chooses to not make its API public.[275] That is, today Quora is much more of a useful website and community than a true platform. Since it's such a new company, it's difficult to definitively predict where it's going. Its site contains tens of thousands of valuable contributions from a bevy of diverse experts. Remember, however, that a useful website and a platform are hardly the same.

---

* For a few of these, see *http://tinyurl.com/phil-gp-linkedin1*.

And my skepticism is shared by others in the know, including Silicon Valley pundit, writer, and entrepreneur Vivek Wadhwa. Wadhwa writes on his blog:

> Quora isn't going to be a Facebook or a Twitter. It is not likely to even catch up with the current market leaders in the Q&A space—Answers.com and Yahoo! Answers (which both get more than 40 million unique visitors a month, compared with Quora's meager 150,000). Unlike Facebook, where everyone socializes, and Twitter, where ordinary people tell their friends what they are thinking, a Quora-like tool is only for those who want to learn what their intellectual peers are saying on, or to research, a particular topic. This is for the tech types—who dabble in technology and dream about things like startups and funding.[276]

This much is certain: Quora certainly isn't as far along the platform continuum as Foursquare, Salesforce.com, and some of the other candidates mentioned in this chapter. It's more of a plank than a platform. It may evolve or its founders may consider different exit strategies.

SUMMARY

Whether these emerging companies and their nascent platforms ultimately become great is anyone's guess. They could stumble. Another company may come along with a better mousetrap. Or the Gang of Four may purchase them at any point. Again, no one can predict the future with any degree of accuracy.

But you shouldn't wait for the verdicts on these growing platforms to come in. Businesses of all types ought to be using many if not all these tools right now—or at least their equivalents. For instance, I use WordPress to run my websites. Quality alternatives exist in the forms of Joomla!, Drupal, Squarespace, and others. The point is not that all businesses should be using WordPress. Rather, all businesses need robust and content-laden web presences.

Waiting for these growing platforms to displace Facebook or Google completely misses the point. These platforms can yield major benefits to your business *immediately*—and may already be doing so for your competition. Conservative businesses that stall will miss the boat—and may not even be around after these emerging platforms evolve.

TWELVE

Coda: A Glimpse of What's Beyond

We've reached the end of our journey. Along the way, we have seen that companies of all sizes have embraced platforms—and seen stunning results. In fact, four of the most dynamic and powerful companies today—Amazon, Apple, Facebook, and Google—can attribute most of their success to the strength of their platforms. Their company founders and current leadership did not wake up recently with platform religion. Rather, at key points throughout their histories, they recognized the primary importance of the platform—and took steps to make theirs as robust as possible.

Just as important, platform companies are never finished. Each continues to expand and evolve its platform in many ways and directions. This book has shown how highly sophisticated technology and the intelligent use of customer data are allowing companies to do simply amazing things through their platforms.

But, in the Age of the Platform, continued prominence and success are hardly guaranteed—something profoundly understood by Bezos, Zuckerberg, Jobs, Brin, and Page. They have built their platforms such that they can add new planks, forge new partnerships, and quickly adapt to sudden technological and business changes.

In this final chapter, we take a look at some of these forthcoming changes. The book concludes by:

❏ Looking at where technology is taking us—whether we like it or not.

❏ Exploring emerging technologies and concepts such as *Web 3.0.*

❏ Examining how powerful platforms will respond to these changes.

❏ Offering a few careful predictions.

Let's see where we are headed.

WEB 3.0 AND BEYOND

> "Technology feeds on itself. Technology makes more technology possible."
> —*Alvin Toffler*

Today's dizzying pace of change shows no signs of abating. If anything, it is likely to accelerate. Although I have no crystal ball, in the next few years, remarkably powerful and exciting technologies will continue to transform our world. Examples include radio-frequency identification (RFID), social search, and facial and voice recognition. Gadgets now used by "early adopters" will mature and become commonplace. Existing technologies will improve by leaps and bounds. For instance, we have only seen the beginning of mobility, as augmented reality, geolocation, and 4G will allow for things previously thought impossible. Appliances connected to the Internet are already here—and in the future we will see "the Internet of Things." You can now buy wearable technology. Coming soon to a home near you: robot vacuums and refrigerators that automatically order milk because they can read the expiration date on the carton.

If Web 2.0 blows your mind, then hold on to your seats. Over the next 5–10 years, the web will become vastly more powerful and efficient. It will become, in a word, *semantic*. We will hear more about *metadata* (data about data) as we progress into the web's third phase—aka *Web 3.0.* The World Wide Web Consortium (W3C)* defines the *semantic* web as:

---

* The W3C is a highly respected international community that develops web standards. It is led by web inventor Tim Berners-Lee.

a Web of data. There is a lot of data we all use every day, and it's not part of the Web. For example, I can see my bank statements on the web, and my photographs, and I can see my appointments in a calendar. But can I see my photos in a calendar to see what I was doing when I took them? Can I see bank statement lines in a calendar? Why not? Because we don't have a web of data. Because data is controlled by applications, and each application keeps it to itself.

The vision of the Semantic Web is to extend principles of the Web from documents to data. Data should be accessed using the general Web architecture using, e.g., URLs. Data should be related to one another just as documents (or portions of documents) are already. This also means creation of a common framework that allows data to be shared and reused across application, enterprise, and community boundaries, to be processed automatically by tools as well as manually, including revealing possible new relationships among pieces of data.[277]

Fascinating books have been written about the semantic web. It's no understatement to say that it will fundamentally change many parts of our lives, especially how we interact with information—*and how information interacts with us*. For instance, simple text-based searches will return data with incredible relevance and *context*, as the Google Squared example in Figure 12.1 illustrates.

When I searched for "Top Men's Tennis Players" on Google Squared, I was not presented with a simple list that included Andre Agassi (my doppelganger) and John McEnroe. Rather, I saw sortable, exportable, spreadsheet-like results equipped with many customizable types of data, including photos.

To some extent, the semantic web is already here. Consider the moves made over the last few years by Best Buy, the U.S.-based consumer electronics retailer. The company dipped its toe in this semantic technologies pool with the goal of "increas[ing] the visibility of its products and services."[278] Even in the early stages, the company has seen amazing results, including a 30 percent increase in search traffic.

top men's tennis players

	Item Name	Image	Description
[X]	Andre Agassi		Andre Kirk Agassi (pronounced /ˈændreɪ ˈæɡəsi/) (born April 29, 1970) is a retired American professional tennis player and former World No. 1. Generally considered
[X]	John Alexander		Combined Men/Women ^ Grand Slams and Davis Cup are not ATP events. Womens Tour. WTA 2011 Season. Live Scores Live StreamsPlayer Sites ... John
[X]	Stefan Edberg		Stefan Bengt Edberg (born 19 January 1966 in Västervik) is a former World No. 1 professional tennis player (in both singles and doubles) from Sweden. A major
[X]	John McEnroe		John Patrick McEnroe, Jr. (born February 16, 1959) is a former World No. 1 professional tennis player from the United States. During his career, he won seven
[X]	Gaël Monfils		Gaël Sébastien Monfils born 1 September 1986) is a French professional tennis player. He is currently the highest ranked French tennis player, and currently ranked

Figure 12.1: Example of Google Squared Semantic Search for "Top Men's Tennis Players"*

Further down the road, things will be either downright scary or very cool, depending on your point of view. For example, a trip to the dentist's office may look like a scene out of *The Terminator*. In 2000, the Journal of the American Dental Association reported that "nanodentistry will make possible the maintenance of comprehensive oral health by involving the use of nanomaterials, biotechnology (including tissue engineering) and, ultimately, dental nanorobotics (nanomedicine)."[279]

The Mid-21st Century

Technologist Ray Kurzweil goes even further—much further. He writes in his 2006 book, *The Singularity Is Near: When Humans*

---

* For your own sneak peak of Web 3.0, check out *http://www.google.com/squared*. Google has since retired Google Squared—at least for now.

Transcend Biology, that human beings will continue to "merge" with technology. In the not too distant future, we humans will become one with computers. Kurzweil extrapolates current and future trends and believes that "nonbiological intelligence will be billions of times more powerful than biological intelligence" by the 2040s.

If you like, go ahead and dismiss Kurzweil as a crackpot. He's anything but. He was one of the first to predict the demise of the former Soviet Union due in large part to technological advances. Kurzweil was no one-trick pony either. In the late 1980s, he looked at current and future trends in the performance of computer chess software. He then correctly predicted that computers would beat the best human chess player by 1998—and he was right again. In May 1997, IBM's Deep Blue computer defeated world chess champion Garry Kasparov in a well-publicized tournament.

With so much technology coming around the corner (at increasing speeds), what does this portend for current platforms—and the Age of the Platform in general?

CONTINUED GROWTH AND EVOLUTION

The Age of the Platform is just beginning and the lead of any one platform is far from safe. Don't expect the Gang of Four to sit idly by as Groupon, Twitter, LinkedIn, and others continue to augment their own platforms. Amazon, Apple, Facebook, and Google will continue to expand in new and unexpected directions, especially where their competition has shown that sufficient demand exists. These companies have used technology in innovative and powerful ways. As such, they are justifiably encouraged by their success—both in terms of breadth and depth. Flubs and gaffes aside, each company is doing many more things right than wrong. In addition, each knows that it will have to expand and evolve to fend off the others.

This is not to say that each of the Gang of Four will compete with the other three in every possible arena. At least in the short-term,

I can't imagine Facebook trying to sell books, ereaders, and music subscription services. Google will continue to do more with hardware, but I can't see it displacing Apple as the *de facto* standard in cool design by the end of 2011. Nor will Amazon or Apple try to out-Google Google. After all, look at Microsoft's struggles in this regard.

Very general predictions about what any one company will do—much less all—are facile. Yes, Apple will continue to be important because people will keep buying iPads, iPhones, and just about whatever else the company introduces. Google isn't going anywhere, at least for the time being. Beyond generalities, however, what does the Gang of Four have in store for us?

For two reasons, it's unlikely that any one prediction will wind up being remotely accurate. First, let's state the obvious: Those in the know at each company keep their cards very close to their vests. And they should. Now more than ever, news breaks quicker and from more sources.

But there's another reason for not trying to predict the specific next moves of such dynamic companies: They often don't know them either. Amazon, Apple, Facebook, Google, and other platform companies are not following intractable long-term plans. Leaders at these companies cannot say *with complete certainty* what they'll be doing in three or five years—and obviously anything beyond that. (Even if their plans came to fruition, they may be executing them in entirely different ways. As Apple and Google have shown, even a term like *cloud computing* lends itself to multiple interpretations.) Yes, the Gang of Four monitors present and future trends—and today makes investments, decisions, and bets based on them. As smart as Bezos, Zuckerberg, and their ilk are, however, they still cannot predict the future. And they're smart enough to know that they shouldn't even try. They can only be prepared for it when it arrives.

The Big Questions

So, is the Gang of Four doing *nothing*? Are these companies taking exclusively "wait-and-see" approaches? Are they being purely reactive? Of course not. At the same time, though, they aren't preparing for every conceivable contingency, trend, and development. Amazon, Apple, Facebook, and Google are operating somewhere between these two extremes, achieving a balance of reactive and proactive moves *through their platforms*. Without their platforms they would take considerable steps back, maybe even to the rest of the pack.

Let's get to the next big question: What, if anything, *should* Amazon, Apple, Facebook, and Google be doing differently? I certainly don't have all the answers, but of this much I am sure: *They should be doing everything they can today to be as prepared as possible for a vastly different tomorrow*. This begs the question: In the Age of the Platform, shouldn't all companies follow that same advice?

Absolutely. But here's the rub: Compared to the Gang of Four, companies that lack powerful platforms have much lower margins for error. They can't swing and miss nearly as often. Platform companies do not need to have everything figured out years ahead of time. And that's one of the main points of the book you have just read.

> A point from Chapter 8 bears repeating here: By themselves, platforms guarantee nothing. They increase the probability of future success, minimize risk and spur innovation, and reduce time to market. All else being equal, companies that embrace platforms will continue to do better than cling to antiquated blueprints.

TECHNOLOGY AND GREENFIELD ORGANIZATIONS

This book has shown that building and maintaining platforms isn't easy. However, perhaps platforms were somehow *easier* to create at *greenfield* sites such as Amazon, Facebook, and Google. (*Greenfield* sites are relatively new and can move with greater alacrity than established, or *brownfield,* sites.) These three companies started with an important and inherent technology advantage over much more mature organizations. Their relatively recent formations and subsequent lack of "baggage," especially on the technology side, allowed them to move very quickly and benefit considerably from their robust platforms.

Apple is the lone exception to this rule. While by no means a new company, Apple embraced new technologies faster and with better results than many of its contemporaries. Despite its age, Apple seems to have young legs. It has blown right past its older competitors.

But there's more to the story than just technology. In the words of long-time computing and technology expert Amy Wohl:

> Amazon, Google, and other web-centric companies built their platforms largely on the cloud, allowing for tremendous scale and speed. Based on their success, subsequent market interest persuaded established organizations such as Microsoft, IBM, and Oracle to move in this direction, too. This happened in spite of previous denials of their interest in the cloud. So established firms, with more of a business focus than the web-centric companies, created and are finally executing their own cloud strategies. However, Amazon, Google, and others have had considerable head starts. Web-native companies did not have to replace or retire antiquated technology, at least to the same extent as old school tech heavyweights.

> Some technologies, such as private clouds, don't require the vendors to retire or replace anything; they're just a new option vendors are offering their customers. The change in attitude is often much more difficult than the change in technology.[280]

Wohl is absolutely right: Technology is certainly an important consideration, but it doesn't explain everything about platform companies and their amazing levels of success. Platforms are about so much more than having "the best" or "hottest" technology.

Yes, Amazon, Apple, Facebook, and Google have built powerful platforms by combining good management with the intelligent use of technology. Their bets on clouds, social tools, and individual offerings have largely turned out well. Beyond these individual bets, they have embraced mind-sets predicated on diversification, experimentation, openness, communities, and mutually beneficial partnerships.

The fallen stars mentioned in Chapter 9 have not been nearly as successful in navigating the same business and technology terrains, and their platforms have suffered as a result. In general, each company's unwillingness to embrace openness, new paths, and collaboration explains much of why its platform has waned. This is much more telling than delaying the adoption of any one technology.

NEXT STEPS

> "Doubt is uncomfortable, certainty is ridiculous."
> —*Voltaire*

This book has introduced the platform as a fundamentally new way of doing business. It has placed a particular focus on four amazing companies: Amazon, Apple, Facebook, and Google. Dynamic ecosystems and communities have driven considerable innovation, profits, and growth at each organization. Moreover, each would not be nearly as prominent today if it hadn't consistently and creatively incorporated new partners and planks into its platform.

There's so much more to say about platforms. It is my hope that this book will start what I believe is a critical dialogue on ecosystems, planks, and platforms. We are in the early stages of this new and exciting time for business, and by no means do I believe this book has addressed these dynamic topics comprehensively. I invite you to continue the conversation at *www.theageoftheplatform.com*, where you will find tools, blog posts, videos, podcasts, and supplemental materials that will help you navigate the Age of the Platform.

You may take nothing from this book beyond a greater awareness of the platform and some important economic and technological trends. You probably learned a few things about the Gang of Four. Maybe I have convinced you of the value of finally improving your company's website, blogging, starting a Facebook fan page for your business, building an app for your company, or selling your products on Amazon.

Perhaps you were already thinking of doing some of these things and you only needed a little nudge—and reading this book provided it. And that's completely fine. But you can—and should—do more with the knowledge in this book. Much more.

Where to Begin

First, harbor no illusions. It's unlikely your company will become the next Facebook or Apple—and certainly not anytime soon. Reading this book doesn't change that. Second, while things happen faster than ever these days, Google—like Rome—wasn't built in a day. However, don't let that dissuade you from building your own platform and planks.

Next, use today's platforms and planks in different ways—and experiment with some of the emerging ones mentioned in Chapter 11. You never know where innovation and experimentation will take you and your business. Facebook didn't start out with 800 million users—it started with one. Apple did not spend billions of dollars on established businesses such as the App Store and iTunes; the company built and grew them over time. Years ago, many influential and ostensibly knowledgeable naysayers dismissed Google as irrelevant and Apple as cute, then dead.* More than a few influential folks demanded that Jeff Bezos of Amazon resign early in his tenure. Their detractors and skeptics are eating a big plate of crow right now—and have been for quite some time.

Finally, realize that there's no going back. Business and technology never rewind. There are those who wish the world would just revert to a simpler time—and many people act like it will. Some are so afraid of failure that they won't try anything new. They think their companies and/or their jobs will be around in five or 10 years if they just keep doing business as usual. They may or may not know about the significance of platforms. More important, they may not *want* to know. Whether they read this book or not, they are going to keep their heads in the sand. This is both unfortunate and dangerous.

In April 2011, I began writing a book that endeavored to be not just informative but inspirational. I hope *The Age of the Platform* has made you consider profound and challenging questions about how you can improve your business, such as:

❑ How can you take advantage of platforms?
❑ How will you use existing platforms to innovate?
❑ In what ways can using platforms improve your business? Your job?
❑ Will you experiment with different planks? Which ones?

If these questions make you feel a little uneasy, don't worry. Embrace the uncertainty. Platforms *require* it.

Now, what are you going to do?

---

* In 1997, über-smart Nathan Myhrvold, former Microsoft CTO, famously said, "Apple is already dead." Whoops.

FURTHER READINGS AND RESOURCES

TRADE BOOKS

Auletta, Ken. *Googled: The End of the World As We Know It*. Penguin, 2010.
> A no-holds-barred account of life at Google, Auletta's account is both honest and comprehensive. Among the many lessons from the book, it's clear that mediocrity and marginal improvements at this juggernaut are not acceptable. In a phrase, that sums up Google—the company and the culture.

Kirkpatrick, David. *The Facebook Effect: The Inside Story of the Company That Is Connecting the World*. Simon & Schuster, 2011.
> Kirkpatrick comprehensively details the beginnings and ascent of this truly remarkable company. It is impeccably researched and an order of magnitude more informative than the movie, *The Social Network*. Particularly instructive is Mark Zuckerberg's early obsession with avoiding the Friendster's fate, which he did by investing heavily in servers and delaying excessive expansion until Facebook could support it.

Martin, Chuck. *The Third Screen: Marketing to Your Customers in a World Gone Mobile*. Nicholas Brealey Publishing, 2011.
> This is an important book about how mobility and mobile platforms are fundamentally altering the dynamics of traditional and even web-based marketing. Location-based services and time-sensitive coupons will cause seismic shifts in who buys what, as well as how and where items are purchased. This book helps you understand why.

Munk, Nina. *Fools Rush In: Steve Case, Jerry Levin, and the Unmaking of AOL Time Warner*. HarperCollins, 2004.
> Many books have been written about arguably the single worst merger in American business over the past 50 years. Unlike some of those other texts, Munk places the lion's share of the blame on Case and Levin.

Stross, Randall. *Planet Google: One Company's Audacious Plan to Organize Everything We Know*. Free Press, 2008.

> Other than Apple, no company has enjoyed such a meteoric rise in the past decade as Google. Stross covers Google's main endeavors, from Google Book Search (formerly Google Print) to Google Voice to Google Docs. Each product or product group is covered in a reasonable level of detail. Stross also provides a solid historical context of Google's challenges, especially in relation to other computing stalwarts (read: Microsoft). In other words, Stross is not so glossy-eyed over Google's success that he overlooks some comparable historical precedents. Not afraid to call a spade a spade, he unapologetically calls Google out for some well-advertised missteps over privacy, copyright infringement, and other snafus. His writing style is very digestible, and I never felt lost reading about more technical concepts, such as cloud computing, indexing the web, or Google's algorithm.

RESEARCH-BASED BOOKS

Anderson, Chris. *Free: The Future of a Radical Price*. Hyperion, 2009.

> Anderson details the evolution of freemium as a business model. He delves into sometimes obscure—but nonetheless important—economic theories. Rather than continue to fill his text with dry economic analyses, however, Anderson moves quite easily into the social sciences, citing the works of scholars such as Herb Simon and Abraham Maslow. Anderson's compelling real-world examples simply jump off the page, making this book anything but academic. The usual suspects are certainly accounted for: Google, Radiohead, *New York Times*, and others provide proof that Free needs to be front and center these days for many company business models.

Anderson, Chris. *The Long Tail: Why the Future of Business Is Selling Less of More*. Hyperion, 2006.

> Anderson's first book explains how the rise in broadband and the web—coupled with the decline in storage—means that the game has changed. It is now possible to find every product,

whether or not it is in a physical store. What's more, cult products can find very productive niches in today's economy. This is one of the most important business books ever written.

Berkun, Scott. *The Myths of Innovation*. O'Reilly, 2007.

Berkun manifests the popular misconceptions about how individuals and companies innovate. He dispels myths such as the Eureka Moment. This carefully researched and example-laden book proves that innovation is much more rooted in hard work and, yes, failure.

Carr, Nicholas. *The Big Switch: Rewiring the World, from Edison to Google*. W. W. Norton & Company, 2009.

In this important book, Carr compares two historical shifts. Companies used to "manufacture" their own electricity but ultimately realized this was wholly inefficient. The power companies were better suited for that purpose. The same thing is happening—and has been for quite some time—with compute power, which is why cloud computing is all the rage.

Christensen, Clayton M. *The Innovator's Dilemma: The Revolutionary Book That Will Change the Way You Do Business*. Harper Paperbacks, 1997.

Few business texts have had such staying power. The same forces that generate companies' success cause them to become complacent. Somewhat paradoxically, organizations need to cannibalize their business models before it's too late—despite amazing levels of success in some cases. This is easier said than done.

Collins, Jim. *How the Mighty Fall: And Why Some Companies Never Give In*. Jim Collins, 2009.

Based on the economic turmoil of 2008, Collins needed to explain why his theories espoused in *Good to Great* seemed to suddenly lack validity. Much like Christensen's book, Collins explains the five stages through which organizations progress. His research indicates that once an organization reaches Stage 4, its demise is a foregone conclusion.

Friedman, Thomas. *The World Is Flat: A Brief History of the Twenty-First Century*. Picador, 2007.

> Friedman's magnum opus magnificently explains the last decade from economic, social, political, and technological points of view. Against that backdrop, he portends a future in which a frictionless economy drives prices lower and lower. It's a scary read for those unable or unwilling to retool their skills.

Gladwell, Malcolm. *The Tipping Point. How Little Things Can Make a Big Difference*. Back Bay Books, 2002.

> Few writers are capable of so effectively stitching together so many seemingly unrelated topics. If you're wondering what the drop in violent crime in New York has in common with the rebirth of Hush Puppies, you'll love this book. Gladwell identifies three types of people responsible for the rapid spread of ideas: Connectors, Mavens, and Salesmen, each of whom plays an important role in the organic spread of products and ideas.

Joel, Mitch. *Six Pixels of Separation: Everyone Is Connected. Connect Your Business to Everyone*. Business Plus, 2010.

> Joel artfully explains how the years of being connected to a handful of folks are now quaint—and over. Today, we're all connected to one another. This presents extraordinary opportunities for businesses that "get with the program" and embrace the Internet, social media, and collaborative tools. No longer do you have to wonder if—and how—you can reach your audience. Joel's excellent book shows that it's never been easier. He explains how you can build a small, niche community and reach your audience effectively and inexpensively. Rife with inspirational stories, this is one of the best marketing and social media books I have ever read.

Keen, Andrew. *The Cult of the Amateur: How Today's Internet Is Killing Our Culture*. Crown Business, 2007.

> Keen's controversial book offers a fascinating look at the normative limits of technology (among other topics). He contends that you wouldn't want a law school dropout to defend you or a first-year medical student operating on you. So why would you want

to watch an amateur video? Why read a book that traditional publishers haven't properly vetted? Keen unapologetically argues for the return of gatekeepers. You may not agree with his book's message, but you simply cannot be neutral about it.

May, Matthew E. *In Pursuit of Elegance: Why the Best Ideas Have Something Missing.* Crown Business, 2010.

Few books leave me wanting more. This is one of them. May skillfully weaves together ostensibly unrelated topics, such as the ending of *The Sopranos*, the paintings of Jackson Pollock, the Sudoku phenomenon, and a whole host of others. Their commonalities? They are all simple and elegant, making them addictive, brilliant, and ultimately successful.

Postman, Neil. *Technopoly: The Surrender of Culture to Technology.* Vintage, 1993.

Postman's classic text takes the reader into fascinating and vastly different realms affected by technology. They include the medical industry, the Manhattan Project, and the psychology of Sigmund Freud. One of the book's main points is that blindly embracing technology's benefits is just as wrong as universally refuting them. Only a Luddite would maintain that technology only makes things worse across the board. Postman forces the reader to ask himself, "Where should society draw the line with technology?"

Ridley, Matt. *The Rational Optimist: How Prosperity Evolves.* Harper Perennial, 2011.

Ridley's central thesis is that we are better off today than we were decades, centuries, and millennia ago. To be sure, technology is more than a little responsible for reducing disease, creating vast sums of wealth, and passing knowledge down from generation to generation. While at times a bit long-winded, it is fascinating to read about how much progress we as a society have made in solving problems and raising our standard of living. Readers with a leftist bent will likely object to some of his proselytizing of free markets, especially in the wake of the global financial crisis caused by largely unregulated financial markets.

Sims, Peter. *Little Bets: How Breakthrough Ideas Emerge from Small Discoveries*. Free Press, 2011.

> Through examples such as Starbucks and P&G, Sims shows that the days of making big, once-in-a-decade bets are rapidly dwindling. Contrary to conventional wisdom, failure is a good thing: It provides valuable lessons, encourages innovation, and eliminates possibilities that simply will not work. The best and most successful companies will innovate by embracing failure, not chastising employees, teams, and departments.

Tapscott, Don and Anthony D. Williams. *Macrowikinomics: Rebooting Business and the World*. Portfolio Hardcover, 2010.

> The authors define five essential principles required to compete in the future: collaboration, openness, sharing, integrity, and interdependence. These principles will allow us to solve massive and seemingly insurmountable problems related to education, healthcare, government, banking, media, and the environment. This is ultimately a hopeful book: Technology can help mankind much more than it can hurt it.

Tapscott, Don and Anthony D. Williams. *Wikinomics: How Mass Collaboration Changes Everything*. Portfolio Hardcover, 2006.

> This bestseller introduced an entirely different mind-set toward solving complex problems. Through fascinating case studies, the authors show how ostensibly disparate groups throughout the globe can work together effectively via technology. These groups not only perform their tasks as well as traditional command-and-control organizations—they actually do better jobs for less time and less money.

ECONOMICS AND MARKETING

Godin, Seth. *Linchpin: Are You Indispensable?* Portfolio Hardcover, 2010.

> Few authors have influenced my thinking as much as Godin, who is a marketing genius—and this may well be his best work. Those who will succeed in this new economy will not be order

takers and rule followers. Rather, the time is ripe for people to take risks and forego traditional paths to success. Lackeys face uncertain futures.

Godin, Seth. *Purple Cow: Transform Your Business by Being Remarkable*. Portfolio Hardcover, 2009.
This isn't 1950. Products and services no longer generate buzz and word of mouth by merely being passable or even good. Godin shows how they have to be remarkable to spread. Every business owner ought to read this book—twice.

Ott, Adrian C. *The 24-Hour Customer: New Rules for Winning in a Time-Starved, Always-Connected Economy*. HarperBusiness, 2010.
Ott introduces a powerful four-quadrant framework that explains seemingly disparate types of customer behavior. Businesses need to understand the "stickiness" of their products—and market and price them accordingly. Time- and attention-starved customers are unlikely to switch products or services if there's no real upside for them, transaction costs are high, and potential for compatibility issues exist. This could not be more relevant today, especially as it relates to great platforms.

BOOK SPONSORS

The following companies made generous pledges to ensure that this book would happen. For that, I am eternally grateful.

INTELLIGIST GROUP

WHERE CAN YOU GO

INSIGHT • VISION • INNOVATION

Who We Are...

Intelligist Group is a team of innovative strategists. In a fast-changing economic and technological landscape, we specialize in unlocking potential within organizations to ensure growth and profitability. Beginning with an in-depth discovery process, we apply a system for helping businesses move past blockages, leverage unidentified or underutilized assets, and identify opportunities for growth.

What We Do...

❑ Investigate ❑ Analyze ❑ Crystallize

"Like putting the point on a pencil, Intelligist Group helped us clarify and crystallize who we are as a business. They changed the way we communicate, internally and externally, and the results have been bigger and better deals for my company."
—Jeff Gomez, CEO, Starlight Runner Entertainment

"Intelligist Group solved a massive problem for us with very creative thinking and simple practical ideas. They were able to tap assets we had lying dormant and had not been paying attention to. Their solutions will save us hundreds of man hours over the next year and thousands more down the road. Brilliant!"
—Deon Douglas, Partner/Creative Director, The Thinking Giant

Website: www.intelligistgroup.com
Email: info@intelligistgroup.com
Blog: blog.intelligistgroup.com
Twitter: @intelligistgrp

ALL YOUR MOBILES ARE BELONG TO US.

www.chaoticmoon.com
hello@chaoticmoon.com

As the world's most proven mobile application studio, we provide everything from initial brainstorming and strategy, to custom development and publishing, to managing your entire mobile presence in any application marketplace. We stand on our history of long-term success by embracing an intense desire to reach further, faster, and longer than ever before.

Chaotic Moon comprises the most talented thinkers, designers, coders, and developers in the mobile media industry today. For more than 20 years we have learned our craft from some of the most innovative companies, such as Apple and IBM. We are award winners, open source thought leaders, iPhoneDevCamp founders, and even doctors. Between us we hold more than a dozen patents and have been interviewed or written for magazines the likes of *Wired, ComputerWorld*, and *BusinessWeek*. For us it's all about our people.

Whether you're a Fortune 100 company or a one-man startup we'll help take your app from a concept to reality. Let us establish, design, and manage your mobile strategy. We will provide custom development on any platform to deliver your new application or resurrect your struggling media.

Consult Your CFO, Inc.
"The Cornerstone of every successful Business."

At some point, every business needs a good CFO.

Whether yours is a small business without the resources to staff a full-time CFO, or whether it's more established and needs specialty services to assist your current team, Consult Your CFO can help.

Consult Your CFO was formed to fill a critical void in the management of businesses at several stages of growth. Young, growing businesses often lack the internal resources to adequately manage corporate finances, so Consult Your CFO offers Outsourced CFO and Part-Time CFO services to these firms. Engagements typically range from weekly oversight to annual reconciliation work. Larger, more established firms often require longer engagements and utilize the Interim CFO services.

Regardless of the need, founder Ken Weil and his team of CFOs and Controllers are available to help with any industry. With an average tenure of more than 20 years in the CFO/Controller realm, each consultant is experienced with the wide variety of business situations that require outside financial management assistance.

Ken can be reached at kenweil@consultyourcfo.com or 410-371-0821.

A HUMBLE REQUEST
FROM THE AUTHOR

Thank you for buying *The Age of the Platform*. I truly hope you have enjoyed reading it and have learned a great deal in the process. Beyond enjoyment and learning (always admirable goals in reading a nonfiction book), I also hope you can and will apply the knowledge in the book to your business. Move your needle.

Perhaps you are willing to help me move my needle. I am a self-employed author, writer, speaker, and consultant. I'm not independently wealthy. I don't have a large marketing machine getting my name out there. My professional livelihood depends in large part on my reputation, coupled with referrals and recommendations from people like you. Collectively, these enable me to make a living.

You can help me by doing one or more of the following:

❏ Write a review on Amazon, bn.com, goodreads.com, or other related sites. The more honest, the better.
❏ Check out my other books: *Why New Systems Fail, The Next Wave of Technologies*, and *The New Small*.
❏ Mention *The Age of the Platform* on your blog, Facebook, Digg, Twitter, LinkedIn, and other sites you frequent.
❏ Recommend the book to family members, colleagues, your boss, friends, subway riders, and other professionals.
❏ If you know people who still work in newspapers, magazines, television, or industry groups, I'd love a referral or reference. Although social media is big, traditional media still matters.
❏ Visit *www.philsimonsystems.com* and read, watch, and listen to your heart's content. I frequently blog, post videos, record podcasts, and create other interesting forms of content on a wide variety of subjects. I also started *www.theageoftheplatform.com* specifically for this book.

You might think doing these things won't have any impact. I respectfully disagree. Amazon, Apple, Facebook, and Google are hardly alone. Millions of people and businesses of all types have built their own platforms. As this book has shown, platforms allow you to reach others in all sorts of interesting and innovative ways. In addition, today we live in a very social world. You simply never know what will spark interest. (Remember the quote at the beginning of the book?)

I don't expect to get rich by writing books. I'm no John Grisham or Stephen King. *Dare to dream, right?* I write books for four main reasons:

- ❏ Although Kindles, Nooks, and iPads are downright cool, I really enjoy holding a physical copy of one of my books in my hands.
- ❏ I have something meaningful to say.
- ❏ I enjoy the process of creating something from scratch. I like writing, editing, crafting a cover, and everything else that goes into writing books. To paraphrase the title of an album by Geddy Lee, it's my favorite headache.
- ❏ I believe my books will help my readers, and make good things happen for me in return.

At the same time, though, producing a quality text takes an enormous amount of time, effort, and money. Every additional copy sold helps.

Thanks again.

—Phil

ENDNOTES

1   http://www.pcworld.com/article/129301/the_50_most_important_people_on_the_web.html#
2   http://www.zdnet.com/blog/btl/eric-schmidts-gang-of-four-who-will-stumble-first/49682
3   http://allthingsd.com/20110531/eric-schmidts-gang-of-four-doesnt-have-room-for-microsoft/
4   http://www.census.gov/econ/smallbus.html
5   http://www.economist.com/node/285614
6   http://l3d.cs.colorado.edu/systems/agentsheets/new-vista/automobile/
7   http://www.pewtrusts.org/our_work_detail.aspx?id=50
8   http://usa.visa.com/download/merchants/visa-bill-pay-insights-newsletter-issue-1.pdf
9   http://www.tgdaily.com/business-and-law-features/53317-facebook-surpasses-google-as-the-internets-top-dog
10 http://gov20.govfresh.com/a-tunisian-on-the-role-of-social-media-in-the-revolution-in-tunisia/
11 http://techcrunch.com/2007/06/15/the-rise-of-the-prosumer/
12 http://techcrunch.com/2010/04/15/nings-bubble-bursts-no-more-free-networks-cuts-40-of-staff/
13 http://allthingsd.com/20110802/exclusive-ning-is-being-shopped-around-at-150m-price-tag/?mod=googlenews_editors_picks
14 http://money.cnn.com/2010/02/02/news/companies/napster_music_industry/
15 http://newspaperdeathwatch.com/
16 http://www.biznessapps.com/how-it-works.html
17 http://www.insidefacebook.com/2010/11/03/facebooks-mobile-products-have-200-million-users/
18 http://www.elance.com
19 http://www.blogtalkradio.com/
20 http://www.usatoday.com/money/companies/management/advice/2010-08-15-advice-el-erian_N.htm
21 http://sethgodin.typepad.com/seths_blog/2011/04/the-realization-is-here.html
22 http://www.rediff.com/money/2006/nov/24bpo.htm
23 http://techcrunch.com/2009/07/22/amazon-buys-zappos/
24 http://polaris.umuc.edu/~njacobs/Acct610/Webliography/lies_damned_lies.pdf
25 http://www.computing.co.uk/ctg/news/1860817/oracle-2010-revenue-surges-cent
26 http://www.cnn.com/2009/CRIME/04/07/sexting.busts/index.html
27 http://www.nydailynews.com/news/ny_crime/2009/04/20/2009-04-20_massachussetts_police_arrest_suspect_in_craigslist_killer_case.html#ixzz0UEKWFvFK
28 http://news.cnet.com/8301-10784_3-9943140-7.html
29 http://www.nytimes.com/2009/03/27/business/media/27adco.html
30 http://www.ycombinator.com/
31 Personal conversation with Mirchandani, 06/01/2011.
32 http://sites.google.com
33 http://www.merriam-webster.com/dictionary/monopoly
34 http://www.economics-dictionary.com/definition/natural-monopoly.html
35 http://www.cato.org/pubs/journal/cjv14n2-6.html
36 http://finapps.forbes.com/finapps/jsp/finance/compinfo/Ratios.jsp?tkr=AAPL
37 http://www.edmunds.com/
38 http://www.google.com/+1/button/
39 http://www.computerworld.com/s/article/9110297/Pentagon_s_IT_unit_seeks_to_borrow_tech_ideas_from_Google_Amazon_other_companies
40 http://www.internet-story.com/amazon.htm
41 http://www.marketwatch.com/story/amazon-posts-first-profit-ever-for-an-online-retailer
42 http://news.cnet.com/2100-1017-245879.html
43 http://www.internetretailer.com/2011/05/10/amazon-replaces-netflix-top-customer-satisfaction-poll

44 https://affiliate-program.amazon.com/gp/advertising/api/detail/main.html

45 http://www.amazon.com/Theodore-Boone-Lawyer-John-Grisham/dp/0525423842/ref=cm_cr_pr_product_top

46 http://www.a9.com/

47 http://www.amazon.com/gp/help/customer/display.html?nodeId=1161404

48 http://www.bloomberg.com/news/2011-02-16/borders-book-chain-files-for-bankruptcy-protection-with-1-29-billion-debt.html

49 http://astore.amazon.com/

50 http://www.amazon.com/dp/B000FI73MA

51 http://www.nytimes.com/2011/05/26/books/bookexpo-america-underlines-industry-shifts.html?_r=1

52 http://itotd.com/articles/295/giving-away-the-razor-selling-the-blades/

53 http://www.investorplace.com/24258/apple-ipad-vs-amazon-kindle-e-reader-market/?cp=msn&cc=synd&cs=investorplace

54 http://www.amazon.com/mobile-apps/b?ie=UTF8&node=2350149011

55 http://www.thedominoproject.com

56 http://mashable.com/2011/02/01/seth-godin-poke-the-box/

57 https://kdp.amazon.com/self-publishing/

58 http://www.mediabistro.com/galleycat/amanda-hocking-scores-four-book-deal_b26297

59 http://amandahocking.blogspot.com/2011/03/blog.html

60 http://artsbeat.blogs.nytimes.com/2011/05/23/agent-and-former-publisher-to-lead-new-imprint-for-amazon/

61 http://www.kickstarter.com/

62 http://www.kickstarter.com/projects/705402671/the-new-small-my-third-book?ref=live

63 http://mashable.com/2010/12/17/kickstarter-ipod-nano/

64 http://cloudscaling.com/blog/cloud-computing/amazons-ec2-generating-220m-annually

65 http://www.crn.com/news/applications-os/226500204/amazon-cloud-revenue-could-exceed-500-million-in-2010-report.htm;jsessionid=6qcAPhELp1er9Vy-CZZSqQ**.ecappj02

66 http://www.techflash.com/seattle/2009/08/Amazoncom_avoids_showdown_over_Kindle_pricing_policy53701757.html

67 http://mashable.com/2009/04/12/amazon-accused-of-removing-gay-books-from-rankings/

68 http://news.cnet.com/8301-27076_3-20057490-248.html

69 http://www.businessweek.com/magazine/content/11_24/b4232041319222.htm

70 http://www.homemediamagazine.com/amazon/amazon-overstock-cut-ties-with-california-affiliates-24375

71 http://www.forbes.com/2007/01/25/apple-microsoft-motorola-ent-sales-cx_kw_0125wharton.html

72 http://tech.fortune.cnn.com/2011/05/18/apple-reportedly-leasing-part-of-a-west-coast-server-farm/?section=magazines_fortune

73 http://techcrunch.com/2011/06/06/apple-15-billion-songs-sold-130-million-books-14-billion-apps-downloaded/

74 http://www.bloomberg.com/news/2011-05-09/apple-brand-value-at-153-billion-overtakes-google-for-top-spot.html

75 http://news.cnet.com/2100-1001-202143.html

76 http://venturebeat.com/2011/05/03/apple-trillion-dollars/

77 http://blog.cd-com/2011/03/is-apple-on-a-mission-to-destroy-optical-discs/

78 http://www.nytimes.com/2011/01/30/business/30unbox.html

79 http://www.appleinsider.com/articles/11/01/07/ces_samsung_eyes_smart_tv_as_center_of_digital_hub_as_it_takes_on_apple.html&page=2

80 http://osxdaily.com/2011/03/18/mac-market-share-around-the-world-usa-15-canada-14-australia-14-and-more/

81 http://www.cnbc.com/id/43294274

82 http://www.bloomberg.com/news/2011-06-07/apple-s-jobs-using-icloud-to-dismantle-the-pc-industry-he-helped-build.html

83 http://www.nytimes.com/2008/03/13/technology/personaltech/
13pogue-e-mail.html?_r=2&oref=slogin&oref=slogin

84 http://www.morphwiz.com/about.php

85 http://itunes.apple.com/us/app/morphwiz/id377345348?mt=8

86 http://itunes.apple.com/us/app/samplewiz/id431031166?mt=8&ign-mpt=uo%3D4

87 http://www.informationweek.com/news/personal-tech/digital-audio/230700088

88 http://www.twitter.com/#!/Jcrudess

89 Personal conversation with Rudess, 07/07/2011.

90 http://news.cnet.com/8301-31001_3-20067614-261.html

91 http://www.apple.com/itunes/affiliates/resources/documentation/itunes-store-web-service-
search-api.html

92 http://www.imdb.com/title/tt0094291/quotes

93 http://techcrunch.com/2011/06/06/apple-15-billion-songs-sold-130-million-books-
14-billion-apps-downloaded/

94 http://tinyurl.com/greatplatform-7

95 http://developer.apple.com/videos/wwdc/2011/

96 http://www.businessinsider.com/chat-roulette-iphone-app-2010-9

97 http://www.wired.com/images_blogs/gadgetlab/2010/09/app-store-guidelines.pdf

98 http://www.macrumors.com/2011/06/09/apple-reverses-course-on-in-app-subscriptions/

99 http://www.apple.com/itunes/ping/

100 http://www.cultofmac.com/bon-jovi-says-steve-jobs-is-personally-responsible-for-
killing-music/86352

101 http://www.nytimes.com/2011/01/30/business/30unbox.html

102 http://www.huffingtonpost.com/2011/03/26/kodak-patent-lawsuit-apple-rim_n_840999.html

103 http://www.rollingstone.com/culture/news/steve-jobs-in-1994-the-rolling-stone-
interview-20110117

104 https://www.google.com/adplanner/planning/site_profile#siteDetails?identifier=
friendster.com&geo=001&trait_type=1&lp=true

105 https://www.facebook.com/notes/facebook-engineering/how-project-triforce-prepared-our-
software-stack-for-prineville/10150177777393920

106 http://www.emarketer.com/PressRelease.aspx?R=1008450

107 Personal conversation with Hickey, 6/20/2011.

108 http://developers.facebook.com/blog/post/108/

109 http://allthingsd.com/20100802/facebook-farmville-now-wasting-a-third-of-your-web-time/

110 http://www.zdnet.com/blog/gamification/farmville-maker-zynga-preps-to-go-public-this-
week-or-next/410

111 http://mashable.com/2010/02/25/facebook-credits-share/

112 http://www.gadgetell.com/tech/comment/facebook-introduces-like-button/

113 http://www.simplyzesty.com/facebook/50-million-facebook-likes-clicked-daily-is-that-9million-
a-day-in-revenue-from-brands/

114 http://www.facebook.com/skittles

115 http://blog.hubspot.com/blog/tabid/6307/bid/9469/20-Examples-of-Great-Facebook-
Pages.aspx#ixzz1Prb1dN7b

116 http://www.facebook.com/thenewsmall

117 Personal conversation with Ware, 6/23/2011.

118 http://ja-jp.facebook.com/blog.php?post=2207967130

119 http://www.facebook.com/blog.php?post=467145887130

120 http://www.allfacebook.com/live-facebooks-awesome-product-announcement-2011-07

121 http://www.theatlanticwire.com/technology/2011/06/roger-ebert-just-latest-victim-
facebooks-censorship-problem/39087/

122 http://allthingsd.com/20100902/facebook-blocked-api-access-to-ping-after-failure-to-
strike-agreement-so-apple-removed-feature-after-launch/

123 http://www.businessinsider.com/why-the-sec-will-force-facebook-to-go-public
-2011-1#ixzz1ACTquX1t

124 http://latimesblogs.latimes.com/technology/2011/06/facebook-sells-225000-shares-to-gsv-capital-corp-ahead-of-anticipated-ipo.html?utm_source=twitterfeed&utmmedium=twitter&utm_campaign=Feed%3A+TheTechnologyBlog+%28Los+Angeles+Times+Technology+Blog%29&utm_content=Twitter

125 http://www.businessinsider.com/meet-facebooks-soon-to-be-billionaire-shareholders-2010-5

126 http://www.insidefacebook.com/2011/06/12/facebook-sees-big-traffic-drops-in-us-and-canada-as-it-nears-700-million-users-worldwide/

127 http://online.wsj.com/article/SB10001424052702304319804576390243972729286.html#ixzz1PpDibmu1

128 http://www.emarketer.com/PressRelease.aspx?R=1008450

129 http://www.reuters.com/article/2011/06/22/us-facebook-winklevoss-idUSTRE75L7NS20110622

130 http://www.google.com/about/corporate/company/history.html#1995-1997

131 http://techcrunch.com/2007/11/30/google-confirms-spectrum-bid/

132 http://googlemade.blogspot.com/2010/11/new-google-product-icons-looks-good.html

133 http://www.readwriteweb.com/archives/the_chromebook_ready_for_the_web_not_ready_to_repl.php

134 http://www.google.com/press/pressrel/applied.html

135 http://www.google.com/adsense

136 http://www.techdirt.com/articles/20060428/0818215.shtml

137 http://thenextweb.com/google/2011/03/28/google-reportedly-partners-with-lg-to-launch-new-nexus-tablet/

138 http://earth.google.com/intl/en-US/licensepro.html

139 http://www.google.com/enterprise/gep/

140 http://www.google-watch.org/gmail.html

141 http://www.pcworld.com/businesscenter/article/189081/google_buzz_criticized_for_disclosing_gmail_contacts.html

142 http://news.cnet.com/8301-30684_3-10452412-265.html#ixzz1PvdESxg3

143 http://www.businessinsider.com/google-pulls-out-of-china-2010-3

144 http://www.businessinsider.com/the-6-delusions-of-googles-arrogant-leaders-2010-3

145 http://venturebeat.com/2010/10/14/google-earnings-q3/

146 http://mashable.com/2009/09/17/facebook-google-time-spent/

147 http://www.washingtonpost.com/blogs/faster-forward/post/google-plus-has-20-million-users-report-says/2011/07/22/gIQATqIPTI_blog.html

148 http://googleblog.blogspot.com/2011/06/update-on-google-health-and-google.html

149 http://mashable.com/2011/08/02/google-plus-25-million-visitors/

150 Slywotzky, Adrian J. *Value Migration: How to Think Several Moves Ahead of the Competition.* Harvard Business Press, 1995

151 Boynton, Andrew and Bart Victor. "Beyond Flexibility: Building and Managing the Dynamically Stable Organization." *California Management Review,* Fall 1991, pp. 53–66.

152 https://secure3.verticali.net/pg-connection-portal/ctx/noauth/PortalHome.do

153 http://www.google.com/press/pressrel/gmail.html

154 http://www.google.com/doodle4google/history.html

155 Personal conversation with May, 6/9/2011.

156 http://www.google.com/webmasters/+1/button/index.html

157 http://www.rush.com

158 http://www.facebook.com/rushtheband

159 http://dealbook.nytimes.com/2011/01/02/goldman-invests-in-facebook-at-50-billion-valuation/

160 http://news.cnet.com/8301-1023_3-20074773-93/facebook-valuation-seen-at-$70-billion/

161 http://www.ning.com

162 https://www.joindiaspora.com/

163 http://www.bloomberg.com/news/2011-03-02/apple-s-steve-jobs-appears-at-company-event-in-san-francisco.html
164 http://www.apple.com/pr/library/2009/08/03bod.html
165 http://techcrunch.com/2010/09/19/facebook-is-secretly-building-a-phone/
166 http://smallbusiness.foxbusiness.com/legal-hr/2011/05/06/3-steps-winning-new-war-talent/
167 http://www.merriam-webster.com/dictionary/frenemy
168 http://arstechnica.com/tech-policy/news/2010/11/google-points-finger-at-facebook-hypocrisy-blocks-gmail-import.ars
169 http://www.businessinsider.com/pivot-startup-2011-2011-5#ixzz1QQBAg6kF
170 http://www.census.gov/econ/smallbus.html
171 http://www.forbes.com/2010/07/28/apple-google-microsoft-ibm-nike-disney-bmw-forbes-cmo-network-most-valuable-brands.html
172 http://www.dailyfinance.com/2010/07/21/the-10-biggest-brand-disasters-of-2010/
173 http://www.bloomberg.com/news/2011-05-09/apple-brand-value-at-153-billion-overtakes-google-for-top-spot.html
174 http://www.nytimes.com/2009/07/19/weekinreview/19cohen.html
175 http://www.americandialect.org/index.php/amerdial/2002_words_of_the_y/
176 http://www.merriam-webster.com/dictionary/google
177 http://www.winelibrary.com/
178 http://www.rovio.com/index.php?page=games
179 http://www.bubbalon.com
180 http://itunes.apple.com/us/app/rain-alert-lite-global-forecast/id337678401?mt=8
181 Personal conversation with Hamilton, 6/26/2011.
182 http://www.webpronews.com/a-penny-for-your-click-fraud-2006-04
183 http://www.webpronews.com/yahoo-click-fraud-settlement-approved-2007-03
184 http://mashable.com/2011/05/20/google-drug-ads-warning
185 http://mashable.com/2010/09/21/google-rogue-pharmacy-lawsuit/
186 http://www.businessweek.com/news/2011-06-25/google-says-ftc-begins-review-of-search-advertising-practices.html
187 http://www.crunchgear.com/2008/06/06/breaking-exclusive-leaked-pics-of-the-iphone-2-thinner-design-check-different-colors-check-video-chatting-check-and-check/
188 http://www.macrumors.com/
189 http://gawker.com/5792583/dilbert-creator-pretends-to-be-his-own-biggest-fan-on-message-boards
190 http://news.cnet.com/8301-31021_3-20022922-260.html?tag=mncol;txt
191 http://www.businessweek.com/news/2011-08-16/google-undermines-samsung-led-handset-makers-with-motorola-tech.html
192 http://news.cnet.com/Microsoft-market-cap-tops-600-billion/2100-1001_3-234802.html
193 http://www.google.com/finance?client=ob&q=NASDAQ:MSFT
194 http://www.hedgetracker.com/article/Greenlight-Capitals-David-Einhorn-calls-for-Steve-Ballmers-resignation
195 http://www.nytimes.com/2011/07/25/business/bing-becomes-a-costly-distraction-for-microsoft-breakingviews.html?_r=2
196 http://www.engadget.com/2011/03/14/microsoft-reportedly-kills-off-zune-hardware-will-focus-on-soft/
197 http://www.businessweek.com/technology/content/jul2006/tc20060731_168094.htm
198 http://www.clickz.com/clickz/news/1711695/survey-banner-ads-most-effective-luring-web-shoppers
199 http://www.guardian.co.uk/commentisfree/cifamerica/2011/feb/07/huffington-post-aol
200 http://www.businessinsider.com/aol-layoffs-start-today-pick-up-steam-as-week-goes-on-2010-1
201 http://www.google.com/finance?client=ob&q=NASDAQ:YHOO
202 http://www.businessinsider.com/tech-deals-decade-2009-12?op=1

203 http://news.cnet.com/8301-10784_3-6071461-7.html

204 http://news.cnet.com/2100-1024_3-5160710.html

205 http://developer.yahoo.com/everything.html

206 http://www.zynga.com/

207 http://news.bbc.co.uk/2/hi/business/4695495.stm

208 http://www.switched.com/2010/10/27/myspace-new-redesign-not-compete-facebook/

209 http://sanfrancisco.ibtimes.com/articles/172011/20110630/rip-myspace-long-live-
     facebook-myspace-sold-for-35-mln-to-specific-media.htm

210 http://www.wired.com/magazine/2011/05/ff_endofauction/all/1

211 http://www.wired.com/magazine/2011/05/ff_endofauction/all/1

212 http://www.pcworld.com/article/122516/ebay_buys_skype_for_26_billion.html

213 http://techcrunch.com/2009/09/01/confirmed-ebay-sells-skype/

214 http://mobile.ebay.com/

215 http://developer.ebay.com/common/api/

216 http://twitter.com/#!/eBay

217 http://www.wired.com/epicenter/2011/04/larry-page-wastes-no-time-reorganizing-
     google-report/

218 http://www.seobythesea.com/?p=342

219 http://en.wikipedia.org/wiki/List_of_mergers_and_acquisitions_by_Apple

220 http://www.insidefacebook.com/2010/12/28/facebook-acquisitions/

221 http://www.businessinsider.com/googles-15-biggest-acquisitions-and-what-happened-to-
     them-2011-3?op=1

222 http://techcrunch.com/2007/10/22/facebook-experiments-with-ads-targeting-peoples-interests/

223 http://www.facebook.com/press/info.php?factsheet

224 http://blog.affiliatetip.com/archives/facebook-flyers-the-next-google-adwords/

225 http://www.marketmango.com/

226 http://www.mypodstudios.com/home/

227 Personal interview with Baer, May 9, 2011.

228 http://www.chrisbrogan.com/how-outposts-improve-your-ecosystem/

229 http://www.facebook.com/Google

230 http://www.youtube.com/user/theofficialfacebook

231 http://www.youtube.com/user/amazon

232 http://twitter.com/#!/GOOGLE

233 http://gigaom.com/apple/apple-finally-on-twitter/

234 http://twitter.com/#!/facebook

235 http://www.readwriteweb.com/archives/looking_for_a_reason_to_jailbreak_how_about_
     spotify_and_google_voice.php

236 http://www.worldwidewebsize.com/

237 http://www.insidefacebook.com/2011/06/12/facebook-sees-big-traffic-drops-in-us-and-
     canada-as-it-nears-700-million-users-worldwide/

238 http://www.foursquare.com

239 http://online.wsj.com/article/SB10001424052748704846004575333222375027784.html

240 http://www.reuters.com/article/2011/06/24/us-foursquare-idUSTRE75N6J020110624
     ?feedType=RSS&feedName=technologyNewsutm_source=feedburner&utmmedium=feed&
     utm_campaign=Feed%3A+reuters%2FtechnologyNews+%28News+%2F+US+%2F+Technology
     %29&utm_content=Google+Feedfetcher

241 https://developer.foursquare.com/

242 http://www.gowalla.com/

243 http://techcrunch.com/2008/05/01/twitter-said-to-be-abandoning-ruby-on-rails/

244 http://www.technologyreview.com/blog/editors/23282/?nlid=1908

245 http://www.technologyreview.com/blog/editors/23282/?nlid=1908

246 http://www.mediabistro.com/alltwitter/twitter-buys-tweetdeck_b8026

247 http://apiwiki.twitter.com/w/page/22554648/FrontPage
248 http://your.twapperkeeper.com/
249 http://www.tweetdeck.com/
250 http://www.hootsuite.com/
251 http://www.tweetgrid.com/
252 http://www.tweetadder.com/
253 http://w3techs.com/technologies/overview/content_management/all
254 http://en.wordpress.com/stats/
255 http://codex.wordpress.org/WordPress_API's
256 http://wordpress.org/extend/plugins/
257 http://www.groupon.com/about
258 http://www.businessinsider.com/groupon-google-deal-falls-apart-2010-12
259 https://www.google.com/offers/home#!details
260 http://www.groupon.com/pages/api
261 http://news.cnet.com/8301-1023_3-20068373-93/groupon-files-its-ipo-papers/?tag=mncol;txt
262 http://www.adobe.com/aboutadobe/
263 http://venturebeat.com/2011/06/21/adobe-subscription-creative-suite-q2-earnings/
264 http://www.itbusiness.ca/it/client/en/home/News.asp?id=63007
265 http://www.salesforce.com/platform/
266 http://developer.force.com/
267 http://appexchange.salesforce.com/home
268 http://seekingalpha.com/article/254576-salesforce-com-poised-for-boost-from-strong-subscriber-growth
269 http://mashable.com/2011/03/22/linkedin-surpasses-100-million-users-infographic/
270 http://money.cnn.com/2010/03/24/technology/linkedin_social_networking.fortune/
271 http://money.cnn.com/2011/01/27/technology/linkedin_ipo/index.htm
272 http://developer.linkedin.com/index.jspa
273 http://developer.linkedin.com/community/apis
274 http://www.quora.com
275 http://www.quora.com/Quora-API/What-kind-of-things-could-be-built-with-a-Quora-API
276 http://wadhwa.com/2011/01/23/why-I-don't-buy-the-quora-hype
277 http://www.w3.org/2001/sw/SW-FAQ#WhatIsTheSW
278 http://www.readwriteweb.com/archives/how_best_buy_is_using_the_semantic_web.php
279 http://jada.ada.org/content/131/11/1559.full
280 Personal conversation with Wohl, 6/6/11.

INDEX

A

accidental lines of business, 164–165
acquisitions strategies, 194–197
Adams, Scott, 174
Adler, Carlye, 233
Adobe Systems, 82, 229–231
AdSense (Google), 118–119
advertising
   Facebook, 93, 198
      Google and, 109
         user authentication and, 95
   Gmail, 125
   illegal, 171–172
   pay-per-click, click fraud, 171
AdWords (Google), 18, 118
Alpert, Phillip, 19
Amazon
   1-Click, 46–47
   Amazon Marketplace, 55, 58
   Amazon Prime, 53
   Appstore for Android, 59
   aStores, 57
   Bezos, Jeff, 43
   BookSurge, 60
   Borders competition, 56
   cloud computing and, 61–64
   customer experience, 45–48, 54–55
   customers
      as guests at party, 47
      site, 54
   customization, 53–55
   disintermediation of others, 63–64
   Godin, Seth and, 59–60
   growth, 43–44
   Hocking, Amanda, 60–61
   IMDb (Internet Movie Database), 57–58
   impulse buys, 52–55
   Kickstarter, 62
   Kindle, 59
   innovations, 165
   pricing policies and publishers, 63–64
   Random House and, 64
   legal issues, 64
   marketing, 48–55
   platform, 44–45
      future of, 65
      planks, 45–63

   RIAA and music in the cloud, 64
   self-publishing, 60–61
   state sales tax, 65
   Stone, Brad on, 65
   video, 62–63
   struggles, 44
   tablet computer, 59
   tags, 54–55
   technology, 51–52
   zShops, 55
Anastasio-Leone, Marissa, 19
Anderson, Chris, 78
Andreessen, Marc, 2
angering others, 175–176
Angwin, Julia, 186
AOL (America Online), 181–183
APIs (Application Programming Interfaces), 78–79
   collaboration and, 193–194
   Foursquare, 223
   Twitter, 226
   WordPress, 227–228
AppExchange, 232
Apple
   1-Click ordering, 47
   Adobe Flash, 82
   Adobe Systems and, 230–231
   APIs, 78–79
   Apple Computer, 67, 69–70
   App Store, 75, 213
   Bon Jovi, Jon, 85–86
   ChatRoulette, 80
   competition, 87
   consumers, simplifying life, 74
   content explosion, 68–69
   critics, 85–86
   developers, 79–80
   digital hubs and, 71–72, 74
   iCloud, 74
   impulse buys, 52–53
   innovation and, 87–88
   iPhone, launch, 74–75
   iPhone 2 leak, 173
   iTunes, 83–84
      MP3.com, 78
   legal issues, 87

MacRumors, 173–174
monopsonist, 34
multiple devices solutions, 73–74
name change, 67–68
partners, 78–80
platform
    future of, 87–88
    planks, 70–84
pornography and, 80
pricing, 86
technology and, 244
WWDC, 80
"Apple is dead...", 246
App Store (Apple)
    approval process, 80
    effects, 75
    In-App Subscriptions, 81–82
    recommendations, 82–84
    Wizdom Music, 76–77
Appstore for Android (Amazon), 59
Armstrong, Tim, 182–183
aStores (Amazon), 57
auctions
    Amazon Marketplace, 55
    eBay, 187–189
    (Amazon), 55

B

Baer, Jay, 208–209
Ballmer, Steve, 179
barriers to entry, 31–32
    virtual, creating, 158–159
Bell, Emily, 182–183
bells-and-whistles trap, 143
Benioff, Marc, 231–233
Berkun, Scott, 163
Bezos, Jeff, 43–44, 47
big company syndrome, xx
Bing (Microsoft), 141, 180
BiznessApps, 10
blogging, 4
BookSurge (Amazon), 60
Borders, Amazon competition, 56
brain drains, 108
brand building, 155–158
    branding across platforms, 214–215
    verb branding, 156–158
Brandt, Richard L., 57–58
Brin, Sergey, xix, 115
Brisman, Julissa, 19
brownfield sites, 243–245
Bubbalon, 161
budgets and growth, 120
bureaucracy, limiting, 192–193

business intelligence, Amazon, 51–52
business model, platform as, 23–26

C

cafelog, 227
Carr, Nicholas, 134
CF (collaborative filtering), 83
change, platform building and, 199–200
change-tolerant organizations, 135–137
Charette, Robert N., 136–137
ChatRoulette, 80
Choi, Geesung, Google and, 177
Christensen, Clayton, 221
Chromebook (Google), 116–118
citizen journalists, 5
click fraud, 171
cloud computing, 12–13
    Amazon and, 61–63
    iCloud, 74
    platform scale and, 134–135
collaboration
    APIs and, 193–194
    building a platform and, 193–194
    incentivized communities, 181
    Microsoft's refusal, 180–181
    platform age, 24
collaborative filtering (CF), 83
communities
    ideas, spread, 140
    incentivized and collaboration, 181
    organic growth and, 140–141
competition, 35
    1-Click and, 175
    angering others, 175–176
    constancy, 39
    increased, 176–177
    Rockefeller, John D., on, 37
complacency and success, 221
consumer and business market
    line blur, 6
Consumerization of IT, 5–6
consumers
    Apple, simplifying life, 74
    business market line blur, 6
    freemium and, 7–8
    Microsoft and, 181
    overwhelmed, 166
    prosumers, 6–7
    restrictions between platforms, 213
    untethered customers, 10
Cook, Tim, 88
coopetition, 149–150
Copius, 108
crosspollination, 211–213

crowdsourcing for decisions, 176
Crowley, Dennis, 223
customer base, 166–167
customer experience at Amazon, 45–48
customer knowledge, 137–138
customers
  bells-and-whistles trap, 143
  crowdsourcing and, 176
  focus on, 141–142
  investing in, 170
  new, 170
Cusumano, Michael A., 87

D

development as a service, 232
digital hubs, Apple and, 71–74
digital revolution, 8–9
Dilbert comic (Adams), 174
discrimination, price, 38
distributed companies, 6
diversification, 153–155
dominate or leave strategy, 154
dynamic stability, xxiii, 135–136

E

eBay, 187–189
Ebert, Roger, 105
ebooks, 58–59
ecommerce and shelf space, 7
ecosystems, platform age, 24
Ehrlich, Jonathan, 108
Einhorn, David, 179
eLance, 11
elasticity of demand, 35–36
emerging platforms
  Adobe Systems, 229–231
  Force.com, 232–233
  Foursquare, 222–224
  Groupon, 228–229
  LinkedIn, 233–234
  Quora, 234–235
  Salesforce.com, 231–233
  Twitter, 224–226
  WordPress, 226–228
enjoyment factor, 37
Enron Online, 189
ephemeral nature of platforms, 178–189
Epstein, Jeff, 234
evolution of the platform, 133, 241–243
expectations in platform building, 215–217
experimentation in building a platform, 197–200
external innovation, 160–161

F

Facebook
  ads, 93
  advertising, 109, 198
  Beacon program, 106
  Credits, 97–98
  customization versus standardization, 103
  dissenting users, 107
  Ebert, Roger censor, 105
  Ehrlich, Jonathan, 108
  email messages, 104
  employees cashing out, 108
  f-commerce, 99–102
  Facebook Connect, 96–97
  Facebook Flyers, 198
  facial recognition, 110
  fan pages, 99–102
  FBML (Facebook Markup Language), 100
  FMA (first-move advantage), 93
  future of, 107–111
  games, 97, 104
  Google and, 109
  growth, managed, 92
  Like button on external websites, 99–100
  lobbyists, 106
  missteps, 104–105
  mobility, 109
  most hated companies, 37
  The New Small page, 101
  opt-out/opt-in, 110
  Ping (Apple iTunes), 107
  platform, planks, 92–104
  privacy issues, 105–106
  public offering (SEC), 108
  Request for Permission, 110
  Skittles page, 100
  tags, 103–104
  user authentication, 94–96
  Wall Street Journal article, 109
  Winklevoss twins, 109
  Zappos page, 100
failure and platform building, 200–201
first to market, 94
flat world, 13–16
FMA (first-move advantage), 45, 93
Force.com, 232–233
Foursquare, 222–224
Fowler, Geoffrey A., 109
freemium, 7–8, 123–124
frenemies, 149–150

Friedman, Tom, 13
Friendster, 90–91

G

games
  Facebook, 97
  Rovio, 160–161
  Zynga, 97
Gang of Four, xix–xx. See also individual
    companies
  elastic demand for products, 36
  hatred for, 37–38
  historical contexts, 28–29
  increases in innovation, xx
  intelligent risk, xxii
  partners, 37
    symbiotic relationships, 38
gatekeepers, 11–12
GE (General Electric) model, 154–155
generalists, return of, 155
geographic monopolies, 32
Gladwell, Malcolm, 140
Godin, Seth, 11, 48, 140
  Amazon and, 59–60
  New Normal, 14
Gonzalez, Albert, 19
Goodman, Ellen, 69
Google
  acting small, 191–192
  AdSense, 118–119
  advertising, Facebook and, 109
  AdWords, 18, 118
  Android technology and, 177
  arrival, 2
  author's uses, 113–114
  Brin, Sergey, 115
  Buzz, 125–126
  China and, 126
  Choi, Geesung and, 177
  Chromebook, 116–118
  click fraud lawsuit, 171
  competition for attention, 122–123
  credos, 129–130
  current state, 127–128
  Facebook and, 109
  freemium and, 123–124
  of, 128–130
  Gmail, 121, 125
  Google Books, 116, 175
  Google Squared Semantic Search,
    239–240
  Google Voice, 123, 213
  GrandCentral, 213
  history, 115–116

iGoogle, 121
innovation, institutionalization of, 120
Microsoft legal action, 179–180
misperceptions, 126–127
Motorola Mobility and, 177
as one-stop shop, 121
Page, Larry, 115
partnerships, 124
personalization, 121–122
platform, planks, 116–124
price discrimination, 38
privacy, 125–126
product icons, 117
revenue, noncore products, 124
Street View, 125
verb branding, 157–158
government
  monopolies, 32
  scrutiny, 172–174
GrandCentral, 213
Great Recession, technology and, 14
greenfield sites, 243–245
Groupon, 11, 228–229
growth
  Amazon and, 43–44
  bottom-up nature, 140
  budgets and, 120
  continued, 241–243
  Get Big Fast, 44
  growing businesses, 170
  managed, 92
  organic, 140–141
  spending and, 141

H

Hafner, Katie, 5
Hamilton, Todd, 161
Harbison, Niall, 99
hardware versus platform, xv
healthy paranoia, 206
Hickey, Colin, 94
Hocking, Amanda, 60–61
horizontal integration, 30–31
Hsieh, Tony, 16
HubSpot, 195–197
Huffington Post, 183
Hughes, Chris, 89
humans merging with technology, 240–
241
HyperArts, 101

I

IBM, xx
iCloud, 74

iFrames, 100–102
illegal advertising, 171–172
iMac release, 69–70
IMDb (Internet Movie Database), 57–58
imitators of platforms, 145–146
impulse buys, 51–55
In-App Subscriptions (AppStore), 81–82
incorporation, 134
India, flat world and, 15–16
innovation
    Apple, 87–88
    Connect+Develop program (P&G), 139
    effects of specific, 163
    external, 160–161
    Google's institutionalization, 120
    innovation and, 165
    internal, 162–163
    Kindle (Amazon), 165
    overwhelmed consumers and, 166
    partner-driven, 161
    partnership and, 138–140
    platform age, 24
    popularity and, 164
integration, 29–31
intelligent risk, xxii
internal innovation, 162–163
Internet
    history, 1–13
    privacy, 19–20
    semantic web, 238–240
Internet Explorer, 179–180
iPhone
    iPhone 2 leak, 173
    launch, 74–75
    Rudess on, 77
IT consumerization, 5–6
iTunes
    Bon Jovi, Jon, 85–86
    MP3.com, 78
    personal information, 83–84
    Ping, 84, 107
    social connections, 84

J

jailbreaking devices, 213
Jobs, Steve, 67
    Bon Jovi, Jon, 85–86
    business genius, 69
    critics, 85–86
    digital hubs, 71–72, 74
    on Eric Schmidt, 149
    innovation and, 87–88
    resignation, 88
    Rolling Stone, 87

Joel, Mitch, xv–xviii
Jungle, 58

K

Kane, Yukari, 109
Keen, Andrew, 11–12
Kelly, Chris, 106
Kickstarter, 62
Kindle (Amazon), 59
    innovations, 165
    pricing policies and publishers, 63–64
Kirkpatrick, David, 89–90
Kodak, xx, 8
Kot, Greg, 9
Kurzweil, Ray, 240–241

L

legal issues
    Amazon, 64
    Apple, 87
    click fraud, 171
    Google and Microsoft, 175
    Google Books, 175
    illegal advertising, 171–172
    Microsoft against Google, 179–180
Leone, Dan, 19
Levy, Steven, 126
limitations of platforms, 169–170
    of, 202–204
    risk and, 207
LinkedIn, 233–234
Little, Mike, 226–227
little bets, 200
Lohr, Steve, 71

M

MacRumors, 173–174
marketing
    across platforms, 214–215
    Amazon, 48–55
    Jobs, Steve, 67
    organic growth and, 140–141
    platform age, 24
Markoff, Philip, 19
Martin, Chuck, 10
May, Matthew E., 143
metadata, 238
Microsoft
    acquisition versus partnership, 180
    anti-trust hearings, 180
    Ballmer, Steve, 179
    Bing, 141, 180
    collaboration, refusal, 180–181
    control desires, 180

dominance end, 178–181
Einhorn, David, 179
    legal action against Google, 179–180
    stock performance, 179
Miletsky, Jay, 204
Mirchandani, Vinnie, 27
Mitchell, Justin, 103
monetization, 8
monopolies, 30–40
    platforms as, 173
monopsonist, Apple as, 34
Moore, Gordon, 5
Moore's Law, 5
Mosaic, 1
Moskovitz, Dustin, 89
Motorola Mobility and Google, 177
MP3.com, 78
Mullenweg, Matt, 226–227
multi-hub universe, 12
multifaceted platforms, 205–206
multiple devices, 73–74
Murdoch, Rupert, 186
music industry, 8–9
Myhrvold, Nathan, 246
MySpace, 185–187
myth of perfection, 201

N

natural monopolies, 33
Neal, Douglas, 6
Netflix, 52–53, 62–63
Netscape, 1–2, 179
network effect, 26
New Normal, 14
New York Times, 10
Newspaper Death Watch, 9
Ning, freemium and, 7

O

Olsen, Ken, 12
Oracle, planning and, 18
O'Reilly, Tim, 4
organizational agility, 167
Ott, Adrian, 148
outposts, 210–211
overseas accounting services, 15–16
overshooting in planning, 201–202
overwhelmed consumers, 166

P

Page, Larry, xix, 115
Parker, Sean, Mark Zuckerberg
    and, 89–90
partner-driven innovation, 160–161

partners
    Gang of Four and, 37
    Google, 124
    innovation and, 138–140
    Microsoft acquisitions, 180
pay-per-click advertising, 171
perfection myth, 201
performance predictions, 17–19
P&G (Proctor & Gamble), 139
Ping (iTunes), 84, 107
planks, 24
    existing, 208–215
    low-cost methods, 209–210
planning
    futility, 17
    Oracle and, 18
    overshooting, 201–202
    performance predictions, 17–19
    profit predictions, 17–19
    vendor lock-in, 18
platform age, dimensions, 24
platform as a service, 232
platforms
    book wars, xv
    borrowing from, 144–145
    branding across, 214–215
    building
        acqusitions, 194–197
        acting small, 191–193
        book back story, xxiv–xxv
        change and, 199–200
        collaboration and, 193–194
        crosspollination, 211–213
        existing planks, 208–215
        expectations, 215–217
        experimentation, 197–200
        failure and, 200–201
        limitation awareness, 202–204
        multifaceted, 205–206
        opportunity seizing, 208
        outposts, 210–211
        overshooting in planning, 201–202
        risk, 206–207
        timing, 217
    as business model, 23–26
    as businesses, 143–144
    change-tolerance and, 135–137
    collisions, 148–150
    definition(s), 22–23
    diversification, 153–155
    ephemeral nature of, 178–189
    evolution of, 133
    extending, 210
    fear of, xvii–xviii

guarantees, 177–178
hardware versus platform, xv
imitators, 145–146
incorporation, 134
limitations, 169–170
marketing across, 214–215
versus monopolies, 30–31, 34–40
need for, 21–22
planks, 24
low-cost methods, 209–210
using existing, 208–215
politics, 150–151
popularity and, 26
presences on different platforms, 211–213
previous platforms, 29
restrictions between, 213
risk and, 56
risk mitigation, 153–155
scale, 134–135, 199–200
versus standalones, 166
stickiness, 144–145
success and, xxi
switching, difficulty, 147–148
synthesis, 146–147
technology and, 26–29
visionary leaders, 146
POD (print-on-demand), 60
Pogue, David, 74–75
policing platforms, 172–173
politics of platforms, 150–151
preemptive strikes, 167–168
presence on different platforms, 211– 213
price discrimination, 38
privacy, 19–20
Facebook, 105–106
Facebook Connect, 96–97
Google, 125–126
Schmidt, Eric, 20
user purchase habits, 106
pro-forma net profit, 44
Product Advertising API (Amazon), 49–50
profits
normal, 34
predictions, 17–19
pro-forma net profit, 44
super-normal, 34
prosumer, 6–7

Q–R

Quora, 234–235

Random House, Kindle and, 64
recession. See Great Recession
regulatory agencies, 172–174
resources
economics and marketing books, 254–255
research-based books, 250–254
trade books, 249–250
RIAA (Recording Industry Association of America), 9, 64
Ridley, Matt, 39–40
Riley, Duncan, 6
risk
intelligent risk, xxii
mitigation, 153–155
platform building and, 206–207
platforms and, 56
safety and limitations, 207
robber barons, 30–31, 37
Robertson, Michael, 78
Rovio games, 160–161
Rudess, Jordan, 75–77
Rush, 84–86

S

Salesforce.com, 231–233
SampleWiz, 76–77
Samsung and Google, 177–178
Scala (Twitter), 225–226
scale of the platform, 134–135, 199–200
Schiller, Philip, 75
Schmidt, Eric, xix
Apple and Google involvement, 148–149
Jobs, Steve on, 149
personal information, 20
on platform strategies, xxii
SDKs (software development kits), 10
Segall, Grant, 37
semantic web, 238–240
shiny object syndrome, xvii
simplicity of use, 142–143
Sims, Peter, 198–199
Skype
eBay purchase, 188
Google Voice and, 123
Slywotzky, Adrian, 136–137
smartphones, 4, 10
social change, 4–5
social networking, 4–5, 84
social web, 4
spam, Amazon, 48–49
spending and growth, 141
stability, dynamic, xxiii, 135–136

standalones versus platforms, 166
stickiness of platforms, 144–145
Stone, Brad, 65
success and complacency, 221
symbiotic relationships, Apple and, 38
synthesis of platforms, 146–147

T

tags
    Amazon, 54–55
    Facebook, 103–104
Tapscott, Don, 44–45
target market, platform age, 24
Taylor, Bret, 109
Taylor, Ivana, 214–215
Taylor, John, 6
technology
    Amazon, 51–52
    Apple and, 244
    brownfield sites, 243–245
    downsides, 13–16
    future of, 238–239
    Godin, Seth on, 14
    Great Recession and, 14
    greenfield sites, 243–245
    humans merging with, 240–241
    platform age, 24
    platforms and, 26–29
    playing field leveling, 13
    for sake of technology, 55
texting intervention, 20
Thierer, Adam D., 33
Time Warner, AOL and, 182
Tushnet, Rebecca, 157
Twitter, xvi, 224–226

U

Underhill, Paco, 53
untethered customers, 10
UPS (United Parcel Service), 93
user base, 166–167
    crowdsourcing and, 176
    restrictions between platforms, 213
users, focus on, 141–142

V

Vaynerchuk, Gary, 11
    investing in customers, 170
    Wine Library, 159
vendor lock-in, 18
verb branding, 156–158
vertical integration, 30–31
video, Amazon, 62–63
virtual barriers to entry, 158–159

virtual companies, 6
    barriers to entry and, 32

W

Wadhwa, Vivek, 235
Wall Street Journal, 9–10, 109
Walter White example, 203
Ware, Tim, 102
Wayne, Ronald, 67
W3C (World Wide Web Consortium), 238–239
web, semantic, 238–240
Web 1.0, 1–3
Web 2.0, 3–13
Web 3.0, 238–241
web portals, 2
Weiner, Anthony, 19
Williams, Anthony, 44–45
Wine Library, 159
Winklevoss twins and Facebook, 109
Wizdom Music, 76–77
Wohl, Amy, 244–245
WordPress, 226–228
Wozniak, Steve, 67, 73
WWDC (Worldwide Development Conference), 80

X–Y–Z

Yahoo!, 183–185

Zappos, 16, 100
zShops (Amazon), 55
Zuckerberg, Mark, 89–90, 109–110
Zynga, 97

ABOUT THE AUTHOR

 Phil Simon is a recognized technology expert and the author of three other management books. He consults companies on how to optimize their use of technology. His contributions have been featured on ZDNet, the American Express Open Forum, *ComputerWorld*, Technorati, *The New York Times*, *The Globe and Mail*, ReadWriteWeb, *Inc. Magazine*, abcnews.com, forbes.com, and many other popular sites.

When not consulting and writing, Phil speaks about emerging trends and technologies. He holds degrees from Carnegie Mellon University and Cornell University.

His main website is *www.philsimonsystems.com;* his Twitter handle is @philsimon. The book site is *www.theageoftheplatform.com*.

OTHER BOOKS BY PHIL SIMON

The New Small: How a New Breed of Small Businesses Is Harnessing the Power of Emerging Technologies. Motion Publishing, 2010

A small seafood restaurant attracts new customers with virtually no marketing budget. An iPad case manufacturer generates more than $1 million in revenue in four months with only four employees. A voice-over company is able to connect thousands of artists with opportunities, all without expensive hardware and software. A law firm increases access to key information while dramatically reducing technology-related costs and risks.

The New Small shows how these companies—and many more—creatively and intelligently use technology to reach new customers, reduce costs, increase internal collaboration and communication, and create flexible work environments.

The Next Wave of Technologies: Opportunities in Chaos. John Wiley & Sons, 2010

This book helps organizations better understand new technologies and their potential impacts. It outlines if, and at what level, these technologies should be implemented to ensure that these companies avoid making the same IT management mistakes of the past 25 years. While serving as a survey of the latest technologies being offered, the book provides a practical focus, and each chapter addresses questions such as how to determine if an organization is ready for a specific technology, how to go about getting it ready, and how to measure success. It also dicusses the key risks and red flags.

Topics include cloud computing, SaaS, business intelligence, open source software, social networks, enterprise risk management, enterprise search, service-oriented architecture, master data management, and others.

Why New Systems Fail: An Insider's Guide to Successful IT Projects.
Cengage, 2010

A Fortune 500 manufacturing company spends millions attempting to implement a new enterprise resource planning (ERP) system. Across the globe, a 150-employee marketing firm builds and tries to implement a proprietary customer relationship management (CRM) system. For two very different companies doing two very different things, the outcomes were virtually identical. In each case, the organization failed to activate and utilize its system as initially conceived by senior management, adversely impacting each business.

And these two organizations are hardly alone. On the contrary, research indicates that more than three in five new systems fail. Many miss their deadlines. Others exceed their initial budgets, often by ghastly amounts. Even systems activated on time and under budget often fail to produce their expected results and almost immediately experience major problems.

Although the statistics are grim, there is at least some good news: These failures can be averted. Organizations often lack the necessary framework to minimize the chance of system failure before, during, and after system implementations. *Why New Systems Fail* provides such a framework with specific tools, tips, and insights from the perspective of a seasoned, independent consultant with more than a decade of related experience.

Lightning Source UK Ltd.
Milton Keynes UK
UKOW051601291211

184504UK00003B/7/P